CHAOS FOR THE FLY

A TALE OF TWO PSYCHES

SARAH MARTIN

For Andrea!
Sarah Martin
AKA Shel Wilson
2022

www.sarahwrites.ca

SARAHWRITES

ISBN – 978-1-778-14670—1

COVER DESIGN: Sarah Writes
Cover Photography: Camila Quintero-Franco via *Unsplash*

first paperback edition

CONTENTS

For Mattie...
You were planned, you were wanted, and
You were loved even more deeply than you were feared.
You were my best friend,
You were my most profound of teachers,
You were my chaos and my freedom.
You **continue** to be my "why".

May your memory be a blessing.

FOREWORD

Before we deep-dive into this tale that's been nearly 70 years in the making, I will keep those first 30 years moving on fast-forward, but I owe you a wee "spoiler alert." For starters, I will refer to stories, memories, and moments — and how those connect and dramatically differ... I will speak often of the spider's web; it's one of my favorite analogies for viewing life, particularly when considering traumatic brain injury. I refer to the Divine as "G-D." We try not to use the full name of G-D in the Jewish faith.

I frequently speak of "two psyches." For me, it means those separate but intertwined psyches that exist within us all, the two psyches between this tale of my son Matthew, and myself — with and for my son. You'll hear me use the words paradox, complicated, and ironies frequently.

You will find some profanity included in the text, and there will be a few racial slurs quoted. This is a *true story* and quotes, where rendered, are literal and unedited. *Was that necessary,* you ask? Yes. As you read through the five books of *A Tale of Two Psyches*, you will recognize why.

You will also find errors in the text, in my formatting, and perhaps with some of my grammar, and for this, I apologize. I was not creating a grand literary publication to be remembered throughout time. Rather, I only wanted to tell the story, forewarn and enlighten others who don't know what they don't know — and provide my son with a positive legacy, despite his many shortcomings and mistakes.

The entire series (five books) is predominantly set in British Columbia, Canada, though there are mentions of Ontario, Florida, and Tokyo, Japan. In British Columbia, much occurred in or near the City of Vancouver and the cities of Surrey and Langley, those being situated proximate to Vancouver. Other scenarios transpired in an area in Central British Columbia known as the "Okanagan." For our story purposes, locations included Kelowna and Kamloops. I have not provided significant locale descriptions; I felt the series already encompassed a lot of information (and pages).

By society's standards, I am one of those with "invisible injuries". I am high-functioning — until I am not. My double vision, my deficient depth perception, my occasional impulsivity, and my ability to mimic good manners when my brain would lead me to "act out", all contribute to that "invisibility" label. It's there, but if you weren't familiar with the indicators, you would never really know. Behaviorally, most will find me quirky (those who recognize TBI, will clue into the fact that I am "affected" — and those same individuals would scold me for calling myself "broken", yet I do). Others will simply not like me. We cannot make all the people happy all the time, and I've finally learned to choose my battles on that count.

I can organize and compose words as I did long before I sustained the TBI, and I can research because I take comprehensive notes, but I cannot tell you what I wrote or researched an hour ago. I suppose, however, that's one of many things I love about writing. It's there for you when your mind has let things go... just like a good therapist.

Since I came into an age of awareness, around the age of 11 or 12 (ironically or not, the same age chronology where my son began his own awareness), it was then I began what led to my adult state of learning, annotating and analyzing, of keeping things straight with journaling. I became a compulsive list maker. Little did I realize that, at that tender age, my "spider's web" had already pre-constructed the foundations necessary to support stories into the future. Time fades our experience and alters or removes our memories entirely. Were it not for the obsessive-level recording of events in correspondence and journaling, my memories would have been erased with the TBI and trauma I survived in 2018.

The accounts you will read are raw and devoid of censorship, whether reminiscent of the dedicated relationship between a mother and son over 44 years — or of the brutal terror experienced and survived because of brain injury, amplified by mental health challenges, addictions, dissociation, homelessness and longstanding patterns of historical gang violence. I have quoted words that were, literally, spoken by my son and myself. You may consider some of the language to be offensive; certainly, the situations that accompanied the language were just that. I have also left my son's written communications unedited — noted in the same context and wording that he expressed them. This is an *up-close and VERY personal* narrative.

A Tale of Two Psyches is a bit of a salute to *Murphy's Law* (which, in its essence, proclaims "Whatever CAN go wrong, WILL go wrong"), but it is also a narrative about how far society's understanding and treatment of brain injury has advanced in 20 years while acknowledging how far we still have to go. It is less of a guide than it is an adventure in awareness, risk assessment, perseverance, and a need for continual re-education.

This is less of a don't-let-this-happen-to-you story than it is a "Don't forget what happened to Mattie and his mom" kind of story. Life's ironic paradox can be so complex that there is no way to make sense of it all other than with the written or audio-recorded word.

After all, you can't make this stuff up. Truth is absolutely stranger than fiction, and to see what's right in front of you is a constant struggle.

DEDICATION

I would be remiss if I failed to acknowledge two of my most enduring friendships, without whom I might not have survived the turmoil, the trauma, and the loss.

Desiree

You have been my rock, my source of strength & renewal for over two decades, and were there with me through Mattie's adult gang involvement, by my side in hospital at the time of his neurosurgery, and through all the thick-and-thin of mega-drama, trauma and successes in those years. You never left me in my greatest hours of need in those transcending years after the event that forever changed my life, and Mattie's. Your encouragement and strength gave me light in a time I could only envision darkness and gave me hope when I only considered it to be a four-letter word.

Eva

You were the turning point for Mattie in the years he thrived post-TBI; he loved you; he respected and admired you. I have been ever-grateful that you have always given me sound advice in the face of undignified circumstances, and have done so with a complete absence of judgment. After profoundly documented historical "failures," you gave me hope in caregiving potential again. I always admired that you approached traumatic brain injury rehabilitation with a focus on the positives, rather than an inundated recital of negativity, shortcomings, and impulsive decisions. You made a difference in SO MANY lives, including Mattie's — and my own.

A Cherokee elder once told his grandson about two psyches that live within every human — two wolves, as he described it. He said the two wolves were always at odds, one against the other. The two wolves were always competing and battling.

The dark wolf wants to control. He is irrational, blinded by anger, and sometimes senselessly destroying or mangling everything around himself. Conflicting emotions of envy, regret, paranoia, greed, arrogance, resentment and ego propel the dark wolf. Conflict breeds confusion and the dark wolf is always lashing out without even knowing why. The light wolf is a nurturer and protector, known for its strategic logic, benevolence, empathy, generosity, and cooperation. It fights only with a noble purpose, and only to provide for and protect its clan. The light wolf lives life, loves life, and protects life.

For as long as the two wolves breathe, the competition between them continues.

The grandson pondered carefully for a minute and then asked his grandfather, "So, if there are two and they are always fighting each other, which wolf wins?"

The elder replied, "The wolf that gets fed and watered is the wolf that wins. Your focus determines the wolf that wins in you."

RISK WITHOUT ASSESSMENT

I 'd not slept for 48 hours, having spent almost every moment at my son's side in the Neurosurgical Intensive Care Unit at Vancouver General Hospital. I'd not been home to shower, and I had not changed clothes. But now, they were "forcing" me to leave, saying I can do nothing here, to go home.

Matt had just undergone a craniotomy for a massive subdural hematoma excision, and the medical staff *insisted* I go home, get some rest and come back. He was in a coma with no chance he was coming out today, or next week — if at all. A prognosis was only mentioned in absolute unpredictabilities. I was running on adrenaline. My son! I couldn't *believe* I had been celebrating my freedom while he was dying?

Ever-strategizing and trying to make sense of that which held no logic, I thought that maybe this presented an opportunity for me to be there for him again, to help him through, to give him the courage to straighten out his life. Maybe there would be hope for him after this. I was going to find a way — if he survived. After all, I am his mother. Who else, if not me? No matter how the atrocities of his lifestyle choices had altered him, I had never known a love so all-encompassing. He was my "why." Despite his troubled psyche, he was the love of my life.

I had to find control over *something*, and I knew sleep was a useless undertaking right now. My neighbor Jeff had come with me after the call came from Ontario; he had remained with me. I made sure he had money for the cafeteria; I bought him cigarettes, and he slept intermittently in the empty waiting room of the NICU. Since Jeff was still amenable to tag along for the "ride" (and what a ride it was)... we took a taxi to the poorest postal code in Canada: Carrall Street and & Hastings Street, Vancouver, British Columbia.

There is a stench in the air in that neighborhood that just never leaves. It seems to seep into your pores. This was the locale my troubled son had made home — or rather, made his bed and laid down in it. It's where paramedics resuscitated him and removed his lifeless body, sirens wailing, lights flashing — and transported him for immediate emergency brain surgery.

The Spinning Wheel, where my son lived, no longer exists. Certainly, there's no travesty in that extinction. It was a surly boarding house of rotting walls, ceilings, and floors... filled with sounds of unsavory ruffians... a dark and filthy environment — with a light bulb hanging from the stairwell ceiling, flickering as though it could extinguish without further notice.

We scaled the steep flight of narrow stairs leading to a sour and disheveled round of rooms. The whole place wreaked of alcohol-induced sweat, foul body odor — urine, vomit, and... wow, was that feces? Yes. Feces. I smelled *human shit.* Somewhere, I could hear flies buzzing.

As one who prided themselves in being able to manage just about anything, I had to admit I had never witnessed the level of squalor that I saw at this moment. It was unfathomable to me that my son lived here, ate here, slept here... that he drank, and worked in the bar next door (less than endearingly known as "Fight Club").

Room 4: that's what I last knew to be my son's room. Since the door was standing open by about six inches, I entered. I did not knock. I never even gave a thought to what I might find on the other side of that door. Jeff, still in the hallway, looked like a deer caught in headlights — wide-eyed and almost looking innocent. Jeff was a gay prostitute; he was not innocent, but the environment we currently faced would take the confidence away from any seasoned-to-life individual.

I examined the room with no small degree of morbid curiosity (such as a bag of over 100 condoms, perhaps a dozen overflowing ashtrays, a bag of silk ties, and two designer shirts hanging in the closet). It was apparent that much was missing (such as the TV, VCR, and bed linens I had given him). I suppose no one had an interest in the shirts left behind because those were all he wore; they had become his "uniform" in this deranged lifestyle into which he had disintegrated. He'd become a mere rendition of his former self, with his "core personality" in absentia. I precariously opened a dresser drawer, thinking to myself that I should have brought some latex gloves from the hospital. Did they ACTUALLY steal his *underwear?* There were two pairs of socks — argyles, both riddled with holes and de-threading at the tops. So, they took his socks, too.

Much to Jeff's chagrin, I began, one by one, to pound on the doors of tenants still sleeping. I demanded information, half out of my mind with rage, with shock and a need to know, with no consideration of the absurd danger I was risking. In hindsight, I'm pretty sure my therapist would call this "dissociation." This was me, doing what needed to get done. I would cross the other bridges when I came to them. To see what's right in front of you is a constant struggle, especially when operating in a "cortisol wash." But hey, behold the turtle: he makes progress only when he sticks his neck out.

THE PHONE CALL

W est End, near downtown Vancouver, BC
It was November 16, 2001. Matt had been independent and living away from me for a sufficient period that I felt I could rent a smaller apartment solely for myself. Yesterday, I had moved into a bachelor suite on the 10th floor of a high-rise apartment building, less-than-affectionately known as "Stack of Fags."

My neighbor Jeff and I had just finished a faux-brick-painted accent wall in my apartment and had mounted half a wall of mirrors. It was just before 10 PM, and we were sitting down to open a bottle of wine to celebrate my independence. Matthew had not returned home for a year now, and our communications struggled. I last saw him on his birthday, November 6th, when he visited my former apartment. The meeting felt strained, and I was confident he was hoping to receive cash from me, instead of the silk tie and fresh shirt I had bought for him. He opened his card and could not have read it in the brief time it took for him to put it back inside the envelope. There was no cash there, so I suppose that was all he needed to know, sadly.

About ten minutes before 10 PM, my phone rang. I almost didn't answer it, as my call display indicated "unknown caller", but feeling elated — I said, "Hello?"

It was my ex — Matthew's father, though I use the paternal phrasing loosely. We called him "Muck." He was never there for Matthew — at birth or otherwise. There was no love lost between us, and Matthew despised his father. His father had been physically and emotionally abusive to me in our relationship. His greatest talents were debatable, being a toss-up between (1) his ability to commit adultery more frequently than any individual known or (2) to consume more alcohol in any given week than anyone else in the local alcoholics' pub. He was what my grandfather, RIP, would have called a "drunk whore hopper."

He also abused Matthew, physically and emotionally, at a time he was especially vulnerable. Matthew never forgave him, and had said for years that he would end his life if he ever had the opportunity. I once said, "Matt — you don't mean that."

"Oh, then you're not as smart as you think you are. I hate the fucker and would like to do just what he did to me, all those years ago."

Muck grunted, "Hey — it's Muck. Do you know where Vancouver Hospital is? You need to go there right now. Matt's in brain surgery. They found a note in his pocket with a number for his cousin here in Windsor, and the cuz called me. Let me know what's going on when you find out."

I think all I said was "Fuck" and don't think I even said "goodbye." I hung up the phone to call a taxi, and within seconds, Jeff and I were in the elevator, headed for the lobby — where a taxi was already there by the time we cleared 10 floors.

"Vancouver General Hospital, please — and can you lose as many red lights on the way as possible? Here's a $50 tip if you can do that."

And he did. It was a 12-minute drive across the Burrard Bridge and down to VGH — a drive that typically would have required 20 minutes.

I identified myself at the emergency triage desk and was told to sit down, that someone would take me into the NICU (Neurosurgical Intensive Care Unit) shortly, adding my son had just come out of brain surgery.

"What is his condition?"

"I'm sorry, ma'am, a doctor will speak to you about that. We don't have updates here at this desk. The doctor will be with you soon. Please have a seat."

His neurosurgeon greeted me in the next half hour, and escorted Jeff and me into the room where Matthew was connected to 10-12 machines... whirring, beeping, whirring, gushing... His head was wrapped in white bandages and his left eye was so blackened and swollen that it looked more like a squash ball than a black eye. I held his lifeless, but warm, hands. He had an odd, large blister on the inside of his middle finger — and I wondered what could have caused that.

I had no knowledge of what had transpired, where or how he had been found — but had spoken to an ambulance crew who had transported him and learned the location where he had been found — and that someone from "The Spinning Wheel" had telephoned. He had been resuscitated at the scene and arrived at VGH with a Glasgow Coma Scale of four — alive, but barely.

I also spoke with Vancouver Police, who informed me that their preliminary investigations showed he had been beaten two days ago and left unconscious in his room at The Spinning Wheel — a skid-row boarding house for men, next door to the bar where Matthew worked (and drank). The bar was known, colloquially, as "Fight Club." Apparently, they reported him to have consumed a 40-ounce bottle of Crown Royal and 6-12 beers daily — seven days a week. He was a perpetual drunk, agitated and violent. He was known to Police, of course.

He had been assaulted at a party on a yacht, where he had run his mouth to the wrong individuals and been selected to learn a lesson. Apparently, he owed a cocaine debt to the same group of people and it was unlikely to be repaid, so the beating represented consequences due.

WHY did no one call an ambulance? WHY was he left in his room to die? WHY did someone only phone an ambulance when he had stopped breathing? WHO was checking on him closely enough to know when he stopped breathing?

It was too soon to know whether he would survive the night, whether he would require a second surgical procedure, or what his overall prognosis for the future would be. We had waited on pins and needles for over 26 hours, with no sleep, no change of clothes, and not even a chance to splash water on our faces. Numb and distraught, I bought a pack of cigarettes from the machine just outside the emergency room, and my 10-year hiatus from cigarettes concluded — just like that.

My friend Desiree had come to VGH to console me and see Matthew's condition, and I had contacted five different clergy members to attend and pray with Matthew in the NICU — a Baptist minister, a Rabbi, a Presbyterian pastor, a Catholic priest, and an Anglican minister. Only the Rabbi did not attend, as predicted (but I still had to try).

Jeff and I were told nothing could be done, to go home and get some rest, and come back tomorrow. There was no chance that Matthew would emerge from the coma, and I was warned I would need my strength and energy for what was ahead. That was when I called a taxi and stormed Vancouver's skid row for answers.

WHAT'S IN A NAME?

I think most of us have had a nickname in our lifetimes... then others of us have shortened versions of our names used endearingly by those who know us best.

My son was born on November 6, 1978, at 10 pounds, 6 ounces — and with dark blue eyes and straight and fine, blonde hair. We designated his legal name as "Matthew Marwood Taylor Wilson III."

Poor guy — the name that rendered countless chuckles through the course of his next 44 years was my doing. Matthew, because it means "G-D's gift." My son, through the years, invariably chuckled himself, adding "G-D's gift to women!" Ahh, the enlightenment that comes to most of us over nearly seven decades of experience. Insecurity breeds boasting.

And the rest of that highway extension of a name? Yes, Matthew was the third "Marwood Taylor Wilson", his grandfather being the first and his father being the Junior.

Few people knew Matthew as a "Third", and in fact, when for whatever reason he heard his name recounted in full — at the end of that "Matthew Marwood Taylor Wilson" he smiled and raised his voice, pointing a forefinger to the ceiling and added "THE THIRD"!

What's in a name? *Quite a bit*, actually — but only those closest to the fold would know the peculiarities and the projected behaviors that led or followed.

"Matthew" was mostly for more serious, even formal, occasions... like in the doctor's office, in the classroom... in the principal's office (which gave us both the expertise in the next step from those frequent flyer occasions, the lawyer's office or the Judge's Chambers). "Matthew" meant business, whether good, bad or indifferent. "Matthew", articulated, could foreshadow an award of excellence, of acknowledging high IQ, or "Matthew" could be recited in Reasons for Judgment at sentencing in a Court of Law.

"Matt" became the shortened version used for expediency, in passing ("Matt, over here, buddy")... or in warning of imminent danger ("Matt! That coffee is hot!")... I used it so much when he was four years of age that my roommate's talking parrot mimicked me for hours on any day! In that piercing, sharp and annoying rendition of repeating "Matt — Matt — Matt!" Rather taken aback that was how I truly sounded, I think that's when I started softening things up a bit and calling him "Mattie" more often than not.

Mattie was endearing. Mattie loved kittens, puppies, and baby birds. My young man loved seniors, and the innocence and trust he saw in many children. He loved seeing good people help people who needed it. He found himself overcome with tears frequently. Mattie would "give and do" for the rare individuals that he trusted and loved, until he collapsed. It was easy for Mattie to be hurt. Mattie was fragile. Mattie was innocent. Mattie was soft and caring.

Mattie was "Matthew's" core personality. He was often called "Big Bear Mattie" through the years of TBI. There is *so much* "in a name." Mattie's favorite movie was "Titanic", with the principal actor he referred to as "Leonardo DiCrappio"; he sobbed with sensitivity every time he watched the movie. Mattie's favorite actors included Adam Sandler, Ryan Reynolds, Dwayne Johnson, Gerard Butler, and Gerard Depardieu (who he called "Gerard Dippity Do").

But "Matt" could evoke horror and terror with his stature alone. At six feet three inches, and an average of 270 lbs, it was easy to see he had the potential to be a force of nature — even if you had only known "Big Bear Mattie." Matt had the adept ability (or curse, depending on how you view it) of dissociation — able to channel absentia with an alternate personality dominance, sometimes with amnesia and sometimes with full awareness and recollection. He could transform with the most seemingly inconsequential of triggers, from Mattie into a "Matt" warranting due care and attention. Matt had no interest in movies; he thought they were a waste of time and were unrealistic, often saying "Truth is *way* stranger than what they do in the movies."

In Japan, because there is no pronunciation equivalent in their language to our "th" sounds, his classmates often substituted more easily pronounced sounds and jokingly called him "Mash-u-potato" or worse, "Mush-u-roomu", resulting in unanimous laughter — and also interrupting the classroom discipline. These became the early "bully events" Matthew experienced in Japan and formed the refusal of mashed potatoes or mushrooms through the years (no mushrooms on his pizza, no mushrooms on his steak — he didn't even want to even hear the mention of those two foods). Mattie got his feelings hurt, Mattie felt rejected, and Mattie cried a lot in his final year in Japan.

"Matt", however, could channel dissociation and unpredictable response with little recognizable forewarning — even at ten years of age, in Tokyo.

Then, the self-proclaimed nicknames — the gang tags... Matt's first "gang tag" was "Q." He was 11. He had created his own gang. Matt adopted the nomenclature from a then-new Star Trek character of the same name... depicted as an all-powerful authority, casting judgment over humanity and enforcing the status quo of his peers, yet Star Trek's "Q" was also a cartoonish agent of chaos who took delight in befuddling straight-laced individuals in control. "Q" was part bully, part teacher, and part comic relief — partly confident in his intelligence but equally uncertain of his perceived value with others. It's not lost on me that Matt likely recognized the conflicting personalities inside his head, and his ability to channel from one to the other, "on-demand" from an early age.

The gang tag that ended with his 2001 TBI was "Primo" — a derelict reference to how he projected the wares he was trafficking at the time – mostly cocaine and lower east side Vancouver prostitution.

So, what's in a name? A lot more than meets the eye, for sure. I like to remember my son as "Mattie", but I would be foolish to delegate my stories, my history, and my memories *solely* to how life was with "Mattie." To achieve balance, and to stay connected to the truth, I have to ensure I know and remember him as Matthew, and as Matt, as well as my beloved "Mattie."

To be unwary is to find oneself unprepared — and failure to recognize Matthew on at least two very distinct psyche perspectives could find one ill-prepared for the limitless potential under that very complex human surface.

"Matthew" could foreshadow expectations of either the extraordinary or the appalling, the exemplary or the forbidden. "Matt" could garner quick attention for recognizing excellence, that a learning experience was imminent, or evoke frequent indications of warning. "Matt" could commission dread and elicit fear. "Matt" could strategize cold horror. "Matt" tilted toward criminality. "Matt" could (and did) dissociate, with advanced capabilities. It was just as important to know "Matt" as it was to appreciate and love "Mattie." Matthew is a tale of two psyches, as much as I am – or YOU are. This is a tale of two psyches — and occasionally, two psyches[2].

ALL WE HAVE ARE STORIES

Be *careful* what you ask for —
What you do and don't pursue.
It's those pursuits, that *action*,
That forms the stories told about YOU.

I n the end, we're all reduced to stories... the ones we tell, and the ones that are told about us. When you think about it, other than with our photographs and a few random memories that fade (or change) steadily over the passing of time, we eventually lose the depth and breadth of all that encompassed and created what we know as "our life." I'm big on stories... as analogies, as history, as memories fondly (or disturbingly) remembered. It's the telling of the stories that truly become our legacy. In the end, we are *all* reduced to stories. Textbooks are nothing more than a collection of *stories*, and no two textbooks (or people) tell their stories quite the same way... THAT's got a lot to do with *perception*... and perception is something we all develop over countless stories told and heard, passed down through ages (or hours). When life gives us challenges, everything we absorbed from every single story is called into every decision we make, every turn we take, and every consequence we reap.

Stories: be careful how you relate the stories you remember — and be very aware of how you tell your own.

A MOTHER'S EARLY BEGINNINGS

This series is less a compilation of stories about me than it is those stories about my perceptions of a life lived with and for my son, Matthew. Where I have needed to recall memories of my own early beginnings, even I (myself) am aware of the fact that I am recalling potentially tainted perceptions — tainted because I was an adolescent or a teen, or recalling from my mind's eye what I *truly believed occurred*. Over time, all memories of my years between the age of four to perhaps the age of 24, when I gave birth to Matthew, are clouded.

Through the years, I determined that truly understanding my son required that I know myself better. So, no story about one can begin without a foundation in the other. It took me 67 years to understand all that, and I suspect if I live to write another five years, I will have an even more enlightened perspective. That's just how life is, for those of us who live it.

For me, I recall life in terms of "turning points." Of course, I've only been able to say that after reaching a certain "age of majority." We only think we see "turning points" in our youth. We get a glimpse, but we can never attain that 20-20 vision that hindsight brings without a certain passing of time.

Turning points shed insights into earlier beginnings. I like the analogy of a spider's web... the one we weave for ourselves... the one we weave for others. We start our weave from our earliest beginnings, and what's left of the web over time serves as a good but ambiguous reflection of our trials and successes.

I can trace one of the most significant turning points in my own memories back to somewhere around the age of 16. That was when I first learned officially that my stepfather was NOT my biological father... that he had adopted me and I'd been born out of wedlock. I have speculated my own theories on that matter, however, somehow just "knowing" that he was not my real father. Case in point, I used to listen to records in my room — and the song that became my mantra from about age 14-15 was one by Diana Ross and the Supremes, entitled "Love Child." I knew, even then.

"So, Mother, why didn't you give me up for adoption?"

Without even taking a breath before she spoke (I'm fairly certain she was holding her breath, ready to pounce), my mother snapped with no small degree of purposeful cruelty, "My luck, you'd have been the evil seed that tracked me down. You'd have been a dirty Jew just like your father, anyway."

Ahhh, that was life, ever "on the edge" with my mother. Today, I can neither call her "mom" nor "mother", as the titles carry an "alien" connotation for me.

I can't think about the woman who brought me into this world without recalling that "evil seed/dirty Jew" comment. And, looking back, it's easy to identify the racism with which I grew up. My mother had become shrouded in scandal in the deep South, bearing a child out of wedlock by a married Jewish man in the middle of the Southern Baptist Bible belt. My step-father proudly served as a Shriner, a Free Mason, and a member of the local KKK.

When someone grows up in this kind of "nature" without "nurture", they often adopt the opposite of what is being indoctrinated in the family home. At least, that became the course of my progression and development. Despite all the religions and cultures that were declared "taboo" in the family home, I developed a growing fascination and interest in so many.

For all the times I heard that the deep South had everything anyone could want, I wanted to leave and experience what I saw in my encyclopedias. I already had some of my own opinions and needed to prove them worthy or wrong.

CHRISTMAS DAY 1979

I can't think about my mother without recalling memories from Christmas Day 1979 — Matthew was barely a year old. By that time, I had already left his father, a man who had proven consistently over time to be a physically & emotionally abusive, adulterous alcoholic. Leaving the environment was the right thing to do for Matthew's future *and* for mine. I had not phoned home to my family in about three months.

Unbeknownst to me, however, was the fact that Matthew's father had phoned in the course of another drunken stupor about a month before Christmas — to enlighten my family expressly with the information that he was black, despite our having kept that information from them until a date into the future. There was no risk that anyone from my family would never visit, and the photos of Matthew sent to them only showed how precious he was, and that he was born with blonde hair and fair skin. My family had always bragged that there was no reason to consider leaving the area where they lived. They invariably elaborated on that, affirming everything anyone could ever hope for, want, or need was right there. They actually judged people for traveling and shunned them for wanting to move away. So, to bet money that we didn't have on the gamble that they would never visit Canada was one of the safest risk assumptions out there.

While I am befuddled by the concept of restricting oneself to such a limited world, I am now sufficiently experienced to recognize the value of blissful ignorance. I equally admire that a foundation for gratitude lies within the realization that what you have is "enough."

My mother answered the phone and with a smile unmistakable in my voice, I shared a jubilant, "Merry Christmas!"

Icy response, for which my mother was infamous, was the buzzkill of the decade: "I thought you might have called before now."

There it was, that dark and piercing foreshadowing, being expertly executed by a pro. I was stunned and speechless already, like a deer caught in the headlights. The Ice Queen continued: "You neglected to tell us you had a nigger baby; but don't worry, that Einstein of a black bastard you married called to let us know".

She continued with what quickly became a rant. "Of course, you never TOLD me you married a nigger and had a nigger baby — because you *knew* it was wrong! I would have thought you would have called before now, but before I tell you to never call again, I'll give you one chance to give up that dark seed and come home to live like a decent person. You FORGET all that nigger shit, and we'll put you in business for yourself, give you a car again and buy you a house."

Well, how's that for ripping off the band-aid? I suppose this gave my mother's twisted psyche an opportunity for vindication. Not only did I have a child out of wedlock, emulating her own shame, but I committed a far more heinous act by having a baby with a black man.

Of course, she would have already presumed that I would honor my decisions to rear the child I had birthed. My mother was as calculating as her cold delivery. I imagined she must rehearse in front of a mirror, ejecting those profuse words of icy cruelty, concocting the perfect facial expression to accompany the delivery. The narrative that flowed next should not have come as a surprise to me, yet it did...

I wasn't sure if I could muster my vocal cords to function, but I knew it was my turn to speak. I cleared my throat and explained, "Mom, I had four miscarriages before carrying this child. I can't ever have another. This was no accidental pregnancy. It was my choice, and I won't abandon him. I love this child and I am going to honor the responsibility."

I *wanted* to tell her I intended to be a better mother than what I'd experienced, but that was not something one said to my mother. I am reminded of a little quote that we often see posted on social media now: "A wise man once said nothing". Well, a wise woman also knew to keep her thoughts to that "inside voice". I let that inalienable truth pass.

"Since when do *you* honor responsibility? I figured as much, anyway. You're dead to me now, so never call here again. And *you hear me, right now*, and commit this to memory, while you're at it: **YOU DO NOT EXIST!**"

And with that, the phone clicked and the "mmmmmmmmmm" of a monotonous dial tone left me stunned, numb, and absolutely speechless.

Every Christmas holiday was foiled for me from 1979 forward. I put up a tree and ensured Matthew had presents until a certain age, then we celebrated the New Year with more meaning, focused on positive change, goals, and gratitudes, rather than "resolutions". We created our own Christmas "tradition" of going to a movie theater to view a new movie release.

Sure, I get it: all the poor decisions and consequences to live with for the balance of a lifetime. She had hers; I had mine. But after four miscarriages, and having been told I would never carry another child if this pregnancy failed, I had not faltered in my decision or in my resolve to bring Matthew into this world.

Hindsight being 20-20, I had clued into that "gravity" concept — of not being able to pull someone up, that the easier way was down with them. Now that I had the baby, with the father in absentia, I recognized I was facing an uphill challenge. I had vowed leadership, guidance, love, financial responsibility and more to this 10-lb bundle of cooing, grinning, poop, pee, and wailing. But babies don't come with a book of instructions, and historically I was unfamiliar with what motherhood *should* entail.

But I knew what I did NOT want to be.

To this day, I hate hearing that "N" word... It makes me literally cringe. I don't even like typing the word to tell this story. I heard it far too much growing up, and I heard it far too often from my son's father. I shake my head now, as it occurs to me once again; that was a word his father should never have used with his son in any capacity, for any reason — ever.

In the years that followed, when I heard the word on television, or in conversations within the home, I left the room. The word spoke to me of everything I wanted to leave behind; it was the antithesis of all I held dear in life. It was a consistent reminder of the family I had left behind, the abusive husband I had left behind... the reasons I had opted to take my freedom and my child into a world that held so much more than pride and prejudice.

A MOTHER'S FIRST MEMORIES

C ounselors, psychologists, and psychiatrists in my day — I've seen my share of them. Most of them began a start-up session with, "So, tell me: what's the first memory you can recall?"

Mine was probably around the age of five... I'd flown with my grandfather to visit my Uncle Hugh and his family in Bradenton, Florida. My grandfather adored me and did his best to protect me from the difficulties of my mother's personality, bless his heart.

That first memory, beyond watching the clouds from the plane and telling my grandfather they looked like cotton candy, was of me with my cousin. He was one of Hugh's children, but I can't remember his name. The child with the ambiguous name was more of a toddler. I sat cross-legged across from him as he fussed about whatever toddlers fuss about. My Aunt Irene stormed in, yanked that toy out of my hand, and thrust it at my cousin. I still vividly remember the look on her face that communicated to me in no uncertain terms that I was an inconvenience, I was in the way, and there was no small resentment for me being there.

The only other memory of that "vacation" with Grandaddy (as I called him then) was of walking through the perhaps one-foot-high uncut, neglected lawn in the backyard, pretending I was a horse (which was my favorite past-time, always playing alone and on my own). With black & white television back in the day and programs like *My Friend Flicka* and *Roy Rogers*, and Tonto and the *Lone Ranger,* pretending to *be* a horse (not riding one) represented freedom to me. I imagined the wind blowing my mane as I galloped over hill and dale and meadow... I was always a lone horse, even inside my imagination. Somehow that strikes me as a little profound right now, having morphed into the recluse that I am, without shame, today.

I remember being admonished when I came back into the house with chiggers all over my legs and feet — the burning itch, the rubbing alcohol and calamine lotion that followed... and the shame of being an inconvenience, still again. And for those who are unfamiliar, chigger is not a racial slur for people from Chile! They are an immature stage of arachnid, more closely related to a spider or tick, however. Often called "Berry Mites", they are not a mite at all. They are so small that they are unseen by the naked eye without a magnifying glass. While not dangerous, their bite will leave one with a powerful, burning itch and red patches on the skin that can become infected if not attended to properly. And they can transform a young and inconvenient child into a focus of negative attention never intended.

I don't remember the plane flight back home, or returning to my parents' home. In fact, only now (six decades later), do I consciously realize that my mother had given birth to a baby during this time: my half-brother had come into the world — my step-father's true biological bloodline. They had sent me away for that!

YOUNG AWARENESS

M y *next memory?* I guess I have it still because it's another formative one. I hold a memory from age six, involving my step-father (whom they had led me to believe was my actual father, of course). At age five, I started school. As I understand from stories shared by my aunt, my mother wanted me out of the house and enrolled in a full-day, five-day-a-week free babysitting service (better known as "elementary school").

I was always bringing home these little pictures I'd drawn or water-colored in 1st grade, writing "I love you, Daddy" on every creation. In fact, that was what elementary school was teaching all of us to do — to create pictures for the family and take them home to be showcased. I took special care and attention to my artwork, that being the only way I knew to express my love and appreciation, only wanting "to be seen" in return.

One day, my step-father came home from work, called me into the parental bedroom, motioned for me to sit on the bed beside him, and gave me a little present... a box beautifully wrapped and encircled with colorful ribbon and a fluffy bow. Elated and absolutely ecstatic, and I still remember the warmth of feeling accepted and appreciated. Was it a necklace, or maybe a birthstone ring? I removed the ribbon and carefully removed the wrapping paper, wanting to respect the details and the trouble he had taken, just to do this for me! I opened that little box, and inside was...

NOTHING.

Absolutely nothing. Right now, as I write this at age 67, I still remember feeling confused. I still can recall the empty sinking I felt in my chest. I still remember looking questionably into my father's eyes, and I still remember his words: "Sarah, let this be a lesson. When you give a gift, always give something of value. Otherwise, you are giving nothing. You've wasted your time and you've wasted someone else's time with nothing."

Because I was a child unable to have friends in my home, I played alone. I was sheltered. In our city, we had one Catholic church. On a day that we drove by that church, I saw (for the first time) nuns outside in full "habit". I was fascinated by the long and flowing black robes, the white accents in contrast. I thought they were elegant. On returning home, and to play outside by myself, I took a scarf, placed it over my head, and began pretending that I was a nun. When my mother heard this, she dragged me into the house by my ponytail and I received a beating — always with a switch from a yard bush with the leaves removed — and she always beat me until I bled. I remember something about the words "cult religion" and "dirty Jew" in there, along with Baptist in the same breath... Another paradoxical response occurred, however — as instead of hating other religions, I retired to my encyclopedias again and learned as much as I could about anything other than the Baptist hell-fire-and-brimstone teachings forced upon me. But the paradox continued... from this experience, I developed a fascination with ethnicities, and from any group of individuals for which my prejudiced family disapproved.

Those beatings (stripped naked and admonished with a switch until I bled) continued until age 16. When she beat my nakedness at that age, however, I clenched my teeth and made no sound — for the first time in the longstanding histories of beatings. Ironically or not, she never touched me again.

Indeed, it was a lesson never forgotten. Skip a couple of years and consider a memory from Grade 4, with teacher Ms. Crawford — a teacher who publically humiliated me in class in front of my peers. That moment changed me — alienated me further from social interactions and added to my distrust of authority figures. Ms. Crawford reminded me of my mother. But I realized, in many later years, in more than one severe crisis with my son, that time and experience *actually* provided me with the empathy I needed to understand how Matthew felt with his own bullying. It gave me a foundation to understand the suffering, first-hand.

Fast forward through to my talent show in Grade 6, winning First Place for singing *Somewhere Over the Rainbow*, and my mother not attending. Grade 6 places us at an approximate age of 11-12. It is at this age that I can track the beginnings of my compulsive-list-making and comprehensive ability to plan and strategize. I enjoyed writing and writing things down. I wanted to *remember* and remember with accuracy. My Grade 6 teacher was "Mrs. Pope." I was not her cherished delight.

Mrs. Pope, who *also* reminded me of my mother, caught me passing notes in class one day to my then-best friend, Belva. Belva was a year older than me and slightly more "worldly". I had created a list of profanity for us — the words, the definition, and an example of how to use it in a sentence! Even then, I had that in a three-column chart form. Of course, my mother was less impressed when the list was delivered to her by Mrs. Pope. I was grounded for two weeks... not that meant much, because I could not have friends over, and I could not visit friends in the neighborhood. "Grounding" at this age simply meant I could not watch TV. I preferred to write, anyway — and to read my encyclopedias.

In my encyclopedias, I read about Russia. I was fascinated by their alphabet. They use 33 letters, and English, of course, 26. So I created a cipher code using the first 26 letters of the Russian language, interchanging letter for letter with the words I wrote in English. From that point forward, Belva and I could exchange communications that were understandable only to the two of us!

It was also at this same age chronology (11-12) that my step-father taught me how to fight. I was being bullied by a boy next door (Michael Murphy) and when I came home with a black eye, my father put a pair of boxing gloves on me (he had been a boxer during his service with the Navy). He told me if that boy ever came at me again, I was not to come home unless I did something about it.

Like clockwork, Mike came after me again. I picked up my father's hammer from the bench in the garage, where I was playing alone, and chased Mike Murphy back home. He *never* bothered me again, and Mike's parents never called mine. I never shared that story with my parents, or with my son — but I include it here because the irony of the situation will become apparent in Book 4 of the *Tale of Two Psyches* series.

So, why share this with you in *A Tale of Two Psyches*? In line with needing to understand myself, I was better able to understand my interactions with my son in later years. These early transitions became my age of awareness, laying the foundation for who I was to become (and who I still am to this day). I could have never imagined how those developmental traits would carry me through adversity, strategic planning, and more in my future.

Then there were the organ lessons pushed on me, with 1.5 hours of practice daily, from age 5 to grade 6, until I excelled at that, too. I performed on television locally, portrayed as a child protégé. For this, my mother dropped me off and picked me up after the performance.

I even promoted myself from regular babysitting (at $1.50 per hour) to landing a job playing keyboards after high school in grade 12 for the *Town & Country Restaurant*. Union scale wages at age 16? $75 per hour! I had an upright piano positioned to my right and a Hammond B3 organ with massive bass pedals and an automatic rhythm attachment with a microphone in front of me. They positioned the equipment on a platform, two steps elevated from the patrons of the restaurant (just the perfect height that they, or their server, could place a request and a tip into the big fishbowl on top of the organ). My family never attended the restaurant to see me perform.

I used my earnings to buy better-quality items for cooking at home. When I made my mother's biscuit recipe, instead of lard — I now used butter. I bought brown eggs instead of white eggs, and cake flour instead of basic flour. The first morning I prepared the family breakfast, my step-father exclaimed, "Sarah, your biscuits are better than your mother's!" My job was done; that was the success I was seeking. And while my mother alienated me all the more, my competitive nature thrived and continued long into my future.

And those shrinks and counselors always asked what was next along my memory lane? Suicide... that began at age 16, though I'd thought about it since the age of 12. That first attempt involved every single pill in my mother's pill drawer and taking a razor blade out of her leg-shaving razor to slice my left wrist. No pity, no attention garnered from mom, though. In fact, she *found it humorous* that I actually thought I could kill myself with the pills in her collection and she laughed at the ridiculous attempt at opening my wrists. They committed me to the psychiatric ward of the local hospital, where I remained for about 30 days, over-medicated and sleeping a lot. Only my grandfather visited.

My mother refused to allow me back home. I suppose the opportunity in the obstacle that she had gleaned from all this was that she had done her time, and 16 years was enough. I get it (though, as a young teen, I didn't then). My grandfather intervened through the Court system and I lived temporarily with an aunt and uncle, a rigidly religious Baptist clan. When that arrangement failed in short order, I lived with the pastor of a local Presbyterian Church. After a few months of that, I begged to return home, promising I had changed, asserting that I had a new focus, and obsessing over how grateful I was for another chance. My mother said no, but my step-father conceded. He bought me a new 1972 Buick Skylark to welcome me home.

But, of course, that didn't last long.

I returned to grade 12 at the school closest to my family's home. I had missed a litany of days (for skipping classes) but my GPA was 98 percent. Because of that, I thought I was exempt from preparing a science project for my Advanced Biology Class. Guess again. Rules stipulated that, after a certain frequency of absences, GPA or not, a science project must be done. If I refused to take part, I would fail my biology class.

Tell me I will fail — that'll be fun. I hired the services of a neighbor, a young boy my age who was good with a camera, to take photographs for my project storyboard after a few months into completing the project. My uncle gave me two male and two female bunnies, with cages, from my uncle, who was a practicing veterinarian. I told him about my project focus and he provided me with hypodermic needles and vials of male and female hormones (testosterone and progesterone). My project title? *Sex Differences in the Brain*. So my little obscure Bible-belt high school felt the stir of controversy, and my mother was appalled with the photographs of bunny genitalia, altered dramatically. The hormones had caused the female to develop a small penis-like structure, and the testicles of the males had disappeared.

Make me do a science project and be careful what you ask for. But I won first place with that and an all-expense-paid trip to New Orleans for my teacher and me — for the International Science and Engineering Fair finals!

And for those who will assuredly wonder — the bunnies went to loving homes. They could not reproduce, but most individuals with bunnies as pets are content with that effect.

So, I was a handful in a passive-aggressive sort of way. But without those childhood experiences, I would have unlikely become the unique personality that I did, and on which my son later depended. Without that childhood, I might never have endured and persevered through 44 years of loving and living for my son — ever determined to be better, and ever determined to persist. My mother made me obsessed with excellence and sparked a competitive nature; she made me a leader; she made me determined to be better than what she'd shown me, and she opened my mind in trying to subdue it.

By restricting my freedoms, she created an ability in me to operate independently and beyond the confines of social constructs.

Childhood abuse gave me the ability to develop the strength I needed as an adult — the understanding of being slighted, of never being believed, of never being enough. Because of that, I always wanted to give my son the benefit of the doubt, a courtesy I had never known. Interestingly, I did not lie — but Matt did, and perhaps my limited understanding of the lessons learned enabled a lot of his future behaviors.

And abandonment taught me the value of being dependable, responsible, honorable, and present. It made me realize the value of loyalty and the importance of family commitment. So in the same context my son said *many times*, through the years, that brain injury made him a better man — my childhood trauma created the foundation of strength and perseverance in me that both my son and I would rely upon in the years ahead.

I continue to believe that we are all *right where we are meant to be*, and we faced the lessons of our past and adapted to them because we would need those lessons throughout our lifetime. Or is it merely semantics? We decide, right or wrong, we experience the consequences of the decision and our life in the future becomes a response to the consequences?

The sharing of this story has shed no small light on how I came to advocate for my son through his mental health struggles, his gang involvement, his incarcerations, his therapies, his institutionalizations, his TBI, his violence, his GREATNESS, his love of life, his humor, his health complications, and his shame.

A Tale of Two Psyches is a legacy of Matthew's life, depicting how he fought to survive and have the courage to come back to living, how he struggled and how, so many times, he *thrived.* This series shares the love and the pain, and it provides an inside glimpse into a family's tragedy, their greatest fears, and their most-profound victories.

VISIONS OF MOTHERHOOD

I learned of my biological paternal heritage in the course of a psychiatric session with my mother. Later, I pressed my mother's sister for details to learn that my mother had dropped out of high school to sing in nightclubs as an entertainer. She became involved with a married Jewish man, according to my aunt. A common practice in that era, my grandparents sent my mother away to avoid the shame of her pregnancy — a "home for unwed mothers." It was then that I could finally make sense of feeling shunned and unwanted; I finally understood why I had felt I was an inconvenience. I felt it because I did not imagine it. Yet, I was grateful to hear the truth. I was 16.

That's a pretty significant "fast forward" there, but I can remember thinking, long before my mother formally disowned me, if I ever had a child, I would vow to be a better mother. I felt had learned the value of love with the withholding of it. I had learned the value of truth by hearing a tardy disclosure.

So, why did I sidestep into memory lane with my own early years? Because a mother and her child, at all ages and through every milestone and setback, become encased in complexity. Every experience in our lives forms the character-building we use for our accession to the next steps we take in life, whether good, hopeful, traumatic, or disappointing. The complexity of my relationship with my mother formed a foundation for my relationship with Matthew. In short, I learned to create the opposite in my life of what had been imposed upon me. I was beaten regularly as a child, but I never physically harmed my son. I was ridiculed and emotionally degraded as a child, but I became careful to never dishonor or harm my son with such responses — based on my own experiences and the pain endured with them. Yet, I failed in other areas, though I tried.

Life weaves a web for us and we fluctuate between navigating the web to victory or becoming entrapped in its sticky predicaments.

LOSING PARENTS WHO WERE STRANGERS

I 've heard a few people reminisce about friends or loved ones after they have died. Of course, everyone wants to speak of their most optimal moments, setting aside any differences in their minds and focusing on the good they could recall.

I had predicted for a long time that if I ever learned of the passing of my mother and of Jackson, my stepfather, I would be devoid of emotion. Whether a self-fulfilling prophecy or the mere logic of having accepted my history while occupied with my present, I was right.

After conducting one of many random obituaries through the years, and eventually reading that both my biological mother and Jackson had passed — mom first and my elder step-father about a year afterward. I felt no sadness, grief, or loss over the passing of the woman I had called "mom." For me, it was like "reading a file." First, I searched my step-father's name... and found his obituary. There were few responses on his funeral home page, but there was a reference to having survived his wife. So, my mother died 11 months before my stepfather passed. I searched my mother's name via Google and located her obituary. Under "Family Tree", there was no mention of being survived by a daughter. They paid tribute to my half-brother and to her cat, Smokey. For all intents and purposes, I did not exist. I had been erased.

Destroy the evidence, destroy the memory. Erase what disturbs your peace. I do not lose the irony of that and who I became over time. I suppose I had also learned that life becomes more tolerable if we erase that which tethers us to an uncomfortable past. Erasing that which disturbed my peace became my *modus operandi* from this time forward.

Despite a "deep" internet search, I found no photographs of my step-father, though I would like to have seen the older man he became. I have no memories of cruelty where he is concerned, only of polite ambivalence — a Southern gentleman with a dry wit and sharp tongue when called to the task. What I DID feel, however, was a profound empathy for how he must have suffered from the passing of his wife (my mother), to have lost a "child bride" ten years younger than he was, to have spent 60 years together, through difficulties and successes. I felt more for my step-father's suffering than I did for my mother's demise. But that was justifiably predictable, given the narrative that stood between my mother and me from the time of my conception.

Through the years, my step-father only spanked me with a belt once, and as irony would have it, that spanking was because I had stolen money from his sock drawer to buy presents for the two of them. So, I had no ill-conceived memories of my step-father. But he had assuredly taught me the most-cutting lesson I'd ever learned about the giving of gifts, and with it, one could conclude we had both missed the actual message to be relayed. Give a gift that has meaning, but not "by any means necessary."

I had a less than optimal childhood, not in the sense of being deprived, going hungry, having no clothes or shoes to wear to school... but deprived in the sense of being utterly lacking in family closeness or connection in the home. Now, at almost 70 years of age, I have endeavored to make sense of it all — to decrypt some understanding for the abandoned child that still lives within me.

We see our history unfold so slowly over time, we cannot feel or know the degree of the progression that flowed from those "turning point" events. What was my evolution from these events? Well, I never abandoned my child. I kept my promise to give him more love and dedication than I had ever known.

But, those lessons interpreted in my youth, also made me a "people pleaser", always doing more than was expected, always autographing my work with excellence, but failing to express and enforce effective boundaries with others until I was in my early 60s. I placed the needs of my child over and above my own, and for that, I bear no regrets — but when things ultimately spiraled out of control, I was ill-equipped for the tragic "cause and effect" that followed.

My life as a mother transcended from one of loving support and guidance to becoming full-blown "battle-ready", self-educating as the days progressed. I can say with 20-20 hindsight, that the lessons taught brought a repeating education until finally understood. In the middle of a continuing crisis, we cannot "see the forest for the trees." I did not know what I was doing, and no speculations about where this journey would lead. I only knew that I was determined to "find a way". A mantra of "be responsible" haunted my daily thoughts.

MONDAY NOV 6, 1978

M attie came into the world on a Monday. His arrival was much like the rest of his life that followed — unpredictable, full of surprises, with more love, gratitude, and adoration than chaos, but chaos ever-present. And like the lyrics of the song by The Mamas and Papas from their 1966 recitations, "Monday Monday":

> Monday, Monday...
> Can't trust that day...
> Monday, Monday...
> It just turns out that way...

Mattie often told me, on my birthday, "Mom, this was the day G-D decided you were important." Well, I've always said the day my son was born was the day I knew my purpose.

In 1972, I had finished high school, with a scholarship, but had become sidetracked by looking for life and had not tried university yet. By 1978, at age 24, I was still a quick learner with a competitive work ethic, however, and owned five taxi cabs in southern Ontario. I was driving the day shift and planning to continue with that until a couple of days before the caesarian section that was scheduled for November 16th. Only now, more than four decades later, does the irony of that date occur to me — November 16th was the date of Matthew's brain surgery.

On November 6th, however, I realized I was going into mild la bor... two weeks early. Back then, to earn $100 in the course of a taxi shift was quite a respectable income. So, I kept telling myself, "One more trip; one more trip", as I wanted to book $100 for the day. Around 3 PM, I had my $100 and drove myself to Met Hospital's parking lot, parked, and walked into the emergency department. I was confirmed to be in labor, my doctor was called and I was prepped for C-section.

I telephoned Mattie's father and left a voice-mail message on the home telephone, saying I was in labor and about to have the baby early. "Come to Met Hospital! You're about to be a daddy again!"

Several weeks earlier, I had requested that my doctor administer a spinal anesthetic for the upcoming C-section. My reasons were twofold: (1) I wanted minimal pharmaceuticals entering the bloodstream of my child, and (2) I wanted to be awake for Matthew's birth.

Not even one sip of alcohol had been consumed during my pregnancy, not one cigarette smoked, no marijuana inhaled and I never took even took so much as a Tylenol or an Aspirin. I was diligent in my monthly medical appointments and my prenatal vitamins, and I ate well.

Matthew was removed from my belly around 5 PM that evening. I got to FEEL him being pulled out (despite the spinal anesthetic) and hear his first cry... When I spoke my first words, softly and carefully, to him ("Matthew — don't cry: no one is ever going to take you from me"), he stopped crying. The name had long been pre-decided. I chose the name because it meant "God's gift". After four consecutive miscarriages, this represented a miracle birth for me (and for newborn Mattie).

I had told my doctor at the beginning of the surgery that I was feeling sensation, that I could feel him swabbing. I actually asked if he could turn the mirror so I could watch him perform the surgery (he declined that request). He simply smiled and assured me I would feel the sensation of touch, but I would associate no pain with it. I certainly identified with the "white-knuckle" pain response when it felt like my surgeon was removing half of my intestinal tract with that baby, however!

I felt the burning stitches being added to my abdomen and asked my doctor if he was done. Once he told me the OR staff would lift me over to the stretcher beside the operating table, I told him, "No worries — I've got this", and raised my knees and moved over to the stretcher! "See!" I declared, "I told you I could feel that"! The attending nurses were astounded; my doctor was less impressed. Turns out I had a high tolerance for anesthetic and its effects had dwindled earlier than expected!

I could hold my chubby little boy, weighing in at 10 pounds 6 ounces and sporting a headful of fine, straight blonde hair and dark blue eyes. "Is his father here yet?" I asked.

"Not yet, but we left a couple of messages at home. I'm sure he'll be here soon."

Matthew's father had called in sick to work that morning (after taking the lunch I'd packed for him for the day and wishing him a good Monday). He was not to be found for days after the birth. He had been in a nearby township, drinking beer and whiskey for the day, with his "affair of the month" and some historical alcoholic cronies.

A series of additional and similar events flowed from this time forward, in addition to circumstances involving violence. I ultimately made an educated decision to conclude the relationship when Matthew was around six months old.

Matthew never received any financial contribution, bonding, or contact from his father, and I did not seek it. I wanted full extrication and an opportunity for a more promising future.

Mattie & Mom, 1979

DEFINING A NEGATIVE TIMELINE

I had graduated high school seven years earlier, with an open-ended scholarship. So, at the time I opted to leave Matthew's father, it only made sense to rally finances and make use of that.

As a single mother, University was, of course, a hardship. I worked part-time and attended classes full-time. Matthew attended most classes with me, but on other occasions, my roommate would spend paid time with him.

My professors adored him, and my peers got a kick out of four-year-old Matthew raising his hand in organic chemistry class to answer a question. Even my employer was fond of Mattie.

As I approached the time of completing my degree, my employer introduced me to a position with a management consulting firm in Tokyo, Japan. Matthew was all too excited to take the adventure! He was seven years of age. I remember when I turned 30, just months before we ventured to Tokyo, he asked me, "Mom, you're 30 now — does that mean you're going to die soon?" Perspective is everything.

Young children are like little sponges. They learn a new language and adapt to another culture in very short order. Within three months of arriving, Matthew was speaking, reading, and writing Japanese on a peer level. He formed words and sentence structures with no accent. It motivated him to learn — to excel. He came home from school each day and without prompting, took a snack and a drink, sat down, and practiced writing kanji, hiragana, and katakana (the three separate written forms of the Japanese language). To say I was proud would have been the understatement of my life, and Matthew's.

I studied formal conversational Japanese at University and thus was mildly prepared. But I spoke to a child or the garbage man in the same formal manner I would address a superior! So, in short order, Matthew was translating for me in the household, in the stores, and in the subway stations. He had friends; he had a girlfriend (age six, a year younger than him) and he was thriving!

He studied Kendo, Judo and Aikido. He was funny, well-adjusted, and involved — until he wasn't.

As the school term closed, the school administration advised that Matthew would repeat grade two rather than be transferred to grade three. Although his grades were exceptionally high (in the 98th percentile, overall), he was being held back because of customs and protocol. A conformist society did not permit Matthew to continue with peers older than himself. Matthew had skipped grade 1 and began his education with grade two studies; his achievement testing had qualified him for a higher level of study. At one point, the principal even said, "Won't you be happier to be in the same class next year with your girlfriend?"

As a parent, we can look back historically and determine just where things *turned*... almost precisely where things went awry. This was not THE turning point, but it was a precursor.

Matt felt humiliated. He was ridiculed in the next classroom and the taunts of "Mushu-roomu", as a nickname, began. He was bullied, and for a few weeks, came home with abrasions or a black eye from his peers. His motivation to study decreased exponentially, and his grades declined. He came home with a "C" in mathematics on his report card one day and I asked, "Buddy, what's up? Math is your best subject? You *love* math."

Unhesitatingly, his response was, "But Mom, I don't want to be better than my friends and make them feel less. I know what it is like to feel different — to not be enough."

Wow, conformity can be a double-edged sword when interpreted by a child with a delicate psyche.

Shortly after that, he came home with still another black eye, but THIS TIME, at the hand of his teacher. He had decided he wanted to leave Japan and try to get to know his father in Ontario. Being unable to vacate my employment contract at the time without sharp financial consequences, I agreed to permit Matthew to travel by plane to Ontario, where he would live with his father. I would arrive in Ontario within six months, and he could decide where he would prefer to live, or whether he would like to split his time between his father's residence or mine.

THEN, the turning point.

TURNING POINT

I spoke with Matthew long-distance, by telephone, every other day. He had told me he did not enjoy living with his dad, that his dad was mean, that he drank too much and there was too much Kraft Dinner and cheap cereal in the house. Sometimes he had to put water on his cereal or eat it dry because there was no milk in the home. There was always beer in the fridge, however. He did not complain extensively, but he was succinct in telling me that when I arrived in Ontario, he would NOT be wanting any contact with his father.

Within two weeks of residence with his father, Matthew attended school one morning with a bright red handprint on his face. His father had struck him, sent him to school with no lunch, telling him to "Fucking figure it out". On disembarking from the school bus, Matt walked directly into the Principal's office and asked them to call the Children's Aid Society, adding, "Because I am not going back to that drunk."

I was consulted long-distance, and Matthew was placed into a temporary foster home — a group home. We continued to speak every second day by telephone, and I wrote to him two to four times each week. I sent gifts to all children in the group home and ensured there were sufficient finances for Matthew's meals, clothing, and dental and medical care, none of which had been accommodated by Matthew's father.

On returning to Ontario from Japan, I found my son unrecognizable — both emotionally and physically. His posture slumped. He exhibited no self-confidence and was argumentative, challenged authority at every turn, and did not "play nice in the sandbox", as one of his supervising staff noted. The second-hand shoes he wore had holes and leaked when it rained, and it was apparent he had not seen a barber since he arrived from Tokyo months ago. His jeans bore stains from spilled bleach and were at least four inches too short for him. He had grown perhaps four inches in height since I saw him last, and apparently, his feet had grown by two shoe sizes. I did not see the warmth of the son I once knew in this persona, yet he hugged me and cried quietly, quickly wiping his eyes as though a bug had crossed his cheeks.

Matthew was, at age 11, out of control. He skipped school classes; they expelled him for fighting. He had sex with a 16-year-old girl at this age, he was smoking cigarettes and drinking alcohol. He was exiting our home at night, unbeknownst to me, to pilfer, vandalize, and run feral with his peers.

Finally, when Matthew's cousin Rocky delivered him to me at home one day, I was told that a little group of thugs in the neighborhood were going to kill him. Rocky suggested I take Matthew very far away from Ontario for a fresh start.

Cue same-day action. I returned to my compulsive list-making, strategized a plan, confirmed the finances required, and began listing items for sale and packing our necessities. All things being an opportunity to learn, I learned impulsive decisions create dependence upon those who bail us out. I had begun my "bailout" MO, which would continue for another three decades, and though I did what I felt was appropriate, hindsight would teach me I needed far more guidance than I knew. What you don't know can fill a book — and *here we are*.

We left six weeks later, packed a U-Haul trailer, and drove across Canada over the next seven days, bound for beautiful British Columbia — our hope for a new beginning, never realizing that sometimes *hope* makes us see what we want to see.

PICKING UP THE PIECES

We thoroughly enjoyed the scenic adventure in the drive across Canada and the special close-bonding time it gave us both. At one point, we called our trip "K-Mart Shopping Across Canada", as we stopped in each major city along the way, rented a hotel room, and went to K-Mart for supplies, some little trinket, or clothing to put a smile on Mattie's face.

We stayed two nights in Winnipeg because the hotel there had an indoor pool with water slides. That was for Mattie; he needed to just relax and be a kid.

Certainly, he had not smoked a cigarette or consumed any alcohol or drugs in the course of our trip to BC. His mood was improved. He seemed happy, hopeful of a better future, and thrilled to be away from Ontario. He seemed more relaxed.

As we got closer to Vancouver, we could smell the ocean air. Matthew had such pleasant experiences and memories from our time in Florida. He was thrilled to be near the ocean again. We both felt elated hope.

We stayed three nights in a hotel room and quickly located a two-bedroom apartment close to the beach, on Vancouver's "west side".

I secured work in short order, as a shipping agent and secretary. One of the best things my mother had ever forced me to do was to take a typing class. Competitive from the time I could speak, I excelled — and employment came easily to me because of it.

THE CAREER PATH LESS TRAVELLED

I secured work as an office manager in Surrey — a suburb just outside the City of Vancouver. We relocated from our densely populated Vancouver neighborhood to a duplex that was positioned reasonably closer to my employment. I was unaware, however, that the Surrey "underbelly" had a dark side and was unwary of the fact that Matthew would have a propensity to gravitate toward trouble. I *thought* I witnessed progress and turnaround in him after arriving in British Columbia, but again, sometimes hope makes us see what we want to see.

Once Matthew had entered school again, the downfall came quickly, and I was at a loss to know how to respond, how to stop it, or how to turn it around. I thought we had been picking up the pieces and starting on a forward foot for the future, and BAM! Murphy's Law struck again. I was trapped in a web and unsure of where to turn. But Matt was trapped, too.

The behaviors I had witnessed with Matt in Ontario were only precursors. Of course, unless such things are attended to without delay — with counseling, potentially with medication, and more – such precursors are foreshadowing events untold. He was using drugs, selling drugs, drinking alcohol, and smoking cigarettes. He was shoplifting but was never caught. Most anyone could have made inevitable assumptions, but I only had time to control what I could, take the next step, hold on to a paycheck and *pray*.

Although I was completely unaware, it was at age 11 that Matt started his own gang. I did not learn of that until court proceedings in 2020, but hindsight invariably offers clarity. It discloses a reality we could not visualize at the moment.

In Surrey, Matthew was expelled from still another school — for fighting, for conduct unbecoming, for threatening peers and teachers. He developed a response pattern of saying or doing something inappropriate in the classroom and just getting up and walking himself to the principal's office. He historically walked into the office, and said "Hi, me again. I've been a prick and I hate this school. Can I go home now?"

Fast forward to his first arrest and his first incarceration, he was charged with assault with a deadly weapon at the age of 12. My son spent almost a full year in a juvenile detention facility in Campbell River, BC — on Vancouver Island. He never seemed to recognize the gravity of his position or the consequences his record would have on his future. In a telephone conversation with me, he had told me, "Mom — please, it's not a death sentence. It's juvie. Get a grip."

I retained legal counsel for him prior to his Trial, but he insisted I not be permitted entry to the courtroom. He did not want me to hear his testimony or that of the victim and witnesses. I agreed to respect that, so I never heard the stories, the details of the violence, and the harm caused to another boy his age until I was reading a newspaper the day after his sentencing. He had gone to the home of one of his gang members, a young boy 11 years of age, had dinner with the boy and his family — and then in the course of a power struggle and argument, Matt stabbed the boy in the chest four times. I held my breath on reading that then, and I hold my breath now on reciting the facts.

Throughout that incarceration, I wrote to Matthew, sent money for snacks from the canteen, and once he had passed a period of exemplary behavior, he visited me in Vancouver. After completing his sentence, he returned to live with me.

The damage to his psyche was undeniable. His response and behavior were worse than ever, having learned new *trade secrets* in the detention unit, and having made new contacts, as well. Matt was uncontrollable. I walked on eggshells. I had missed so much time from work, I was fired from my job. Seeing so many repeat patterns of behavior, seeing him skip school classes, still again, seeing him expelled from still another school, it did not take long to realize that I was going to need access to lawyers.

What also never registered with most parents of children active in multiple sports was *multiple head injuries*. Matthew's participation in martial arts, soccer, football, boxing, basketball, rugby, and baseball resulted in head strikes, sometimes with unconsciousness and other times just being coached to get back out there and "go again." These years saw coaches using phrases like "man-up" or "don't be a pussy." Twenty years later, we are more aware of the consequences of recurring head injuries; back then, not so much.

Needless to say, his propensity for aggression and violence saw additional head trauma. By the time he sustained the significant traumatic brain injury in November 2001, he was primed for recovery disaster.

I responded to an advert in the *Vancouver Sun*, soliciting a legal secretary, arranged an interview, and presented my resume, with no British Columbia legal experience outlined, but a decent rendition of scholastic achievements and work-ethic letters of reference articulated. The position, for which I had zero experience, offered a salary of $2,000 per month. The lawyer asked why I was there!

"If you give me an opportunity to learn and prove myself capable, just direct me minimally and see what I can do, I will work for you for $1,400 per month. You can discharge me if I make a mess. If I do not fail — and I won't — at the conclusion of my three-month probationary period, then I would ask for a salary of $2,500 per month." The lawyer agreed.

That became the meager beginnings of a career in personal injury, municipal, and employment law for me, with ready access to lawyers and medical experts for decades to follow. Looking back, other than deciding to move to the other side of Canada, it was one of the most astute decisions I had ever made in response to an extreme crisis.

I needed another lawyer for Matt within a few short months of him completing his first juvenile custodial sentence. His next charges? Aggravated assault, and assault causing bodily harm. He had picked up a peer gang member and used him as a catapult, head-first, into a concrete wall. The young man suffered a traumatic brain injury. As irony would have it, during Matthew's incarceration at Forensics, years later, he would find that same young man, with a TBI almost as debilitating as Matthew's, there in the institution. Matt and the young man had to be carefully be kept distanced, each for their own protection. In those later years, the word "karma" was coined by many corrections and medical personnel.

Matthew spent almost another year in a juvenile detention center, this time in Chilliwack, BC. I often wondered if he had access to steroids in that unit — because he went in thin and lanky but emerged looking "jacked."

Matthew, exiting a
Chilliwack Juvenile
Detention Unit, age 13

Fast forward to age 14 when, post-incarceration, Matthew was living with me again. It was at this age that Matthew decided he did not want to be "a dog on his mother's leash." Those were his words, and I would hear him use the same phrase later, as a brain-injured adult.

He rented a few apartments over time, with gang peers, but was evicted at every turn – for non-payment of rent, for not taking care of the properties, for allowing garbage to amass inside the apartment, for multiple complaints and subsequent police attendance, and more.

He often broke into my apartment while I was at work, stealing electronics and food from me. I had learned to never leave cash in the home. Each time, I would return home from work to find my apartment door wide open.

Once, I arrived home from work and saw two Vancouver Police Department cruisers outside my building. Matthew was not living with me at the time (age 15 now). I remember thinking, "At least I don't have to worry about THIS involving Matt"... only to park my car and enter my building and see a huge plate-glass window in shards, with blood on the stairwells and walls from my floor to the first floor. Matt had broken into my apartment again, apparently fought with another gang member, sent that young man "flying" through the plate-glass window, and fled the scene. No charges were ever brought. Snitches get stitches; no one gave witness. This was the first time I would hear the phrase that would repeat through the years to follow. Matthew was now "known to Police."

It was on this premise that Matt continued on his gangland downward spiral, never incurring further charges for several years. This marked the time when Vancouver saw the Canuck's Riots of June 1994. A police officer, who already knew my son by name, telephoned me at work one day, asking me to visit the station after I finished my shift. Matt had been arrested for participation in the riots. The constable said he had some video footage I would find interesting.

It was one of many shameful and degrading attendances at local police stations, often the Vancouver Police Department but occasionally involving the Surrey RCMP, as well. Video footage showed my son about ten feet up a pole on Granville Street, drunk and swinging a bottle of Crown Royal, shouting "Fuck the Police" and as out of control as any movie actor would be in an apocalypse scene. I later found Global News coverage and various photographs affirming my son's participation. The photo below is of my son, behaving badly front and center on Robson Street in those riots. Matt was 15.

He attended four different secondary schools, expelled from each one for aggression, conduct unbecoming, and non-attendance. On every occasion, I chose a new family home, as it was the only manner in which I could ensure him another opportunity to pick up the pieces and continue his education. He played sports in every single school (football, basketball, soccer) and, despite proving to be adept, he failed at team camaraderie. His issues with authority and his propensity to crime were not to be assuaged. Despite a sharp and analytical mind with a memory for numbers like a savant, he left school in grade 11.

I continued my career in litigation and my friendships with lawyers on a litany of levels.

TILT

In the years from 1995 to 2001, ages 18 to 24, Matthew was in a loop best described as a "tilt." With a "tilt", you become intoxicated with power and frustration. ANYONE can "tilt." I believe these instances formed the basis of his ability to channel his empathy and emotional pain into another persona. I even heard him say, more than once, "I don't know who I am, but I'm not myself."

Matt suffered from PTSD that began in these early years, though it was never acknowledged or discussed. Even today (and as I write this, it is 2022) we have only a rudimentary understanding of Post Traumatic Stress Disorder, its mechanisms, and the effective treatment response to it. Twenty years ago, we knew much less.

When triggered, his eyes would dart about in public, he would not sit with his back to a window. He would not sit on a chair or sofa near a sliding glass door or window in anyone's residence, and he would not allow his bed to be positioned in front of a window. He suffered from frequent night terrors, involving him being killed, him killing his father, or him killing me. Dissociation can be a response to temporarily circumvent acute PTSD: if you can't deal with a situation, you escape to another level inside your mind. You tilt. I saw this in him regularly.

We were predominantly estranged during these years, with short-lived intervals of him finding himself trapped, in trouble, and hungry — leading him back to the family home. His gang personas, and handles, were reflected as "Q" and "Primo." "Q", age 18 to 22, was the "disruptor" and "Primo" was the trafficker and pimp (age 22-24).

The community in which I lived and worked at the time was population concentrated, but "small." Word traveled quickly, especially anything worthy of scandal circulation. A neighbor asked me one day if I was aware my son was trafficking cocaine. I laughed! But she told me she was serious and she could prove it. I took the bait.

That night, my neighbor invited me to her apartment and called a number for her "dealer." I positioned myself in a bedroom next to the living room and locked the door. I heard the entry buzzer engage and heard more than one person enter, with nominal grunts and pleasantries exchanged.

"SO, what's it gonna be tonight?"

My heart sank — that was my son's voice. He sold her an eightball of coke and I heard him snorting powder up his nose, as he demonstrated the product was safe. Then he left. He had been accompanied by a very large and threatening man, who apparently served as Matt's bodyguard. In the years that followed, I never disclosed to him I had set that trap to learn a savage truth.

As Primo, he also worked as an enforcer.

NINE ELEVEN

T uesday, September 11, 2001. None of us beginning this day could have suspected it would be a day to be forever held in global infamy.

I was still home watching the news on TV, downing the last of my third cup of coffee, just before 10 AM. A surreal video clip on TV portrayed what must have been a movie trailer — two buildings in New York City systematically "accordion-folding" down upon themselves, disintegrating into a cloud of grey-black dust. I remember wanting to make a note of that movie, as it would be one worthy of a view. THEN, I realized this was not a movie trailer; this was breaking news! There had been a terrorist attack in New York City. I stood there stunned and in absolute disbelief, along with the rest of the world.

I wondered if Matthew had seen the news? Heck, I didn't even know if he had even *watched* the news these days. I didn't know if he did anything beyond drinking, drugs, and wreaking havoc. Actually, I wondered what Matthew was doing these days. Was he keeping a low profile? Was he eating? Was he safe? I wish I had some way to reach him, but he had not given me his most-recent telephone number.

I wondered if he ever thought of his Mom... Seeing those Twin Towers collapse certainly made me grateful we were not in New York City. I remember having considered it at the time we opted to travel to Tokyo. Almost as if it was to be some gruesome foreshadowing, my world (and Matthew's) was about to collapse like those twin towers. The tragedy of Nine Eleven would be the last pre-morbid memories Matt would recall when *his* tables turned and collapsed.

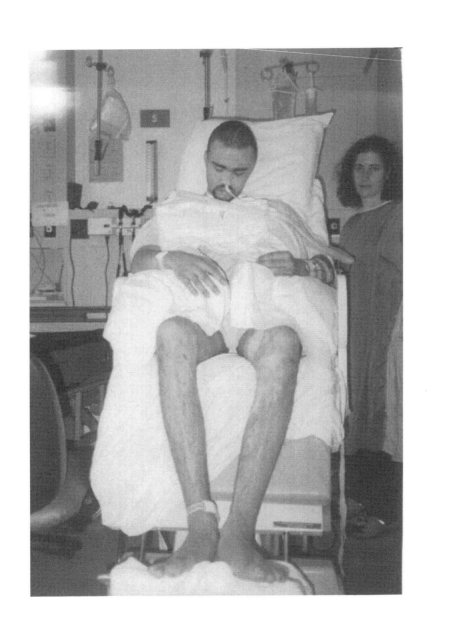

GET SOME FOOD IN 'YA

V ancouver General Hospital, June 2002... Matthew was down to 150 pounds — a 6-foot 3-inch skeletal version of his former self. His neurosurgeon had warned that there was a very good chance he would not survive. The next warning came in words of perhaps needing to return him to surgery, for still another subdural hematoma evacuation, which thankfully never became necessary. After that, I was warned that his brain function might not return, and if he survived, he could be left incapacitated; I was told I might need to consider removing life support.

I made a comment to Matthew's surgeon on the same date as that photo, "My hope is that he will never return to the lifestyle that caused this." I was operating on "blind faith" that he was going to recover from this; he was going to turn around and defy the odds as he always had in life.

The neurosurgeon looked at me with incredulity that I simply did not understand, adding, "Ms. Martin — he will not return to that life; he is unlikely to return from the coma. If he does, he will be left forever altered. He has sustained a very significant traumatic brain injury."

Then, once Matthew was transferred from the hospital to a rehabilitation facility, I was told his life expectancy could likely be predicted to be about age 35.

Once he'd emerged from the coma, he was continually hungry. I was unaware that the "governor" for hunger, impulsivity, and so much more was disengaged in my son's brain. So it was only natural, I suppose, that I wanted nothing more than to see him improve, see him thrive — I loved seeing him eat and enjoy food. After all, once he could walk again, he was going to be a "walking miracle." Mom was here and dedicated to helping – a reluctant hero, but here for the rescue operation.

He ate *everything*; he WANTED everything. His appetite was voracious, but in very short order, I learned the wisdom of constructive, monitored feedings. One day, he had consumed all the food on his hospital tray, three candy bars, three cookies, four containers of Jello pudding, half a pizza, and some sushi — and without warning, he literally *hurled* food in regurgitation. It was like a scene excerpted from "The Exorcist" — I'd seen nothing like it then, and I've seen nothing like it since. I remember a rather crusty, senior registered nurse rolling her eyes, saying, "I *told* you not to feed him more." She turned and slithered out of the room. It took almost two hours for two aides to clean the floors, change the bed linens and disinfect the room after that.

I never fed him like that again. I don't think the nurse ever spoke to me again, either.

MANAGING THE UNMANAGEABLE

The years that followed, 2002 through 2009, are hazy. That timeframe has been difficult to recount with any graphic detail or guaranteed accuracy. There was a litany of failed residential placements, failed group homes — each collapse of hope, each aborted attempt resulting in Matt's return home for residence with me. I never thought twice about it. It was my responsibility. I stated on almost every occasion, "Who can I ask to assume the risk if I, myself, am unwilling to try? If his Mom can't prove to the world that there is something worthy of hope inside, who *will*?" If not me, who?

This is how people end up living on the streets. This is how people end up dying invisible... dying in solitude... with no one to grieve or honor them... I took motherhood seriously. My son did not ask to be born; I brought him into this world, and I was determined to see that he knew he was loved, knew he was wanted, knew he would not be abandoned. Morbid humor strikes at every turn: I keep remembering how Matthew used to say, "You brought me into this world, and you can take me out." Wow, that humor falls flat on the crowd now.

When I initially brought him home from GF Strong, completely unaware of the gravity of what could *and would* be ahead of me, I had no advice, no guidance, no binder of suggestions for caregiving to a brain-injured adult male. I was merely told to supervise and watch him closely, to return to the hospital should seizures occur, and to be prepared that his navigation would be precarious (left brain injury, right body deficits; double vision; vertigo; absence of peripheral vision; frontal lobe disinhibition; severe memory loss, and unknown states of dysfunction). But what did all that mean, really?

With hope at the forefront of these undertakings, even after the first precarious month, I did not know it was not okay to leave him at home alone (no one warned of that). He seemed more functional than he was, but I can only make that assessment with 20-20 hindsight. At the time, I thought he was faring better than he really was — likely, because of the miracle that his survival represented. But he wandered, he knocked on doors, and he made women uneasy. In short order, my landlord asked me to move.

In that same timeframe, less than 90 days from his hospital rehabilitation release, I took him to watch a gymnastics performance, walking over bleachers to find a seat. As I recollect that situation today, I am appalled by the depth of my ignorance. I did not know the risk at which I placed my son, with his double-vision, his absence of depth perception or peripheral vision — and completely unaware that he was not "in his head" yet. Matthew had no memories of those early months after release from the rehabilitation facility. I think his first memory landed around the year 2003, about 1.5 years after his TBI.

I can almost hear my therapist asking me to elaborate on things I know I *did right*! I taught him how to read, write, walk and communicate again. I taught him to pee sitting down — not for the obvious and selfish woman's household delight of never having a toilet seat left up, but because his vision was so deficient, he could not aim. In the early weeks and months after rehab, he also fell down a lot — and falling *anywhere* presented significant risk and reinjury, but falling in the close quarters of a bathroom almost guaranteed a fall would include striking his head on something.

Matthew chose to continue the practice for his entire adult life. In fact, he invariably complained when men left a toilet seat up — and provided lectures of disrespect to women on a regular basis!

It takes a community to recover from brain injury, and I cannot even remember how I began contact with the Acquired Brain Injury Program. But eventually, Matthew was assessed and placed into his first residential care setting... which started on a successful footing, until the owner opted to no longer continue residence in the home, hired a live-in worker as a replacement guardian, and altered the structure in place and the house protocols. Matthew was moved from a lovely bedroom on the main floor of the sizable home to a cold, damp, and less-kept bedroom in the basement. Matthew did not respond well to a change in structure, and ultimately, the placement failed — along with 17 others over the course of his caregiving history.

Why did so many placements fail? Well, for starters, Matt was a big boy. At 6-foot 3-inches, and with weight ranging from 368 to his average weight through the years at 270 lbs, he was a force with which to reckon. On the one hand, his development was arrested, probably around the age of 11 or 12. He presented child-like, endearing, cuddly even — until he wasn't. Back to "What's In a Name?", Matt was the polar opposite of Mattie.

When Matt could not achieve his goals of securing cigarettes, snacks, or marijuana from others, he resorted to aggression, threats, intimidation, and bullying. His audience bore no exceptions — he equally manipulated staff, management personnel, and other TBI survivors. He took ready advantage of those with disabilities such as Down Syndrome. Matt preyed upon the weak, the compassionate. Conversely, Mattie was preyed upon.

The first eight to nine years of TBI found him unilaterally removed from residential care placements and day programs, repeatedly. In one home, because he was denied more cigarettes, he threatened the two women who owned and operated a day program; I received a call at work to pick him up or he would be arrested. The two women were locked inside a room in their facility, seeking safety from Matt's aggressive demands.

In another home, he was removed because he threatened other clients living there. When one young man with Down Syndrome refused to provide Matt with a cigarette, Matt picked him up by the shoulders and slammed him against a wall. "Give me your fucking cigarettes or I will hurt you. You don't want me to hurt you, do you?"

Still another placement failed because Matthew was sexually abused by a caregiver. We could not deal with the extra stress that litigation brought, along with the intrinsic TBI tango of disasters and crises that flowed. Life was wholly crisis management in those years.

Brain injured from the age of 24 forward, Matt lost his "prime manhood" years to sexual dysfunction. Given his historical criminal propensities, he was identified as a "high risk" deviant from the time of rehab at GF Strong Rehabilitation in Vancouver. Medications were structured to curb aggressive behaviors with a sedating effect, but also to achieve a chemical castration response. Hindsight being 20-20, as it invariably is, I cannot help but wonder if they held any consideration on a "fast-forward" basis. I mean, what was going to happen when frustrations rose to the surface? I believe that the medical practitioners of the day get through just that — the *day*... with some consideration for the weeks and months ahead. However, I suppose their responsibilities merely sat with "the day", the immediate need, and protecting those who would provide caregiving for this damaged and unpredictable young psyche.

Do what you can to get done what needs to be done, right now — and cross the other bridges when you come to them. That was the challenge for medical personnel — and for me. Those years between 2002 and 2009 saw several decompensation events for Matthew, all precipitated by either marijuana use or benzodiazepines. Every single time — no exception.

2006 rendered his first adult criminal conviction and first adult incarceration. Found NCRMD ("not criminally responsible because of mental disorder"), Matthew spent 18 months at the Forensic Psychiatric Institute — home to the criminally insane. FPI can best be described as a real-life "loonie bin" — BC's Cuckoo's Nest. 2009 saw the "mask slip" after cannabis, benzodiazepine medications, and a solitary occurrence of alcohol consumption at a poorly managed group home.

The years that followed can best be described as trying to manage the unmanageable.

WHEN THE MASK SLIPS

What precipitated Matt's first assault against me in 2006? He had been home visiting for the weekend and did not want to return to his residential home care. Things had been declining. Matthew had been having issues with regulating the number of cigarettes he smoked, often smoking three packs a day. That's 60 cigarettes in one 24-hour period, eight hours of which he spent sleeping. He was a chain smoker, lighting the next cigarette with the butt of the last.

Given his very limited income through a "Persons With Disability" pension ($120/month as "comfort monies" for his cigarettes, movie outings, snacks, haircuts, and clothing), it fell to me to pick up the slack in his finances (or have him exist without, which would have placed Matt and his caregivers in precarious, higher-risk circumstances). His caregivers and I developed a plan, to which Matthew contracted and agreed to adhere, where he would be systematically provided with ten cigarettes per day. He could not self-monitor, so the distribution had to be provided every hour. He learned to smoke a half-cigarette at a time. Case in point, if we let him manage his smoking, make his own decisions, and gave him ten cigarettes in the morning, they would all be smoked before lunchtime. Cigarettes proved to be a temporary consolation for his frustrations, impulsivity, and aggression, but the control system was mandatory.

It was just before 9 AM, and I was making another pot of coffee in the kitchen when an agitated Matt demanded — said he NEEDED, another smoke. He did not want to return to his group home. He had already had two cigarettes since 5 AM. I gently denied another cigarette, adding to just "Hang in there, buddy, there's another one coming at 10 o'clock." No voices were raised; no argument ensued. There was no anger and no discord. There was only Matthew, looking slightly wild-eyed and desperate for a smoke. I recall him saying something, but noted that his voice was altered. The voice was colder, deeper, calculated, and horrifying — but I can no longer recall what was said.

In the next second, I never saw the punch coming, but I crumpled to the floor in a pool of blood from a sharp fist to my head. I kept running the minutes that followed through my mind... there was no heated exchange of words preceding the event; there was no argument... just the denial of an early smoke, his dread (for whatever reason) of returning to the group home, and BAM! The shortest distance from fist to the floor was through my face. Matt kicked me, and kicked me, and kicked me some more. I screamed, all the while, "Mattie — PLEASE stop. Mattie, STOP!"

As quickly as it had begun, it stopped. I could not stand and I had trouble breathing. I was in pain and thick, black and sticky blood covered my kitchen floor. My son walked to the sofa, tears welling in his eyes, picked up his favorite stuffed animal (a plush little Rottweiler puppy, about two feet long), and dialed 9-1-1. I tried to get up from the floor but still could not stand.

"*Mattie*, don't call the police. Buddy, don't call."

But it was too late.

"Hi, I've been an evil man and I've hurt my Mom real bad. You need to come and get me." He was out of his head, and now he was back.

In what seemed like mere seconds, two RCMP constables were breaching my door and cuffing my son, reading him his rights. I implored them to ensure he was not placed into an upper bunk at Surrey Pre-Trial, advising them he was severely brain-injured, has double vision, no depth perception, and vertigo. I let them know he has limited sensation on the right side of his body (as he sustained a left-brain injury) and is wholly deaf in his right ear.

Later, I was told that he had been assigned an upper bunk and that he had fallen and fractured a leg.

In trying to maintain control, advocacy, and rehabilitative progress for Matthew, I had lost the battle... I didn't keep him out of jail. I could pick up the pieces from a group home gone sideways and I could redirect a negative impulsivity encounter with him, given the necessity. But I could neither contribute to nor control the fact that charges were laid and a prison term seemed inevitable. *Incarceration* might even mean I'd lost the *war.*

Once in the prison system, parental/caregiving control and guidance are abandoned. It's denied, along with any semblance of empathy or sympathy. Brain injury is ignored in the criminal justice system, and there is no treatment or consideration offered for it. In the criminal justice system, violence cannot be met with sympathy. Violence is to be deterred... consequences are to be imposed.

I get it. I'm not one of those tree-hugging moms with a glitter peace sign on a half-cap-sleeved t-shirt. But I am an advocate. After all, I became a paralegal years ago because I knew I would need lawyers for my son that I could not afford. I was also cognizant of the inevitable reality that I would need to learn advocacy from the grey areas in between the conflicting aspects of TBI and the law.

So I turned my mind, as I'd done for Matthew so many times over the years, to viewing this objectively — like I was reading and analyzing a file. His mask had slipped; and despite there being no debate from any source that he was unqualified to make his own life decisions, he *had* made a grave life decision and the consequences of his actions were creating another narrative altogether for him now.

With there having been no voices raised, no argument, no anger, and no discord that fateful and tragic morning, what was Matthew's justification for the attack? For 18 months, he told RCMP, his lawyer, and a full complement of medical staffing that he became angry and hurt his mother because his mother called him a nigger that morning.

Wow. Not only did that broadside my heartstrings, but it also took my breath away... left me with a sinking, empty void near my heart, and robbed me of any words. I couldn't help but consider that all those professional adults must have, at least, *wondered* if there was any truth in the storytelling. And if it *were* anything other than conjecture, what a horrific injustice to any child, whether adult, brain-injured, or otherwise.

But that never happened. There were no racial slurs in our household — EVER... not then, not before that time, and never afterward. Even with the proliferation of rap music played in the car, viewed on the television, and heard in the gym, I was purposefully careful to *never* sing along using that slur. In fact, the only time I ever heard that word used in my son's presence, other than from his peers, came from the mouth of my alcohol-crazed ex-husband, Matthew's father, and Matthew resented and despised his father for it.

Sometimes you never realize the value of a moment until it becomes a memory. Had Matthew dissociated from his core personality to a gang mentality to pressure for cigarettes? Clearly, he was not forward-thinking in those moments, but clearly, there was an evil presence lurking just under the surface. Two psyches, alive and not so well.

THE CUCKOO'S NEST

M atthew spent the next 18 months at the Forensic Psychiatric Institute, often referred to as "Colony Farms," as it originally provided farming and cultivating duties for its resident patients — much in the same way that we used to see the *chain gangs* performing road construction. Colony Farms was less than affectionately referred to as "The Cuckoo's Nest," and for good reason. It was the "loonie bin" — the nuthouse.

All patients are referred by the courts or BC Corrections for psychiatric assessment, treatment, and rehabilitation. Their mandated goals include restoring an individual's fitness to stand trial or reintegrating them into their communities while ensuring public safety.

Their patients are the most severely mentally ill people in the province. All live with complex mental health issues, most often with psychiatric disorders like schizophrenia, sociopathy, or bipolar disorder. For many patients, such mood disorders are complicated with PTSD, pre-existing violent propensities, addictions, and personality disorders that render them anxious, paranoid, or fearful. Most have also experienced trauma. Colony Farms is a residence for the criminally insane.

From the first allotment of approved visitations, I was committed to visiting him as frequently as was permitted. Telephone calls were permitted early, and he called me every few days, and I ensured I was always available and present for those calls.

I cannot recall how long it was before I could actually take him out of the facility for a few hours, but I did so as soon and as frequently as they would permit. In short progression, visits were expanded to overnight, and then to a weekend at home with me.

I worked for a lawyer in Port Coquitlam who expressed concerns over my intention to visit Matthew. When visitations were ultimately permitted and scheduled, the lawyer told me one day, "Sarah, you know — he is going to kill you one day. You need to step back from this and let the chips fall where they may. Let the system take over; they have the expertise. You don't."

I got that a lot from people. I got it from caregivers, too. But I continued to stand by my thinking that if he *was* deserving of help, and a mother could not assume the risk, how could that mother ask someone else to take a chance? I knew his "core personality." I had witnessed him thrive. Certainly, I had witnessed the opposite of that, too. If I could not assume the risk, how could I possibly ask a health authority to fund someone else to assume it? If not me, who?

By the time his Review Board Hearing arrived, we had established a historical pattern of success and his mental health was deemed to be stable.

I asked to be made a party to the proceedings and represented him as best I could before the Review Board after the lawyer assigned by Legal Services sat there and never spoke a word, other than to identify himself as counsel. As with other matters of advocacy, I presented my *curriculum vitae* and multiple letters of reference. One such reference letter is transcribed below:

January 11, 2008

TO: THE BRITISH COLUMBIA REVIEW BOARD
Re: Matthew and his Mother Sarah Martin

I have known Sarah since we worked together at XYZ law firm in 1994. I also know Matthew's pre- and post-brain injury personalities.

Prior to his injury, I found Matthew to be selfish, hostile, and surly. In fact, I did not like him at all and avoided seeing Sarah at her home when he was living there with her.

Since his injury, however, I find Matthew is a totally different person. He is a child to me and has childlike behavior and manners. He is very open and frank and loving. I much prefer this new-and-improved Matthew, although I realize his behavior is directly related to TBI.

I have seen Sarah and Matthew interact with each other on many occasions now and I find their relationship to be inspiring, gentle, and loving — everything a relationship between a parent and child should be. I have never seen Sarah be harsh with Matthew and I have seen nothing but love coming shining through from Matthew.

Matthew is quick to trust and likes everyone. I feel he needs to live in a home where he is supervised all the time – the same as a young child would be. I do not believe it is in Matthew's best interest to be kept in an institution, as I feel he will be preyed upon. Sarah always has Matthew's best interests at heart and places his needs above her own at every turn.

Matthew was granted an Absolute Discharge, rather than a Conditional Discharge.

I thought the Absolute Discharge was a victory. In fact, I thought it was the *goal*. I directed my presentation to the Tribunal with that goal in mind. I learned, however, in rather short order, that the Conditional Discharge might have been the preferred directive. In fact, the funding authority changed its protocol for resumed funding for a brain injury survivor after this Absolute Discharge decision. In the immediate future of that timeline, no funding was resumed for Colony Farms patients achieving Absolute Discharge. I am unaware whether that premise continues to this day, though I understand the rationale for the decision.

So, what's the defining basis for denial of refunding? With a *conditional discharge*, should there be any repeat offense, it was a sufficiently simple remedy to bring the patient with recurring mental health complications BACK to Colony Farms. With an absolute discharge, if further issues involving violence or aggression transpire, the patient returns to the criminal justice system for assessment and sentencing consequences, and no consideration is given to traumatic brain injury as extenuating circumstances for the crime(s) committed.

Matthew was never found NCRMD again, though he returned to Colony Farms for another assessment in 2018. But that is another story. I'll get to that in due course.

He was terrified of ever needing to return there. It was the type of environment where people screamed throughout the night, where impulsivity ran wild, and some patients were drugged to the point of stupor and drooling. Matt called it "The Cuckoo's Nest" frequently through the years ahead. Despite a markedly deficient memory, he never forgot his experiences at Colony Farms. The thought or mention of the facility brought him back to obsessive smoking and shaking his leg.

BIRTHDAY 2009

After a period of behavioral improvements, Matthew's visitation privileges were increased. The facility sought to "test the waters", with family interactions and community response. He came home for a birthday visit from Colony Farms in 2009.

Mattie and Mom 2009

I took him out for a fresh haircut, new clothing, birthday cake, and sushi!

I had rented a three-bedroom apartment in Coquitlam, mere minutes from his location at Forensics... After furnishing and renting two bedrooms to local students, I could live rent and utility free, at least. One grieves the loss of their privacy but celebrates survival and the creative endeavors to continue it. Once again, we do what needs to be done.

If no one else could assume responsibility, the task fell to me. My inner-voice mantra continued, "Be responsible. If not me, who?"

STRANGER DANGER

A ddictions and traumatic brain injury — what a gruesome partnership.

After achieving an Absolute Discharge at his Review Board Hearing in late 2009, the health authority had placed Matt into a Langley group home. At first, the "honeymoon period" went fairly well, with Matthew testing staff boundaries and seeing how far he could get with bullying for cigarettes with other residents. From the fourth day there on-site, I was getting regular telephone calls. Staff sought advice on how to best handle the behaviors that were surfacing, and when things escalated over a few short weeks and his behaviors had become alarming after being caught with a McDonald's "Happy Cup," half-filled with vodka, staff presented me with an ultimatum.

The urgent call came to my office on a Friday, saying Matthew needed to be removed, to be taken to my home for a weekend detox, or he was to be vacated from the premises. He could no longer continue residence there unless I stepped in to triage the situation.

As I had done so many times through the years, both before and after his traumatic brain injury, I left work early, driving from downtown Vancouver to the outer limits of Langley. Staff barely spoke to me as they ushered Matthew out the door to my car. There was no sympathy; there was no empathy. I told them I would provide an update on Sunday and return him to the home in the late afternoon, on Sunday.

I don't think there was any conversation between us during the roughly 30-minute drive from Langley to my Surrey apartment. Certainly, there was no apology forthcoming from him. I chose not to interrogate him, as I knew what had transpired and did not want to enable gaslighting or more conjecture.

Weekend detox included a B-12 injection in the arm, about four liters of filtered water each day, walks in the fresh air, good food, positive conversation, television and music in the home, card games, and a couple of games of Monopoly. By Sunday, he was looking a lot better. He was still not conversant and there was no humor or his typical quick-witted response.

His anxiety was amplified, apparent in his incessant leg-shaking and an absence of wit or laughter. He looked distracted, and a little too "wide-eyed." He did not want to return to the group home. This was a pattern. With every caregiving placement failure, he became horrified at the premise of returning.

He did not like the female registered nurse who managed the home, and he did not like many of the residents. While I concurred that the manager of the facility had "personality deficits," that was not something I shared with my son. I had smelled alcohol on her breath more than once when I picked him up, and once she had neglected to give him his evening medication. She was angered with having to return to the home to accommodate his medication. Her words to me over the telephone, slurring her words, were mocking, "OH — *POOR* Matt — his meds are late. Wow-wee." Truly, you just can't make this stuff up.

His primary indicators of impending anxiety "about to overflow into something more" continued with increased leg shaking and eyes darting about in distracted thought. It was almost as though he was expecting impending doom. In hindsight, I suppose he was; I was as yet unaware. I did not recognize this, per se, as a *warning sign* for sudden decompensation — but then again, there were no warning signs in 2006 either.

By around 2 PM, I was exhausted — to the point of feeling physically ill. I had slept little since Thursday night and asked Matt if he minded if I laid down for a few minutes. He said "No worries." adding he would just keep watching TV. I went to my room and laid atop my bed, and did not close my bedroom door. A few minutes later, with my back turned to the door, Matthew knocked gently and asked if he could come in and lie down. I did not turn around, but said "Sure, buddy." He laid down behind me and extended his right arm around me. I thought he was about to give me a hug.

But there was no hug forthcoming. As I turned, his right hand and arm directed a 12-inch butcher knife to my throat. He had quietly and discreetly taken that knife out of my kitchen drawer, strategized to use it, and deceptively (and purposefully) invited himself into my room.

I believed this to be another psychotic break — another dissociative state. His demeanor had altered. He was mutating into that same personality I saw in him a couple of years ago, before he spent 18 months at Forensics. I can only speculate that his damaged mind saw an opportunity to control the narrative, to ensure he did *not* have to return to that group home. I could merely speculate that he did not know what he was doing at that moment. My only alternative was to respond with split-second precision.

I turned and rapidly grabbed his right arm with my right hand, holding him back with all my strength. But given he outweighed me by about 100 pounds and was almost a foot taller, the struggle was intense. As I felt myself losing the tug-of-war as he guided the force of his arm and the knife closer to me. I recall thinking, "If I don't do *something*, he is going to kill me." I grabbed the blade with my left hand, as I continued to withhold him with my right hand and keep him from taking the knife toward my throat again.

Then, he spoke — in that icy, deep-voiced fugue state I had heard before. It was the same voice that had repeated in my night terrors for two years. "Let go of my arm; I won't hurt you." It again was like something out of a scene from the *Exorcist*; I was not hearing the voice of my son. He was in full dissociation — not in his head. This was a stranger in my home, and the phrase "Stranger Danger" popped erroneously into my befuddled mind.

As I took hold, the knife blade sliced the palm of my left hand, and the blade broke completely away from the handle. With the forceful struggle momentarily relieved, Matt fell backward, and I lunged for the door to freedom.

Running around to the front of the house, I opened the door to my landlord's premises and stumbled in. The wife was stunned; blood dripped from my hand, and my handprints were on her front door. A neighbor phoned RCMP, but before they could arrive, Matt had taken my wallet, cash & credit cards, my cell phone, and my vehicle. He drove away.

Matt did not have a driver's license.

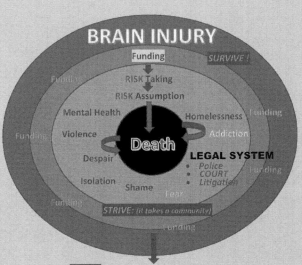

THRIVE: Essential Services *(it takes a community)*

Care & Supervision
Physical Rehabilitation
Psychiatric Monitoring
Psychological Counseling
Family Counseling
Nutrition & Exercise
Life Skills
Socialization
...MORE...

THE FIRST FACE OF ADVOCACY

A dvocacy wears two masks. It requires two entirely separate purposes to achieve a primary goal — the primary goal being to keep the survivor alive... to avoid or at least delay untimely death or further disability.

Some days, you are fighting to recite all the progress that has been achieved, and how it was accomplished — setting out the two steps forward and lessening steps back of the dance that comprises traumatic brain injury.

Other times, you are fighting to have the horrors and impulsivity, the dangers, and loss of control recognized by professionals. In those times, when control is lost and decompensation takes on a life of its own, you *beg* for help after having just recently *implored the same professionals* to realize and trust a process for funded caregiving.

It is easier for frustrated and overworked personnel (caregivers, medical staff, etc.) to send a survivor to jail because dealing with the issues is counterproductive, high-risk, and costly. BUT, they always exit from jail at some point. Ill-prepared, on the streets, conditioned to more negatives learned while incarcerated.

WHAT THEN?

It didn't take long for Matt to falter after the first violent conviction that cost him 18-months of incarceration in Forensics. On the surface of things, most of us would think that a near two-year sacrifice of freedom, loss of autonomy, distance from beloved family and friends — and missing even the sight of blue sky, the smell of fresh dew in the morning, or the feeling of green grass beneath one's bare feet, would be sufficient to compel a vow to *never* suffer this again. But TBI and mental health, particularly clouded by a fog of addiction, make an unpredictable outcome at the best of times. At the worst? Well, you can't make that stuff up. Fiction is founded on bizarre truth. I will get to that part of the story soon enough.

After relentlessly advocating for his improvements and his release from Forensics, strategizing and implementing plans for a new start from this point forward, Matt faltered with cannabis and benzodiazepines and broke his solemn vow to never consume alcohol again. His eight months incarcerated at Surrey Pre-Trial for that triggering indiscretion found him "released to the wild," on his own, with no money or sufficiently protective clothing for the elements.

The next chapter of advocacy became one of fighting the system to hold him, assess him, and provide for his safety and the safety of the community. Of course, the goal is still to keep your survivor *alive*.

After no shortage of communication, verbal and written, Matthew was admitted to the psychiatric ward of Burnaby General Hospital in mid-January 2010.

THE DARK FACE OF ADVOCACY

Today is Valentine's Day, February 14, 2010. I am struggling with encroaching sadness today and am facing the reality of having a hard time continuing to care for Matt. I feel incredible guilt for allowing myself to admit that.

So many days are incredible, but many are less than that. He has recently stolen money from me again and he tried to sell my sectional sofa today while I was at work. I discovered he had shoplifted a candy bar three days ago... and I found the metal seal from a screw-top wine bottle on a throw rug in my home. There is never any alcohol in the apartment, and we do not have people over. I clean floors and shake out rugs every two days. So where did it come from? Of course, Matt does not know... and neither do I.

I realize "this is TBI" and all this is part and parcel. And I *know* I have so much to be grateful for and that he is doing so very well otherwise, and that he has come *so* far. And he *needs* me; he depends on me.

But I am so indescribably tired. I am overwhelmed and fear I cannot manage all this much longer. There has been no further update on residential placement from the Health Authority (all I hear is "they're on it").

I surmise that because I am (literally) on it and *in* it, they are holding this on the back burner. There could be a measure of "We told you so" in these delays, as well. I will never be privy to whether that is paranoia or valid intuition. It's akin to someone living in an unsafe apartment and asking for advocacy for something better, but never receiving access to a better living accommodation because they *have* a home — and the homeless are "more desperate" for lodging.

For those unfamiliar with traumatic brain injury, know this: there is no prediction, no cure, no solitary and effective treatment, and no sole category of conditioning and structure that applies. For as much as an expert has developed expertise, educated, and spent decades in the jungle dance that is TBI, there are just as many convolutions, exceptions, and maladies. It's a professional case of "You don't know what you don't know, and what you don't know can fill a book."

If a TBI survivor has no consistent support, the narrative becomes easily circumvented to over-medicating and a blurred frenzy of institutionalizations. But, Matthew had an actively involved, educated mother and Committee — one with just enough of a legal background with a few connections to make a medical practitioner at least lend an ear to listen and heed historical information. Of course, I maintained comprehensive and organized documentation, including but not limited to emails, medical reports, medical records, caregiver reports, recorded and transcribed telephone conversations, journaling of daily events, and more.

Not only could I have never advocated for Matthew through his life from age 11 to post-TBI, but I also could never have been capable of writing the memoir that you currently read. Without the written word, without the voluminous records maintained and stored over almost countless moves and relocations, I would be wholly incapable of recalling much of the past, must less placing dates, names, and consequences to the events.

As I now age more rapidly, I have days where I cannot remember if I ate four hours ago, or what I did the day before. I still commit to keeping a journal of my activities, my thoughts, my medications, and more — every single day. I would not enjoy a true quality of life without that, and I would be at higher risk of losing my autonomy in short order with the decline of failing memory.

Now, I had to reverse-engineer my Advocacy Intervention to see him confined to psychiatric assessment and supervision. But again, for those who don't know — getting a psychiatrist to consult with a person with high-level traumatic brain injury is, well, like searching for the proverbial needle in a haystack. It is an arduous task and one with which many simply stop trying.

I did not give up. I had made a promise on November 6, 1978, to never abandon my son. The next contingency plan began with citing the "hazy years" by gleaning organized records and conferring with three criminal lawyers for opinion (two paid, one unpaid: advice articulated between the trio was identical). Now, at least, I was qualified to converse with the experts.

Enter stage left, my letter below to the chief psychiatrist at Burnaby General Hospital on January 19, 2010, after discussions ensued over how they thought they could simply return Matt to Forensics. "Absolute Discharge" became the "fly in the ointment" once decompensation had escalated to a crisis level.

Burnaby General Hospital Psychiatry Department

Dear Dr. R:
RE: Matthew XXX, <u>Psychiatric Admission & Transfer</u>

Thank you for taking the time to contact me for more information as to a general timeline regarding the above-noted patient. I confirm you have within your medical chart a copy of the 2006 Supreme Court Order of Committeeship, appointing me as Matthew's Committee of Person and of Estate.

I confirm I have also clarified that Matthew is <u>not</u> a candidate for entry into the Forensic Psychiatric Institute ("FPI"). He has entered a guilty plea through the criminal court system, and his probation order is from the Provincial Court of British Columbia.

They granted Matthew an absolute discharge after completing 18-months with FPI in 2006 — no conditions; no options for return or help on an out-patient basis. For Matthew to re-enter FPI, he must (1) commit another crime and (2) be assessed and confirmed as not criminally responsible by way of mental disorder ("NCRMD"). Three experienced criminal lawyers have confirmed this information.

I again respectfully submit that the *only* workable placement for treatment & assessment and a mandatory critical medication review (with observation) is a transfer to Hillside Psychiatric Centre's provincial bed system in Kamloops. I have provided contact information for individuals familiar with this case file at the BC Neuropsychiatry Program, UBC Hospital, BC Mental Health and Addictions, and the Fraser Health Authority.

General Timeline
I confirm this is not an exhaustive timeline, but it will give you a consensus of what Matthew (and his caregivers and funding personnel, and I) have experienced over eight years.

Family History

PATIENT'S FATHER & GRANDFATHER
Matthew's grandfather was a long-term alcoholic, exhibiting irresponsible and abusive behaviors through the years. He is deceased, having died of complications from cirrhosis of the liver.

Matthew's father, currently age 66, is an alcoholic, uneducated, and abusive. My son did not know his father until he attempted residence with him after leaving Japan in 1989. Matthew was physically and emotionally abused by his father and was removed from his residence. His father could never maintain employment beyond one to three years at any interval and has made it emphatically clear that he is completely disinterested, uninvolved, and estranged from Matthew.

PATIENT'S MOTHER
Mother is university educated and employed as a practice manager/senior managing paralegal in personal injury law.

During pregnancy, the mother consumed no cigarettes, OTC, prescription or illicit drugs, or alcohol. The father was, however, violent with the mother during the pregnancy.

The mother left the father when Matthew was six months old.

The mother lives with a diagnosis of C-PTSD, determined as reacting to stress with depression because of the son's misfortune/misbehaviors, with historical evidence of the same from early childhood. Psychological counseling has been consistent with the same physician for over 18 years and is determined to have assisted. The recent assaults by her son amplified her PTSD condition, but she continues to work effectively in a high-level, professional capacity.

Following an "all of which is respectfully submitted" sign-off, and no less than six additional conferences with medical personnel, lawyers, and institutional management, the darker side of advocacy was, once again, a success. This was invariably "subject to change, without notice, of course.

Matthew was transferred by ambulance and committed to Hillside Psychiatric Hospital in Kamloops, BC.

And, my thoughts return to questions posed to me in therapy through the years. "Describe what you feel when you see mountains and forests for miles." I realize the psychologist was seeking an answer reflecting peace and tranquility, or freedom... but we learn in law, every quickly, that we never ask questions in a courtroom or during "Discovery" to which we are less than confident of the response.

My response was that I see treachery. My mind goes to being alone there and wondering how I will strategize survival and an escape to safety. I see dark advocacy.

Three steps forward, ten steps back. Dark advocacy was the warranted response to Matthew's dark psychosis and a medical system still navigating how to deal with brain injury and mental health components, but the "shades of grey" and unfortunate treatment decisions that flowed from the next institutionalization simply exposed yet another angle from which to assess a complicated psyche.

PARADOXICAL REACTION

For those unfamiliar with standard treatments for agitation and anxiety, the "traditional" first treatment response is to administer a benzodiazepine pharmaceutical. These drugs are commonly known as "tranquilizers," with popularity falling predominantly with Ativan (Lorazepam) and Valium (Diazepam) in a clinical setting.

Some physicians, in a non-clinical setting, suggest or prescribe cannabis. Case in point, Matthew's pre-morbid addictions included alcohol and cocaine — but never cannabis. He did not avail himself of marijuana products until 2002, months after his TBI. His then family physician prescribed cannabis for him but retracted the prescription a week later when behavioral issues surfaced in Matthew. Twenty years ago, the risks of psychosis in brain injury survivors were neither discussed nor readily recognized. This effect certainly became apparent in Matthew in short order. Of course, once an addict has tasted the waters, an addiction response is triggered. For Matthew, marijuana joined the ranks of "primary behavioral triggers," along with cigarettes.

Matthew's first two violent offenses perpetrated against me were triggered by cigarettes, marijuana, and alcohol.

But the safety of a clinical setting is often a paradox within itself. Matthew, himself, called the scenario an "oxymoron," when reflecting on his 18 months of incarceration at Colony Farms. Having been hopeful for psychiatric treatment and progress in the care of Hillside Psychiatric, managing the unmanageable fell again to benzodiazepine drugs as a primary response to Matthew's escalating behaviors.

Now readily accepted in the medical and brain-injury communities, benzodiazepine treatment often results in paradoxical reactions in susceptible individuals causing an increase in anxiety, agitation, hallucinations at the onset of sleep, aggressiveness, hyperactivity, irritability, hyperactive behavior, amnesia, insomnia, and exacerbation of seizures in epileptics.

Marijuana has also since been determined to produce a paradoxical reaction in brain injury survivors, with an increase in seizure activity. Twenty years ago, the research and information were simply not available.

Another ten steps back...

So, what's the big deal with a few cigarette butt violations and some tranquilizers, you ask? How did things go so awry as to find Matthew in a Kamloops jail shortly after arriving at Hillside for therapeutic care and attention?

Hillside is a locked, guard- and video-monitored facility. Anxiety and fear provoked Matthew's smoking compulsion. Feeling threatened and entrapped, his behaviors intensified quickly into bullying, verbal threats, and physical violence. When isolation only worsened the behaviors, as punishment, they denied cigarettes. This merely resulted in Matthew observing and developing a plan of action to vacate the facility. He told me weeks later that he felt he had absolutely nothing to lose.

He learned that if he placed an object in the egress path of the doorway when other patients exited to smoke, he could exit via the doorway when guards were not observant. Frequently, he was detained and restrained for picking up cigarette butts in the courtyard. He was oblivious to the warnings of such contagion as tuberculosis or hepatitis, choosing risk over abstinence.

Eventually, Matthew was charged erroneously with sexual assault, and despite being no stranger to my son's expertise in conjecture, I believed him when he denied any such actions. I retained one of the best criminal lawyers in Kamloops, Matthew entered a plea of "not guilty," and the matter proceeded to Trial.

Trial witnesses disclosed Matthew had been administered significantly large dosages of both Ativan and injectable Valium. Expert testimony for the defense (Matthew) affirmed under oath that in cases of TBI, benzodiazepine drugs often triggered a classic "paradoxical reaction." In short, instead of achieving the desired level of "tranquilization," the pharmaceuticals induced aggressive or violent behavior with amnesia.

Being privy to this information led me to my next step in advocacy. It was highly likely that Matthew would see charges dropped at Trial, and would exit a Kamloops jail into a community with no safety net in place, incapable of providing shelter or meals for himself, and unable to access medication or other services easily. It was going to be critical that he return to my home while I pursued a resumption of his funding and a group home or residential care placement.

PARADOXICAL PLANNING

M atthew's legal counsel informed me that the test for permitting Matthew to return to the family home would be a "high bar" to overcome. I needed a plan, a schedule, a contingency plan, and more. So, I again used the written word (and the career in law that had become so necessary in response to my son's early criminal infractions) in advocacy for my son.

April 19, 2010

TO: XXX, Crown Counsel
AND TO: XX, Defence Counsel
Provincial Court of BC
Kamloops, BC

Dear Sirs/Mesdames:
RE: Matthew X, DOB XXX

I write to you with respect to the forthcoming Trial of the above-noted accused, scheduled to proceed on Monday, May 3 2010 in Kamloops Provincial Court.

I am Matthew X's mother and Committee of Person and of Estate. I have attached a true copy of the 2006 Order of Committeeship for your records.

Matthew suffered a traumatic brain injury 8.5 years ago (in downtown Vancouver) because of gang retribution — a savage & violent attack. He was in hospital and GF Strong Rehabilitation for seven (7) months. He has undergone comprehensive rehabilitation over the past 8.5 years and given the extent of his organic brain injury, he is exceedingly high functioning. As such, Matthew is a permanently disabled person and will have his PWD pension (approximately $860/month) reinstated when released. As his Committee, I will manage all funds on his behalf and will supplement other financial needs as required.

Once Matthew is released, I will have him return to live with me in the family home. I have gone to great expense and inconvenience to move to a rural area where he can easily access counseling services and, over time, integrate into the Sardis community.

I am ready, willing, and able to provide the proper support structure, safe & healthy residential environment, and continuing rehabilitation for my son. The following represents my preliminary systematic planning, organized on Matthew's behalf.

The Family Home: The family home where Matthew will live with me is a new condominium, located approximately a 10-minute drive from Cultus Lake. Matthew will have his own private bedroom, as the condo is a two-bedroom unit with a den. I have attached photos of the family home for your reference, as well as one photograph of Matthew as he presents himself when living with me (well-groomed, alert, etc), which is in contrast to his present appearance while held in KRCC.

I maintain an organized and clean family home, free of drugs and alcohol. My home is free of violence and discord. The home is safe, relaxed, and clean. My next-door neighbor, with whom I socialize occasionally, is an RCMP constable.

About Me: I am a personal injury paralegal and have worked in this capacity in British Columbia alone for 22 years. I have attached a copy of my *curriculum vitae* and verified income of $80K per annum. At no material time have I found myself unemployed. I have also provided six letters of reference.

I am stable, in good health (emotionally and physically), and fully aware of the risks inherent in accepting my injured son into the family home. I have availed myself over the past 8.5 years of continuing education regarding brain injury care and rehabilitation, behavior modification, physical rehabilitation, and more. I am also a personal trainer and competitive bodybuilder and was the individual responsible for having provided physical rehabilitation to Matthew immediately following his brain injury (coaching him on how to walk again and more).

I volunteer on a regular basis with a local Brain Injury Association and have spoken at brain injury conferences. I am familiar with many of the "players" in brain injury rehabilitation and maintain regular contact, both in advocacy for my son and as an integral component of my employment.

I am presently working in Surrey with a sole practitioner, and have almost concluded that employment contract. My final day at that job will be May 19, 2010. I will then have a six-week holiday, which I will spend with my son camping, fishing, attending church functions & activities, implementing an exercise program for him, and more. In July, I will work for a local Chilliwack law firm, which is a mere 10-minute drive from the family home.

The Plan: It is "common knowledge" that a great deal of carefully coordinated and implemented structure is required to achieve successful rehabilitation and community integration for an individual such as Matthew. I have collaborated with various experts, such as forensic psychologist Dr. H; the president of the local Brain Injury Association, Ms. P; Mr. S, formerly the head of brain injury funding and rehabilitation for ICBC; forensic psychiatrist Dr. H, a highly successful and qualified expert in residential care & community integration for male, forensic-based brain injury victims — Mr. S, and more) in my plan to have Matthew live with me and provide a structured program for his continuing rehabilitation and community integration.

I have arranged the following for Matthew, in anticipation of his returning to the family home:

- Once released from Kamloops Regional Correctional Centre ("KRCC"), I will drive him home (from Kamloops to Sardis). I will take the next two days off work to familiarize him with the family home, his general neighborhood, and the activities in which he will be involved on a structured basis. He will meet the life skills worker on his first day arriving in the family home, who will provide care to Matthew while I complete my existing employment contract. The first week spent together will be slow and simple.
- Their generalized activities will initially be as follows:

Monday—Walk with 2 dogs; out for coffee; make lunch together at home; drive to some destination for another walk

Tuesday—Attend with Probation Officer; out for coffee; walk with 2 dogs; make lunch together at home; train at the gym; out for coffee

Wednesday—Visit SPCA; volunteer for dog-walking; out for coffee; make lunch together at home; watch a movie at home

Thursday—Walk with 2 dogs; out for coffee; grocery shopping with a list; put groceries away at home; do laundry; out for coffee

Friday—Walk with two dogs; out for coffee; make lunch together at home; out for a movie; out for coffee

Then, for the last week of May and the full month of June 2010, I will take vacation time from work. I have enclosed a charted daily plan for his care and activities.

In July, when I begin a new paralegal contract in Chilliwack, the life skills worker will resume full-time supervision with Matthew.

<u>Contingency Plan in the Event of Decompensation</u>: Should Matthew decompensate again, there is also a plan in place for that contingency — in that Matthew would be accommodated with expedited admission to Chilliwack General Hospital's psychiatric ward, thereafter transferred to Hillside Psychiatric Centre in Kamloops for treatment. Matthew has been accepted into the BC Neuropsychiatric Program there and Hillside (and the BC Neuropsychiatric Program) maintains an "open-door policy" for his expedited return in the event of decompensation. He can avail himself of residential treatment there for up to two years. Before discharge, Hillside's social worker(s) would confer with Fraser Health Authority mental health workers, after which time he would be returned to Chilliwack General Hospital for pre-arranged community placement.

I have given significant consideration to what is the best course of planning for my son's continuing rehabilitation and community integration, and I have consulted with multiple professionals in the course of my planning to effect educated decision-making.

I have been in written and telephone communications with my son since he entered KRCC. He and I have spoken almost every day by telephone since his entry. Matthew and I have a close and healthy family relationship and I am his <u>only</u> family and advocate. His father lives in Windsor, Ontario, and has been estranged from his son for two decades. He is irresponsible and has been a longstanding abusive alcoholic.

I am confident that I can provide the best caregiving and community reintegration protocols for Matthew, and I am dedicated to his continuing advocacy and am pleased to answer any inquiries you may have in the circumstances. I can be contacted at either of the telephone numbers noted on this letterhead, or through my existing employment with XYZ Law Group, where the switchboard is open from 9 to 5, on weekdays.

Thank you for your professional consideration in this matter that will shape the course of the future for Matthew.

Yours truly,
Sarah Martin

———⊲⋈⊳———

The sexual assault charge details? I never knew the full extent until the Trial proceedings were underway. Testimony from more than one Hillside staff affirmed Matthew had been seated in the facility's cafeteria when a female patient came to his location, bent down, and whispered something in his ear. When she bent down, Matthew placed his right hand on her left shoulder; when she brought her head up to leave, his hand slipped from her shoulder down her chest and across her left breast. Testimony confirmed it was an involuntary movement, and not one intended as a sexual affront.

The chief psychiatrist from the facility left the courtroom before being called to testify. All charges were stayed and Matthew was released to my care, again. The day before Trial commencement, the same psychiatrist reminded me of the two-year "open door policy" for further treatment at the facility, however — once charges were dismissed, I was advised that Matthew was no longer welcome there and would not be granted an opportunity for further treatment in the future.

Oh, how the paradoxical reactions abound.

HOME AGAIN

I was grateful to converse with Matt during a courtroom break. His anxiety levels were, understandably, "off the charts" and he had been particularly upset to see some of the Hillside staff in the courtroom, though grateful some of them testified truthfully.

His ability to focus was questionable, noting the incessant leg-shaking and restlessness with his hands and eyes. I needed him to understand what was about to happen, hoping to put him more "at peace" and that all was going to be fine.

I told him, "Once your Trial finishes, the Kamloops jail will release you. I will drive you home." After that, the plan is that:
- I will re-establish your PWD pension
- I will rent a furnished suite for you in Sardis (that's Chilliwack, just the good side, which is near me)
- I will supervise your finances and your medication intake twice a day and will ensure you always have your medication prescriptions filled on time
- I will ensure you always have cigarettes, within the agreed-upon smoking of ten cigarettes per day
- I will take you grocery shopping
- I will take you to attend a probation office until you learn to travel there on your own.

MONDAY MAY 3, 2010
Matthew was fully acquitted at Trial. We retrieved all personal effects & medication from the Kamloops Regional Correctional Centre ("KRCC") before exiting the city.

We navigated the Coquihalla Highway (BC's own *Highway to Hell*) back to the Lower Mainland and encountered severe blizzard conditions. It was a slow and treacherous journey home. We witnessed at least eight motor vehicle accidents (two quite major) but arrived home safely.

Matthew and I shared some incredible bonding conversations the entire drive home. He was elated and grateful for his freedom again.

He loved the condo and the area. "Buddy, what are you MOST happy about?" I asked.

"Mom, I can smoke now and have a bath — and eat cereal whenever I want to. Oh! Is that okay if I have some cereal? I sure missed it."

We had some concerns about the status of the pre-existing Court Order and that had him worried, as it mandates an original address for residence. Matthew obsessively kept reading the Order and began leg-shaking and crying. I told him everything would be fine and let him smoke at will. I called Craig, his lawyer, and also the lawyer for whom I worked. Craig was prepared to bring an application within days to vary the Order. We were told not to worry.

Matthew smoked nearly a full pack of cigarettes after leaving KRCC and before going to bed at home in Chilliwack. I am only providing gentle reminders of his smoking frequency, hoping to wind down the quantity smoked over a few days.

His behavior has been impeccable. He is very grateful to be home — to be free, but visibly nervous about making any mistakes. I have been trying to convince him to relax, reminding him he is home. He is safe, and I love him unconditionally and am here for him.

He went to bed at 11 PM and slept through the night, up at 5 AM on Tuesday morning.

TUESDAY MAY 4, 2010
Mattie already had his bath, clothes on and coffee made when I awoke around 5:30. He was in noble spirits — motivated, thrilled to be free, and wanting to start his day! It concerned me, slightly, that I had heard none of his movements in the apartment.

We attended with his probation officer. I telephoned the former Burnaby PO as well. It would seem that all is now fine with the Order (now stating to "reside as directed," as in directed to live at the family home). He has been told to report weekly to his Chilliwack probation officer.

The Burnaby PO wanted to refer him to the Forensic Outpatient Clinic in Surrey, but I advised that would place him at extremely high risk for decompensation. I elaborated on some history of funded caregivers violating protocol through his 8.5 years of TBI, taking him into the "taboo zone" of downtown Vancouver, where he sustained his brain injury and where there continued to be individuals who would recognize him. Each time this protocol was breached, Matthew suffered severe anxiety and some form of decompensation. I articulated that once my vacation time began (off work in two weeks), I would make every possible concerted effort to have him enter Chilliwack Mental Health for monitoring.

I also advised we would attend to secure a family physician (Dr. S) at the Clinic on Monday evening (Dr. S's next evening attendance there). We must ask permission to become a patient. I will request (1) prescriptions for Mattie, (2) referral for bloodwork for Mattie, and (3) referral for bloodwork for myself. Certainly, if I do not take care to maintain my personal health, it would be an injustice to my son.

We also attended with the Ministry and later picked up Mattie's cheque, grateful to have had no complications or delays.

We walked the Rotary Trail, alongside the Vedder River, for about 25 minutes; he loved the walk, although his balance was terrible. He did, however, giggle all the way, as he does when elated and relaxed. His legs were sore afterward, and he said he loved that, too. It occurred to us both that he had not been for an outdoor walk for over two years. Wow! What sad consequences for irresponsible behaviors due to brain injury!

He retired to bed at about 9:30 PM, extremely exhausted with a bit of a headache. Despite being in excellent spirits, positive, hopeful, and exceedingly happy, he continued to be fearful of making any mistakes all day but slightly improved over the course of Monday. We prayed before he slept.

FIRST, IT IS AN INTENTION.

THEN A BEHAVIOR.

THEN A HABIT.

THEN A PRACTICE.

THEN A SECOND NATURE.

THEN IT IS SIMPLY WHO YOU ARE.

OMINOUS INEVITABILITY

M attie told me he awoke around 3 AM, but moved himself to the living room, turned on the TV, and went back to sleep. I never heard him moving about. I recognize it as respect and appreciate it, and am saddened and concerned about his inability to sleep well. But I am also apprehensive that I slept through it all, given our history.

We had coffee & breakfast together and then reported to Probation in Chilliwack (took three minutes). I took him home. Carly, his life skills worker, arrived and promised to call me if there were any concerns or issues. I went to work.

Mattie and I spoke by phone my entire drive home from Surrey to Chilliwack (perhaps a one-hour drive). On arrival, he met me outside and we ventured out for sushi. He was excited to tell me about his wonderful day, although he smoked too much. Oh well; we'll work on that later. He spent most of the day with Carly at her place and had a blast. They ordered pizza!

Mattie went to sleep around 10 PM, exhausted & with a headache. We prayed before he slept.

MAY 6, 2010
Mattie awoke around 5 AM. When I arose around 5:30, he'd already had his bath, made coffee & had a couple of smokes. I never heard a thing; again, this gives me some angst, though I admire his motivation, organization, and respect. He was particularly tired, however. I went to work; he went back to sleep. Carly took him out from 11 to 5. He was great with Carly, though he over-smoked again. He asked her for cigarettes. Yikes.

They went to the mall, visited the SPCA, walked the Rotary Trail, and met her parents and the parents of her friend. All great.

He had a terrible headache and showed signs of exhaustion (I gave him two aspirin). We both retired to bed at 8:45 and prayed before he slept. He seemed exhausted but thrilled.

MAY 7, 2010

Mattie was still asleep when I arose at 5:30! He had slept through the night. He had no headache on arising and presented as very perky! When I went to work, he went back to sleep — and called me when he awoke (around 9:30). He had his bath, made his bed, and washed his coffee cup (without prompting).

He's excited about his outing to Hope, BC today, with Carly. It's the area where *First Blood* was filmed and bears a significant history from the days of the Gold Rush, and more. Allegedly, there have been Sasquatch sightings in Hope, as well.

All things considered, Matthew is doing remarkably well, although I recognize we are in another "honeymoon" period. He is testing boundaries, both with me, in the home, and with Carly. But I want to focus on the positives. As for cigarettes, we simply play that by ear for now, with no zealous restrictions, just gentle guidance to his own adult awareness and logic. There will come a time when we will direct to more self-discipline in a week or two, but it is important to effect that gradually and cautiously.

JUNE 2010

Matthew had one incident of what I will call "sleepwalking". I awoke one morning (6 AM) to discover that the bag with bottles of medication had been removed from the fridge, and his sedation medication (Zopiclone) bottle removed. That bottle was left open with its cap off. It would seem that perhaps one or two of the tablets were missing, but I cannot be certain. Is he taking this to get high? Is he taking this because he wants to sleep without nightmares? No matter what, it constitutes wrongful drug abuse and needs to be carefully monitored. Zopiclone, though not a benzodiazepine, reacts in the brain similarly to a benzodiazepine. It would seem that he was not attempting to sneak medication; rather, it would appear that he is so preoccupied with needing or wanting to sleep soundly through the night that his subconscious mind has him sleep-walking to medicate. From that day forward, all medication was locked and hidden, and no longer stored in the fridge. From that day forward, I also stored my personal medications in a coat pocket in the back of my closet.

JULY 2010

We had a couple of incidents over Matthew soliciting cigarettes and being unduly friendly with a woman who lives next door at the condominium complex. We are on the ground floor and there is an open-concept patio, making for easy access to all resident entries and patio walkways. He was told she would not give him a cigarette, and when she accepted a telephone call and turned her back – she turned to see him stealing a cigarette from her pack (which had been left by her on her balcony).

When I arrived home from work that day, Matt told me that the woman had accused him of stealing cigarettes. I broached the subject with her, and she was polite but defensive. She told me that Matt had been there on more than one occasion and described the theft incident. Matt called her a liar, and I sent him home. The woman is a Royal Canadian Mounted Police member and teaches firearms training at the gun range nearby.

This presented as a déjà vu for me from Matt's historical past, adept at conning me into believing his pattern of pathological lies and then intimidating the wronged party to make them walk away. This behavior of skilled manipulation, entitlement, and demand for immediate gratification at the expense, intimidation, and inconvenience of others is disconcerting. I realize that trouble lives just under the surface with my son, and I need to be alert and wary.

Environmental Changes

Matt lost his motivation to attend the nearby recreation center and walk the Rotary Trail. He stopped at the same time a chap named Rob (from the church and gym) ceased contact. Rob had been involved in Matt's life for almost a full month, with daily contact of some capacity. Matt seemed to adore and respect Rob and said he valued his time.

When Rob abruptly halted all contact, Matt was devastated; he cried often. The rejection affected Matt adversely. He told me he *thought* he had a good friend in Rob, but again, someone else has walked away and left him stranded. After all this, Matt did not want to return to the recreation center, his reasons stated being (1) it was too hot there and he could only stand to work out in the very early mornings, and (2) he did not want to see Rob, as Rob had hurt his feelings deeply.

I had asked myself, however, is there more to this than "meets the eye"? Is there something that Rob and others are not disclosing to ME? If so, it would be part of a recurring "MO" with Matt's honeymoon period and resorting to problematic behaviors.

Traditionally/historically, IF I find out, it is long after the situation has transpired and in a timeframe too late to do anything to remedy or correct it, with Matt or with others in the community. It is an exhausting premise that leaves me in the "shamed parent" category in every community we've ever lived.

AUGUST 31, 2010

There was another incident of alleged sleepwalking, at which time it was suspected that Matthew smoked two cigarettes in the wee hours of the morning. The empty cigarette pack was tossed onto the deck floor (this is something he has never done). The cigarette pack had been stored in a drawer inside the kitchen desk. I question myself if the incidents of "sleepwalking" were ever truly that? Rather, I suspect that Matt purposefully arises in the night to snoop, to smoke. Now, I wonder if he exits the family home? Certainly, if he smoked on the patio and left an empty pack of cigarettes on the deck, it is unlikely to be "sleepwalking". I want to give him the benefit of the doubt, but I think I do that too often. I understand *why* I do — as I was falsely accused of so much as a child and despite having truth when I denied many accusations; they did not believe me. That has carried through to my adult life and decision-making with my son. I am uneasy with this realization, for my own shortcomings, and for the risk of having Matthew running feral in my peaceful little neighborhood.

SEPTEMBER 6, 2010

When I had to discharge Carly of her services with Matt, I scrambled to locate a more-experienced life skills worker. Carly had exhibited some inappropriate interaction with Matthew, giving him extra cigarettes in contraindication of our written protocol and planning, and worse — smoking marijuana with him. He had also told me they held hands in public! Oh my.

I sought out and hired another life-skills worker for Matthew -- a lovely gentleman named John. What an absolute blessing this gentleman has been. He presents SUCH a profoundly excellent example for Matt (calm; no profanity; patient; kind; intelligent, good sense of humor). Although I have had to pay this expense personally (as the Acquired Brain Injury Program has denied Matt any consideration of funding or caregiving assistance since I removed him from institutionalization, despite documented evidence from professionals confirming he has been consistently non-violent, non-aggressive, and cognitively improved), it has been worth every financial sacrifice to have John on board.

SEPTEMBER 7, 2010

Matt was up at 6:30 AM and asked me if he was "off". I could not see it, but I told him that if he FELT he was "off", then perhaps there was some reason for it. He insisted he had slept well. Important to note is that, historically, when decompensation was foreshadowed with off-moments and changing behavior patterns, Matt was aware. Many times, he felt it and mentioned it often before I noticed it.

We had coffee together and after walking me to the door when I left for work; he told me he was going to return to bed. That was his "usual."

He phoned me at 7:30 AM, stating he could not sleep and was getting up and ready to go. I reminded him his chore for the day was to do laundry & run the vacuum. He confirmed he had not forgotten.

At or about 3 PM (when John D had left for the day), Matt phoned. He had been quite diligent with his check-in phone call protocols, and I was hopeful we were on the right track again and that I was not observing another episode of his expert manipulation and covert tactics.

I asked if he had run the vacuum, and he said yes. He added he would take a nap, as he was tired.

He phoned back about five minutes later, to say he had not exactly told the truth – that John had *offered* to run the vacuum for him. Matt did not do it himself.

I asked if he had done the laundry, and he said yes.

My instincts suggest to me that Matthew is dishonest. I will speak to John. This is apparently not the first instance of John running the vacuum; this is inappropriate. Matt has a longstanding history of manipulating others to do his assigned tasks for him, frequently feigning "I have a brain injury, and this is really hard for me", or "I am so tired, but I don't want to disappoint my mom."

When I arrived home from work, I found Matt's behavior and body language slightly "off". It was nothing serious, but simply not his usual positive and loving self. He could not recall what they had done or eaten during the day but remembered they went to Starbucks.

He told me he had talked with a man at Starbucks and was swearing with this man in public. He said he completely forgot that John was sitting at the table next to him and he felt embarrassed when he saw his worker sitting there and said, "I'm really sorry." Matt describes John's response as having said, "o-KAY" but in a tone that communicated it was unacceptable and there was likely nothing he (John) could do about it. I suspect that the man at Starbucks triggered Matthew into a moment of dissociation, taking him to another level of his past behaviors — to another personality response. I would be remiss if I said that I was not exceedingly concerned with this turn of events.

Matt had washed a load of laundry, but he had not removed the clothing from the dryer, folded it, or put it away.

Careful to remain gentle, but direct, I suggested to Matthew that "the Starbucks' response" was unacceptable and did not speak well of us, collectively, as a family. I told him I believed it represented something inside of him that showed he was still at risk of being drawn to trouble and inappropriate people. I used the example that I would *never* strike up a conversation with an individual openly spewing profanity in public.

If his improvements actually trigger a pattern of decompensation, I find myself with mixed emotions about his continuing improvements. There is such an insanely delicate balance necessary to monitor his behavior because of the brain injury. Does higher function lend itself to behavioral downturns? Will his desires for independence overrule logic?

I am feeling (again) that he may be on his way to instability, which could again present "Stranger Danger" for me, or individuals in the community. While I suspect there would be more warning indicators surfacing if decompensation was imminent, I cannot deny the reality of historical incidents. After all, I never predicted or imagined the two prior assaults could have occurred. I do have legitimate concerns for what I think I recognize as early warning signs and know I will need to be alert. I must be relentless in my observations and document them carefully.

I am grasping at straws here and sure wish I had some advice from a professional. For now, this is my plan:

Changes to Be Effected
1. Return to a structured & consistent exercise program, including the gym and regular walking.
2. Regular church attendance (we did not attend this past Sunday, because my budget did not permit me the luxury of gas for the trip to Agassiz).
3. Continued participation in the ABI Support Group on Thursday mornings.

SEPTEMBER 8, 2010
This morning, Matt arose at 6:30, gave me a hug, and went

for his morning half-smoke; I suggested he might want to take his medication before having his cigarette, and he complied. He returned and went straight to his room to sleep again. He did not say goodbye to me, nor did he wish me a good day. This is undeniably a continuing "off-baseline" behavior pattern. If Matt were an adolescent or teen, the behavior would be of no concern. But he is a brain-injured adult with some serious underlying propensities to be monitored, and with a history that cannot be discounted. I will have to listen closely to his voice patterns when I speak with him later in the day.

He phoned me at 8:20 AM from his bath; he was groggy, and thus "off" in this capacity. I could not assess with confidence whether there were behavioral changes in his voice. I am actually wondering whether he secured marijuana again. After all, I do not know if he has been slipping out at night while I sleep — and wandering the patios and yards of neighbors. His response in the past, when he has side-stepped with cannabis use, was what I am witnessing now... lots of sleep, slurred speech, not saying goodbye, failing to say I love you, being dishonest, and more.

Still trying to encourage independence and responsibility in gentle increments, I mentioned he should walk his dog to Sardis Park after the bath, and he seemed to think that was a good idea. I reminded him NOT to stop and chat with neighbors; just to mind his business, walk his dog and return home. I reminded him that John D would arrive at 1 PM today.

I also reminded him we had agreed that there would be no trips to Starbucks for one week and that we would discuss that matter further next Tuesday. There had to be some sort of consequences for Matt's inappropriate behaviors in public. I had asked Matthew, after the Starbucks' transgression, what *he* would do if he had a child who had done the same thing. Without hesitation, he said, "I would tell him no coffee at Starbucks for a week." Matthew's decision was implemented. John D was aware.

I had a discussion this evening with Mattie. I printed him a copy of something I had found on Facebook. There was no artist or designer attributed to it. We read it together and talked about what it meant afterward.

"Mom, this is great. It's so true, though it's stuff I never thought about. It's really scary if you only read the first one and the last one — "First it's an intention... Then it is simply who you are.""

I commended him and told him we have to think about our intentions before we do something. He interjected, "Mom, I guess it doesn't matter what I meant to do, it only matters what I *did*. I think you've told me that before."

I gave him a personal example, adding that when I am angry and want to snap off a rude email in response, I first ask myself, "What do I hope to accomplish with this?"

"Good idea, Mom. That can save you from embarrassment. I don't email anyone but you, but if I thought about what I was going to say before I said it to you, it could save ME a lot of trouble. But I don't plan most things – they just spit out of my mouth because my brain is on pause or in high gear, with nothing in between. I constantly embarrass myself."

I then guided him to look at this from a POSITIVE perspective.
"What do you mean? Positive? I don't get it?"

I suggested he think of it from a fitness perspective – walking, weight training, saying no to sweets, eating cleaner foods, making better choices – going for the calorie burn, and not being lazy or procrastinating. I asked him to read the little poster again.

"Wow, Mom — you always say there are two sides to every coin. Thank you for teaching me and for knowing I can still learn. I love you, Mom. Thanks for never giving up on me." And he added, "Thank you for letting me live with you again, Mom. Don't give up on me yet, K?"

SEPTEMBER 9, 2010

Today went well, without incident. On such days, I find myself almost holding my breath, waiting for the next issue to drop. I live life in a perpetual state of being prepared for anything — or so I think. It's better described as a state of ominous inevitability.

When attending the ABI Support Group in the morning, however, Matt was quite emotional — crying loudly (sobbing) on two occasions, because of extreme feelings of the empathy expressed by Esther and other survivors (in their communications of understanding many of the symptoms he had faced through the course of his own brain injury; he was so relieved to hear that others experienced many of the same things, and he became very emotional). He has largely felt he could not discuss his issues, because "Nobody likes a complain-freak", but I keep stressing to him the importance of communicating — because *some* challenges can be overcome, and others need to be acknowledged and strategized to find another way. "That way, everyone (especially you) can work around the issues and find a way that works for YOU."

He told me he felt trapped inside his body. "Mom, my brain is constantly on pause. I know stuff, but like you say sometimes, 'I can't access that information.' It's right there, I *know* it's there, but I can't reach it. And if my brain is not on pause, it is working overtime."

I told him that might be called "racing thoughts." "Exactly! My thoughts are either doing nothing or they are racing like they're gettin' paid for it. And I always feel I have this 'silent scream' inside me. But, hey, don't worry; I don't scream. I just handle it. But it's there, Mom. It's really there, and I hate it."

"Do you feel that 'silent scream' when you are happy? Like when you are having sushi, petting dogs and cats, watching a comedy at the movie theatre?"

He thought for a second and admitted, "No, but that good stuff can't last forever. I have to return to my head and what's in it or NOT in it, and it makes me crazy. It makes me cry a lot, but I don't want to keep being a pussy. My PO told me I have to man up. I am a man, you know — even if everybody calls me a man-child. That makes me feel like I am retarded."

"Buddy, not a good word to use."

"Yeah, I know. The truth hurts."

And my heart sank again. He lives in a state of ominous inevitability, too.

MISSING IN ACTION

Today is September 10, 2010. When I awoke at 6 AM, I noted Matt had already smoked a full cigarette (he was sleeping in his room, door closed).

He arose at 6:30 and I asked what was up, and he said he had a smoke at 5 AM. I carefully asked, "Why, buddy? I thought we had an agreement that you would not smoke before 6 AM?"

"I had a nightmare."

This marks the first nightmare he has had since returning home from institutionalization.

I asked what he dreamed, and he did not want to tell me. I told him it was important, so I could monitor him and help him, and he said he dreamt he had killed his father with a knife. He added, "That really upset me. I mean, I hate the man; but I should not be wanting to kill him. I hate my murderous thoughts."

I noted he had slept with his fan off (no white noise). He said he had been cold (understandable, but I could not help but wonder if he had turned off the fan, which typically helps him sleep soundly so that he could get up, sneak around or out, and readily hear whether I was up and awake inside the home).

There were multiple sirens at or about 5 or 5:30 AM this morning, and I also awakened with a nightmare (likely triggered subconsciously by the sirens in the seconds before waking fully). My nightmare involved Matthew frightening someone's child and, in the dream, they were seeking to have him arrested; I felt helpless to assist him in my dream but also was concerned & afraid of his psychiatric condition. Wow, even my subconscious mind is on high alert. I suppose it should be.

The early morning sirens may explain Matt's nightmares, but coupled with the recent behavior fluctuations, I must be careful to monitor this closely. I could be over-reacting because of my apprehension, but believe there are some changes occurring with him. At the moment, I have concerns, but I don't want to overreact. I will remain vigilant and continue to document all events.

Matthew could not get back to sleep after I left for work; he phoned me at 7:25 AM (I was driving to work) to let me know. Note to self: this is another recurring pattern, for whatever reason. I wonder if he is feigning a need to sleep, simply to distract from his true motives and intentions?

I phoned him when I arrived at work, and (again) I sensed something different in his voice, though not readily identifiable; he is "slightly off." I feel his niceties are fabricated and forced. My first impression is that this is an educated, feigned, and mimicked behavioral response. But, I am also concerned that I am merely over-reacting out of my anxiety. The last thing I want to do is unjustly "jump to conclusions" and cause Matthew more harm.

At or about 10:20 AM, I phoned to check my voice-mail messages (I had my cell phone off as I was very busy in the office, and both lawyers for whom I work are in this morning). I told Matthew earlier I would check my messages regularly and would check back in with him.

He had left a voice-mail message saying he was taking his dog to the dog park and that he would be back by the time John D arrived (which Matt knows to be 12 noon).

I have called about 20x since 10:45 AM. It is presently 11:55 AM and Matt is still not answering. I also cannot reach John D to warn him that Matthew may be "missing."

Given Matt's recent behavior changes, and now the nightmare of last night, I am extremely concerned that he is showing signs of deterioration. I am now considering whether I wish to continue with his residence in the family home at this point. I have not felt comfortable or safe when sleeping, and I have been blocking my door with a vase and multiple pillows every night. Over the last five months, I have not had a good night's sleep.

Now 12:17 PM, Matthew is still missing. John D phoned me at 12:10 asking where Matt might be, and I filled him in. John agreed to walk to Sardis Park to see if he could locate Matthew; he told me the Starbucks incident only lasted about two minutes this week, but Matt's reaction to being denied an outing to go for coffee on Wednesday was more serious. John said he was disturbingly determined to go for coffee, but John told him I had given instructions saying it was not to happen.

I had left a voice-mail message requesting an urgent return telephone call from Chilliwack Community Corrections at 12:15. I need to know what the procedure will be if Matt has gone AWOL.

Sadly, John D resigned, apologizing profusely but adding he did not feel he could guide Matthew, and frankly, after seeing the stark contrast in his behavior in Starbucks and his rage for being denied the opportunity to attend for daily coffee, he was afraid of Matt. He wished me luck and told me to be safe.

Matt had reported to his probation officer and advised, "I'm not fucking going home. I am a grown man and I don't want to be a dog on my mother's leash. If I want to smoke, I want to smoke. If I want to have coffee at Starbucks, I want my coffee, and I am going to smoke weed if I want to smoke weed." This was the same probation officer who shared a joint with him previously, so the behavioral regression now made sense. I asked the PO to secure my apartment keys, as I could not have Matthew return to the family home now. He said he would do his best, adding he arranged a bed for Matt at the Salvation Army homeless shelter in Chilliwack. Matthew had to arrive by a certain time and had to exit the facility early morning. He would roam the streets by day.

Matthew telephoned me around 7 PM; it was already dark outside. He spoke in an altered voice, and I realized he had dissociated. "Come meet me at the homeless shelter and I will give you your fucking keys, but I want my fucking meds. Do you hear me? I want my fucking meds *now*."

After driving to meet him, on arrival he threw the keys at my car and threatened to hurt me if I didn't hand over his meds "right now." I handed the medication blister packs to him through the lowered window of my car, afraid to exit, and he ripped them from my hand and stormed away, shouting, "The picture of me you created in your mind is not my responsibility! Fuck you, bitch; fuck you very much, you fucking cunt!"

I don't know whether I was more stunned or brokenhearted. The mask had slipped again, and I was revisiting a personality with whom I was horrified.

THREE STEPS FORWARD, THREE STEPS BACK

M atthew spent a week homeless on the streets of Chilliwack, still reporting to his probation officer and arriving in time for entry to the Salvation Army Homeless Shelter each night. His PO convinced me to give Matthew another chance in the family home, and Matt signed an agreement clarifying the simple, still unchanging rules of the home. No drugs, no alcohol, no visitors, wash your dishes and put them away after each meal, and follow the law.

He has returned to train with me at the gym, and we take regular walks together. I hired another life skills worker to supervise him and keep him occupied through the day, and that seems to have gone well enough. I continue to keep medications and cigarettes locked away.

NOVEMBER 6, 2010
Today is Matt's 32nd birthday! We have already had our usual coffee together at 6 AM and spent that time reminiscing the day he was born. We spoke of how we have *wanted* to spend his birthday together over the past several years but lost those opportunities because of his institutionalization. Case in point, he was in a mental hospital this time last year. We both remarked on how much progress had transpired in a year.

It has already been a day for being grateful for his birth, & the testament to the progress he has achieved — in transforming into a far better individual than he was before his brain injury and toward becoming the person he is endeavoring to be. He's back to bed for more sleep (as he does, every day, brain injury requires consistent, regular sleep for repair) but we will begin the day again when he wakes up again!

NOVEMBER 11, 2010: Remembrance Day

When Matthew is stable, he is happy every day of his life. It's apparent in the hundreds of photographs taken over the years.

This photo, however, makes my heart sink. It is a clear indicator of the shifting of his right eye. We should have the results of the CT scan by December 6, 2010. TBI: three steps forward, two steps back. It is my belief that cannabis resulted in more seizure activity for him, and his eye has shifted because of that. This is only my educated speculation, however. I felt that when I mention cannabis in the same context as seizures and decompensation, health care providers are refraining from rolling their eyes. I have witnessed firsthand, however, the disconcerting effects of his cannabis use.

NOVEMBER 16, 2010

Today marks the nine-year anniversary of Matthew's brain surgery. He doesn't seem to associate the date with significance. I'm grateful for that. I hold significance for so many dates, and for events and people whom I would rather not really remember. It haunts me. I am grateful that with so many other maladies and confusion conflicts, this is one that does not plague my son.

Matt had a successful day today, with no hugging and less childish mannerisms in his voice. He's accepting redirection well and is again putting forth serious efforts to bring himself to a behavioral level closer to his chronological age. So long as he continues trying consistently, I can continue with my own efforts on his behalf.

I cannot deny, however, that this has been a hard road. I keep thinking "I'm too old for this," and then the paradox of my resentment for that woman from the funding agency telling me that at 46, I was an aging parent. Ahhh, we all eventually come to understand the expert assessments of the ones with the money. "Follow the money" takes on an entirely different perspective!

NOVEMBER 17, 2010

My Facebook check-in today stated, "Well, it was another productive day for Matt... and a very tiring one for me. But, work is good and I'm thankful every day that I love what I do. It is a pleasant break from being a primary caregiver and advocate, 24-7. And after a good day's work, I look forward to coming home to the only family I have."

DECEMBER 5, 2010

Well, today is my birthday. Matt saved his hard-earned pennies and bought me a John Legend CD! I don't really care for John Legend's music, and I would never disclose that to my boy, but Matt loves the artist — so I will cherish the CD!

He also made me a birthday card, expressing his love and thanking me again for his freedom. It was the most pleasant birthday I've had in years since Matthew was distanced from me for the last four consecutive birthdays because of institutionalization. I realized he had spent more of his adult life institutionalized than free.

He told me not to worry about getting older, adding "Birthdays are good for us — the more we have, the longer we live!" I note that his memory continues to function best with idioms and rhyming, as it did when he first came home to my care from GF Strong Rehabilitation in 2002.

I've been experiencing some health concerns again, with symptoms surfacing for a while now, and have some significant breathing issues, which are worsening. The doctor will give me a report in two weeks. Poor Matt is so terrified; I try to make light of everything for his sake — but it is disconcerting.

Matt found a photo taken in November in his jacket pocket and gave it to me (sporting his heavier-than-normal "Movember" mustache). He's posing with his friend "Thom" from the Drop-In Centre.

I cannot help but note that his "friend" Thom seems very uncomfortable. I think this is a man that Matt often pressured for cigarettes and weed. It was more common than not for Matt to pose in photos with individuals exhibiting this type of expression. Mattie was endearing; Matt was a precarious approach on the best of days.

DECEMBER 18, 2010
FINALLY got the results (today) of Matt's CT scan of November 13th. There are no significant changes from last year's CT. Unfortunately, however, this doesn't give us any insight into why his right eye has shifted. His eye continues to be off-centered and his double vision is worse than it was two months ago.

His TMJ injury continues to present issues, though he does not complain about this either. He only mentions it when he frequently says, "I'm sorry about my jaw clicking." In public, he is very embarrassed by it. The appearance of the shifted eye particularly humiliated him. I think his perception of it is far worse than the reality, but that's what we do to ourselves, isn't it? We always see it as worse than it is. He will not venture into the community most days without dark sunglasses in place.

DECEMBER 24, 2010
Well, we had to begin our Christmas Eve with a lecture in the family home. Lessons for children never stop, no matter the age. But, not wanting to focus on the negative over time, Matt and I are also reminiscing about what 2010 has brought for us as a family. We've decided that 2010 was a year of FREEDOM, for Matt and for me.

It is nice to have four consecutive days off work now. After our Christmas Eve brunch, we will take a country drive. That always reminds us of why we live here, because of the beautiful, rugged, mountain-filled terrain and the peace that nature brings. After dark, this evening we will take a drive to view Christmas decorations.

Matt has progressed to a level of semi-independence this year and has proven his ability to live responsibly in the family home — out of institutionalization. We measure brain injury recovery one day at a time, but he's had nine months of (hard-fought) success. I pray this can continue for him, as he is a good man, at his core, with a very kind heart; when he is stable and devoid of cannabis use, he is endearing, compassionate, and funny.

JANUARY 1, 2011
And, we begin another new year! Matt and I have reminisced and stated our gratitudes for 2010, agreeing that we both saw 2010 as a year of freedom for both of us: freedom from institutionalization & the prison of inappropriate meds for him, and freedom from bad employment for me — now being blessed with a job I can hopefully enjoy to retirement. Certainly, I have never been so fortunate to work with such a brilliant lawyer as I do now. 2010 was a hard year, but a significant year in the end.
Our New Year Resolutions for 2011:
— Collectively (both of us): lose weight; eat clean; live life with more balance
— Matt: become more independent & age-appropriate
— Me: tone down my Type A personality and learn to work fewer hours; to achieve a balance in my life and to be more "mindful of the moment."

JANUARY 4, 2011
Matt has taken a turn for the worse... He left the family home again today. I think he is in limbo between brain injury and wanting to be a grown man and having marijuana regularly. I have taught him everything he needs to know to live on his own, so hopefully, he can survive this. It is painful to let a child leave the nest a second time... but alas, I must let the eagle fly and hope he can thrive.
Despite the anxiety and concern over Matt, I am trying to focus on the positive. I have been busy with the new job, but it is absolutely wonderful. It is so nice to work for a lawyer that expresses their appreciation for the effort and quality work product delivered. I

have known little of that throughout my career. It is also incredibly rewarding to work with a lawyer who is at the top of their game, confident and quick-witted! This gentleman is assuredly *the* most intelligent individual I have met in my lifetime. I'm very blessed to work with him.

JANUARY 6, 2011

They committed Matt under the *Mental Health Ac*t this evening. He's in terrible condition, and a medical team will begin with a medication review and then undertake neurological studies. Because his eye shifted some five weeks ago, there could be some neurological changes, which is not good news. My suspicions were accurate: cannabis *does* trigger seizures in many brain injury and stroke survivors.

At any rate, he's safe, and the community is, too. He had unfortunately become quite dangerous in his confused, psychotic state. RCMP intervened, but no charges were laid. The irony is not lost on me; this is a scenario where the public would be enraged with no charges pursued and no arrest mandated, but it was a morbid blessing for him to have still another "chance."

Matthew proceeded peacefully to Chilliwack General Hospital, where he was transferred by ambulance to Abbotsford Regional Hospital — as they have a more extensive psychiatric department there. I was told I would receive a call once visitation was permitted. But I read the triage notes from the nurse for a dose of enlightenment.

"We just want to make sure your Mom is safe."
"Don't you worry about my Mom, she's tough as nails. She can take a punch, too."

How confusing and horrific this must be for him. If this is half as debilitating for him as it is for me, it is catastrophic.

WHAT IF?

Matthew spent six days and nights in the psychiatric ward of Abbotsford Regional Hospital. I visited him daily. There was no humor, no laughter, no endearment, and almost no conversation — but he seemed grateful for my visits, for the snacks, coffee, and cigarettes I brought him.

Sadly, they unilaterally released Matt from Abbotsford Regional Hospital yesterday. I am shocked that they did not phone me — knowing the seriousness of his TBI and the resulting disability residuals, aware that I am his Committee of person and estate, and knowing I had visited him every day he was there. They gave Matt a bus ticket and the address for the homeless shelter in Abbotsford.

I am stunned. He didn't even know where he was when he phoned me. "Mom, they gave me this paper for some address in Abbotsford — I guess I am in fucking Abbotsford? I thought I was in Chilliwack. Will you come to get me the fuck out of here? I'm sorry to ask you, but I don't know where in the fuck I am, Mom."

So, for now, he is in the Abbotsford Salvation Army Homeless S helter... I am trying to find him proper accommodation, as he has no other place to go. I cannot permit him to return home, as his mood continues to be one of disrespect – clear from the tone of voice and the profuse profanity. I perceive him to be out of control. And if I allow him home again, there will be no opportunity to resume funding and placement for him. No good deed goes unpunished.

JANUARY 13, 2011
They returned Matt to a Chilliwack shelter, as Abbotsford has a significant drug & alcohol problem & they thought it to be far too much of a risk for Matt. If he can remain stable on the streets until Tuesday, he has a long-awaited psychiatric assessment scheduled. He can then go into specialized housing with 24-7 supervision, funded by Mental Health and the Acquired Brain Injury Program. One hour at a time, I continue to have hope for my son. This time, however, it's not making me see what I want to see.

JANUARY 17, 2011

Matt has stabilized again, though he is still a resident at the homeless shelter by night. He spent the entire day with me on Saturday and again on Sunday, and it went well. Each night, I spend a couple of hours with him & give him dinner, then return him to the Shelter. He has a psych assessment tomorrow.

But, I ask myself — has he actually *stabilized*, or is he realizing that manipulation and impulsive behaviors are getting him nowhere? Am I witnessing kindness and feigned stability as manipulation right now? If that is the case, then what I am observing represents 'strategized discipline from Matt, which would reflect a far higher cognitive response than anyone else acknowledges, making him very dangerous.

JANUARY 29, 2011

Matt still has no assisted living placement and is simply taking one day at a time stability-wise. He's teetering on a precarious edge. He has needed psychiatric commitment for over 30 days now; it is shocking to see hospitals just release brain injury victims to the street. I suppose there is also the possibility that the triage staff considers him to be just another problem adult with no interest in improving or accepting help. They treat him as an addict, rather than a brain injury survivor. Ten years of TBI crisis, victory, and more crisis — and the medical system continues to operate in a void where TBI is concerned. I realize I am torn as a loving parent, and that hope makes me see what I want to see, but I also cannot dishonor my commitment to him from birth.

WHAT IF I am "the one" that stands between him and folly leading to premature death? WHAT IF I am the missing link in his progression to leading a peaceful and content life? I face a sticky predicament in that spider's web, navigating my path to become a reluctant hero and hoping that the rescue doesn't bring me down into the vortex. We are all hostages to what we love.

We Rise and Fall More than a Bakery

F inally, there's some success to report at last. As of February 13, 2011, funding was back in place for Matthew and they moved him into an assisted living one-bedroom suite on Friday, with caregivers & professional rehab program in place. Since that time, I've been so tired that all I could do was sleep at 7 PM each night. I am grateful to have some opportunity to tend to my own needs, at last. First: rest, 2nd back to the gym, 3rd drop weight, 4th socializing! Matt is safe again. We've dodged another bullet.

FEBRUARY 20, 2011

Matt has been in his new, assisted living accommodations for nine days now. Apparently, he was a bit of a handful the first few days, but he seems to have settled in well for the past three days. He is going to Church today: great news. He reports he will go to a different church over the next four Sundays and decide which one he likes best. I encourage him to make his own adult decisions on this, and more. I am glad he is making this assessment for himself again.

After his TBI, I took him to church almost every Sunday. He had asked me "What religion are we?" and my response was that was something he needed to decide for himself, as an adult. We attended multiple congregations then, and his consensus was fascinating for each:

- Baptist: "They are cruel and prejudiced."
- United: "They don't teach anything."
- Catholic: "Pretty inside, but too confusing and too much kneeling (I can't do either)."
- Judaism: "Too strict and I would never be good enough. You're not good enough for them, Mom, and you keep getting hurt by it. I can't follow all that. They judge *you* because your father was a Jew and not your mother, and that's just *wrong*."

- Jehovah's' Witness: Really nice people, really friendly, good message and great cookies and coffee, "But, I can't hand out those magazines"
- Seven-Day Scientists (what he called 7th Day Adventists): "I don't know what they were talking about."
- Anglican: "That's my choice. They are nice, they are calm, and they keep saying 'Peace be with you', and we can all use a little more peace."

MARCH 3, 2011

It would seem that Matthew is improving day by day. He is about to be enrolled in a vocational program, with a goal of part-time work soon. And "they" said nine years ago he would never be capable of walking, learning, or integrating into the community. AHH, the difference the "F" word makes (FUNDING)!

MARCH 6, 2011

I need a distraction and some ability to focus on myself for a change. After all, unless I am optimal, I cannot be the advocate that Matthew needs.

I have decided to compete in amateur bodybuilding one last time. The goal is to do a contest in November 2012. There is one scheduled for Matthew's birthday — so this is to be a present for him. I am amazed at how many people are so supportive of this. One of my friends told me it was amazing. "I am glad you are going to compete again! You are so happy and so much fun when you are bodybuilding."

Even Matthew was thrilled at the decision, asking, "Will I be able to watch you from the audience?"

That was when I told him this was to be his birthday present for 2012. He cried.

MARCH 11, 2011

Well, one week of dieting and I am already feeling a difference. It is tough getting used to being hungry, but I've started off hard-core rather than easing into it. Darn Type A personality of mine! Life continues to be good. Matt is doing exceedingly well. His workers are qualified.

It feels like time to do something for myself now. I will move from my studio/bed & breakfast rental on April 30th. It has been quite convenient, living next door to my office — and the room I have is amazing, as is the soaker tub! I also wanted to state that Matthew could not return to live with me, and this arrangement gave me that opportunity as an honest disclosure. But, I end up working extended hours all too often, because of the proximity to work... And I feel I "want more" now.

I look forward to being able to cook again and to have friends over! It's interesting that whenever I am dieting, I love to cook for others! I look forward to buying furnishings & decorating again, too. The three-month stay at the B&B studio has been good for me... but it is time to move on, now that I've de-traumatized from Matt's downfall to rise to the top again!

APRIL 11, 2011

How very peculiar; I am still not totally healthy again yet. I have felt ill for eight weeks now. Life, however, continues to be good. Matt is safe & stable, and I am slowly moving forward to find my own life again. I'm a work in progress, but at least I am working on it!

APRIL 13, 2011

I had a lovely visit (dinner & a movie) with Matt last night; he is improving still and doing well. It amazes me how positive he has been in recent days. Once again, he said, "Mom, I have such a great life." I am pleased to see he doesn't let severe disability get the best of him. I learn from him each day and feel blessed to still have him in my life.

MAY 9, 2011

Today is Mother's Day. It has always been one of my favorite holidays, as that is what I have most wanted to be (and be good at) for over three decades. Today, Matt and I shared a lovely day just talking and observing nature at Cultus Lake. It has been so nice to choose simple over complex, and just get to know my newly developing son's mind better. I am grateful for his continuing stability.

MAY 11, 2011

Last night, Matt wondered how I ironically knew he was doing a particular something — while talking to me on the telephone from his place. I jested, "I have a camera installed secretly in your place." He didn't skip a beat with his retort, saying, "Then how do ya like me naked?!" I am hoping quick wit is a sign of cognitive improvement for him! And I hoped he was not strutting around his home in his birthday suit!

He told me about meeting a potential girlfriend, and having been successful in getting her telephone number! Apparently, he called her twenty times the first day! So, a little motherly advice tonight included a suggestion to, perhaps, WAIT three days to phone her; then wait ANOTHER three days! He is so very lonely but unable to understand that frequent calling results in the opposite of endearment.

JUNE 29, 2011

I have been enjoying some time off work. I have explored a lot of trails and done some low-level hiking! It's always interesting to see how a little exercise, clean nutrition, and releasing a modicum of stress will do that for you in such a short time! I have dropped ten pounds already!

JULY 6, 2011

Well, I'm loving life again... Matt seems to improve and present as more positive than ever, which makes it easier to tolerate the inevitable stress that still lurks around the corners!

The additional great news is that Matthew's life skills worker took him fishing two days ago — to see if that could be something that interests Matt since he has been apathetic and disinterested in everything post-brain-injury (besides eating and smoking)... Matt claimed to love fishing and is going again tomorrow! I could not be happier! On Saturday, I will take him to Fred's Fish & Tackle and let him choose a rod, reel and some bait!

Matt saw an addictions counselor today & really was grateful for the opportunity. He said he talked about everything that was "pissing him off" and the counselor told him he had nothing to worry about, adding that he should be very proud of himself and his progress. Matt is also journaling every day now, which is utterly remarkable.

JULY 7, 2011

Today was a very stressful day at the office with unnecessary & immature politics. That nonsense is getting really tiresome — and fast. I wish people could just mind their own business and be civil to one another. I am grateful my boss is great to me and appreciates my work; he is, undoubtedly, the most incredible mind with whom I've ever worked. Now if only two petty, insecure & bitterly competitive women could find things in their life for which they should be grateful, rather than thriving on the anxiety they rain down on others. But alas, no good deed goes unpunished. Women in law firms the world over share these scenarios in the workplace. But the fact remains that a narcissist will dislike anyone who can out-perform them, out-charm them — or out-think them.

But, to focus on a positive, Matthew had still another incredibly positive day. And I received word that I had "won a battle" that began a year ago when a physician over-prescribed the dosage of all of Matt's medications by 60%. I wanted the doctor reprimanded by the College of Physicians and Surgeons, and now he has been.

JULY 8, 2011

Trouble in paradise, again. The honeymoon phase has concluded, though I am unsure whether it is the honeymoon phase with another inadequate residential home care provider, a honeymoon phase with Matthew — or both.

Reports are often slow to "trickle in" from new placements, but now I have been told that the fishing equipment purchased was a waste of time and money. Matt only wanted the fishing outings so he could solicit marijuana and extra cigarettes from others. He put his pole into place, stuck it into the ground with the line in the water, and walked away. He was told he could not join the group for fishing again, as they could not adequately supervise him.

The honeymoon phase of journaling lasted five days. He proved to be capable but unmotivated.

JULY 10, 2011

After a meeting with the agency that provided Matthew's current residential care home placement, I was told that the agency knows well that the woman homeowner is a problem *but* because there are so few homes available, they don't know what else might be out there. I have requested another placement, as I see increasing risk scenarios for his decompensation.

The agency reported Matt describes the homeowner, in telephone conversations with them, as "She's a fucking bitch."

She has refused interaction with Matthew for a full week now. The agency has determined that she is listening to his telephone conversations from a secondary line in the home.

Matthew had only ONE interaction with her last week (Thursday) when she delivered his meds at 8:30 PM. I was on the phone with him, so I heard everything that transpired. I wish I could have recorded the exchange between them. She knocked on the door, Matt said (politely, with no tone in his voice), "Come in" and she entered and snapped, "Take your meds NOW — right now." Wow.

In 9.5 years of brain injury, Matt has *never once* failed to comply with medication; he's had a self-created "mantra" for years, "I love my meds; my meds keep me alive."

This woman is baiting him to act out — to failure. It is the most bizarre situation I've seen, especially because he understands his precarious position of needing a stable placement. Given she is well-compensated for providing meals, medication, and a bachelor suite downstairs, I am left still further confused. I truly don't "get it."

Tomorrow, Matt's cousin, Rocky, arrives in Chilliwack for a visit. I am hopeful this will be an uplifting and motivating surprise for Matthew. Rocky has not seen Matt since the brain injury.

We roll with the punches, and every next journey is as unpredictable and diverse as the last one. We rise and fall more than a bakery.

THE COOLDOWN, THE FRYING PAN & THE FIRE

I have taken three vacation days from work again, and *this* time I am going to have fun (rather than catch up on chores, shopping, and sleep)! I took Matt's cousin, Rocky, to Chilliwack Lake and then showed him Cultus Lake, after which we walked some of the Rotary Trail (darkness encroaching with a mosquito bonus sent us home). We ate dinner around 10 PM and then slept soundly.

Matt will see Rocky tomorrow. Both Rocky and I are excited to see the reaction!

JULY 28, 2011

We have so many wonderful things in our lives now, recontact with family, reconnection with someone Matt loved many years ago... a new car... stable and tolerable employment... relatively good health (considering)... Now, if only Matt can remain stable.

A few days ago, Rocky said Matthew may well "fly the nest," with difficulty at first, but once the wings adjust, he believes this will work out for the best. He used the example of a loon coming off the lake and heading into a flight — a clumsy mess initially, but then ok. I have to have faith in that, too... as we are now at the end of Matt's rope...

Matt has some serious issues lurking just under the surface; while I am doing my best to focus on the positives, the potential, and to learn from the past, I recognize my son is hanging on by a thread, behaviorally. I believe what I have been witnessing, for weeks, is expert mimicry. Rocky has identified it as well.

Three days ago, after an outing to Hope, BC, we returned to Chilliwack. I needed a couple of items from the grocery store, so I shopped and left Rocky and Matt in the car. When I returned some 15 minutes later, the mood was *off*, though Matthew cheerily greeted me with a resounding "Welcome back!"

Rocky only explained what had transpired in those minutes later in the evening, after Matt had taken his meds and retired for sleep. He was both alarmed and held an altered opinion of Matt afterward. While I was in the store shopping, a man had parked two cars over from ours and had left his trunk open as he went into the store. Matt's personality, and his vocal structure, transformed. "Rock — dude — let's rip that guy off, the dumb fuck left his trunk open." Rocky told me it was at that moment when I returned and Matt cheerfully greeted me with, "Welcome back."

He never spoke freely or amicably with Matthew again. He told me to watch my back, "There's something very wrong with my cuz and I don't think you or anyone else is safe for long around him."

Despite Matt's failures of three days ago, he seems to be back on track again. At least outwardly, he is polite and cautiously well-mannered again. He may live independently in another two weeks, as there has been no success in securing a residential care home for him. I pray he is ready for that step — as it will be sink or swim.

Time and time again, Matt's overwhelming desires for independence have been accompanied by cannabis consumption. The rapid decompensation that flows from that is almost invariably a disaster, followed closely by institutionalization. With marijuana use, one hundred percent of the time, he wreaks havoc, personally, in the home, with caregivers and funding personnel, and with the community. Three steps forward, two steps back. The dance is so frequent that one cannot speculate where the rhythm will lead next.

The current residential placement is languishing. Historically, Matt has proven to be a capable and pathological liar. We now face a "he said/she said" scenario with funding personnel (and any prospects for an alternative placement), although the agency holding the current contract is well aware of the caregiver's shortcomings. The woman has continued to push buttons for Matthew and bait him into misbehavior. She continues to listen in on his telephone conversations and has even entered his room to wake him up at night, angrily demanding to know if he took his meds. She has twisted stories of Matthew's response in the household so much that I bought a nanny cam inside a teddy bear for his room. If for no other purpose, I wanted to know when I could and could *not* believe my son, being all too familiar with his uncanny ability to manipulate and deceive.

But this woman is a "piece of work." The following is an actual copy of a letter received from the woman *at my office on September 16, 2011*, months after Matthew left her residence. Attached to the letter was a printed copy of an online article that had been written about me — telling the story of my first weight loss journey to a bodybuilding stage, from 1999 to 2000. It was one of the most-bizarre occurrences with any caregiver. She was, however, another alcoholic. That marks to alcoholic home managers we've witnessed to date, and as I write this now — I can confirm that in the years to follow, we experienced two more. Of course, these homes were annotated on the list of "bad placements." Truly, one can't make this stuff up (and remember: this is a true story). The good news, however, is that the woman never received another homestay.

Her career as a residential caregiver ended as quickly as it began, thankfully.

JULY 30, 2011
Matt's residential placement has now officially failed, though it lasted longer than I would have predicted. At all material times, the home offered no support — only a place to sleep, shower, eat and have his medications managed twice a day. Workers transported him for supervised community and program outings. Four months in, he has improved measurably & significantly because of his program attendance, independent life-skills workers & structure. And despite a terrible homeowner who has relentlessly baited him to failure, he has not acted out in any serious capacity. There has been no violence or aggression, though he has spoken to me privately that he is diligently withholding what he feels stirring inside. That alone represents a measurable improvement.

AUGUST 4, 2011
Matthew was transferred to a new residential care setting in Abbotsford. Because of the proximity to Abbotsford Regional Hospital, and Matt's negative memories from his time in their psychiatric ward just months ago, he did not want to go. I had to explain to him that the homeless shelter and being homeless on the streets by day were not in his best interests. He never asked me why he could no longer return to live with me; he only assumed he knew the reason. "Mom, I know you've had enough of my bullshit and I am so sorry I screwed up again. I wish I could come home, but I get it."

It was more than that, however. I did not share with Matt that I had no *choice* but to take this stance to achieve continuing funding for him. If I were readily available to assume the risk of his care, there would be no need for the ABI Program to fund his caregiving. There is a need to fund caregiving because I have been so litigious in my advocacy for my son. Matt just has to keep his head on straight, and I have to remain diligent and professional.

He will, at least, have the continuing benefit of the positive programs and respite workers through the same agency now, which has significantly helped him improve these past four months. One step forward again and we live to dance another performance.

It was a splendid day today — for Matt because he lives in safety to try another course, and for me, because Matt is finally safe again. I hope I can condition myself to relax again and have some faith that my son is going to be just fine. Finally, I don't have to worry over every waking hour that Matt is decompensating simply because a homeowner didn't like his personality, his sarcasm, or his sharp tongue in response to gaslighting and bullying.

AUGUST 9, 2011
A few weeks ago, I suffered a minor stroke. Two days ago, I had a TIA. I continue to have a hard time with post-TIA symptoms, as I am not bouncing back as I did after the first one a few weeks ago. I am particularly disoriented and yet unable to multi-task beyond two items at a time (I usually work with four to six items on the

go at a time in the office). Manual dexterity in my left hand is still problematic, and my balance continues to be impaired. I suppose there has been too much stress for far too long, and I'm not 40 anymore; heck, 50 sounds young to me now. I am facing a wake-up call in my aging years.

I did not tell Matthew about my health conditions, as there is nothing he can do to help — and worrying him unnecessarily would serve no purpose. In fact, it could destabilize him. I will focus on myself and give him access to edited information to allow him to focus on himself.

AUGUST 12, 2011

I am physically better today. My doctor's orders were to rest at home, in between having comprehensive testing undertaken. I will know next week whether I am diabetic. My first round of bloodwork suggested a need for glucose tolerance testing. A heart condition, stroke propensity, hemochromatosis, PTSD, COPD, and now maybe diabetes... My body is not holding up to extreme stress anymore. High blood pressure and sleep apnea just don't say "Life is for the living!"

AUGUST 17, 2011

Matt's new caregivers allowed him to have his own little kitten today! I thought Matt had been ridiculously happy over the past two weeks — but I have *never* heard him as happy as he was today! The prediction of the day is that he will be extremely responsible and will take excellent care of his *daughter*, as he calls her! I can't wait to hear what he's named her!

I am looking forward to the weekend! I will take Matt to see the Othello Tunnels in Hope (after he gets a fresh flat top haircut from the RCMP barber)! We both look forward to venturing out in the Jeep — and hoping the weather will be great so we can take the top off (and hoping I can figure out how to get it back on after that)!

AUGUST 18, 2011

Matt has now had about nine consecutive perfect days. Utterly a mazing... no misbehaviors, no problems, just continuing progressive improvement! The responsibility of caring for his kitten has proven good for him. I believe he has craved the ability to feel responsible, to have a purpose, to have some control over his life decisions — to work toward independence (or semi-independence).

And what did he name his kitten? Drum-roll, please: "Sara!!" He is spelling it differently from my name, but I thought that was sweet! He said I was his best friend and the new female in his life was second — quickly adding, however, "But G-D is first, Mom."

He always added that G-D is first; it made me proud.

AUGUST 24, 2021

Work stress is taking a serious toll on me now. I absolutely cannot withstand much more. I was so emotionally & physically exhausted after working another 11 hours yesterday, that I could not stop crying last night. This morning, I am nominally improved. These are dire straits I'm facing now, and I feel I'm headed for a breakdown. At all costs, I must avoid that. Fall down six times, get up seven. Time to dust myself off and muster a smile; I won't accomplish anything positive by having my private pity party. As Mattie always says, "Nobody likes a complain freak."

AUGUST 27, 2011

I took Mattie out for a day trip today! Our adventure placed us in the patch of a big toad, a chipmunk, a black bear 20′ away from us (we were in the Jeep), and a lot of bees & mosquitoes! We saw a gigantic cave in the mountain and I told Matt that when I was young, I would have wanted to climb up and see what was inside. "Mom, I worry about you sometimes!"

We also stopped on the side of the road, got out of the car ("Mom, you're crazy!"), and patted a couple of baby Holstein cows on the way back. That prompted Mattie to ask about becoming a vegetarian again.

It was a beautiful day. Matthew is back at his residence, and I am taking my farmer's tan to the bubble bath!

AUGUST 29, 2011

I have dropped 19 pounds in four weeks, 15 of it in the last three weeks. Seeing the scale motivated me to work harder at the gym today. I took a day off work for medical testing today and had another carotid Doppler ultrasound. Those results should come back in four to five days. Very curious to know how my blood is flowing in there and avoid any more mini-strokes (or a big one, of course). My stress levels have declined significantly with Matt's stability, and exercise and nutrition have been consistent. Better to start late than to never begin at all.

SEPTEMBER 6, 2011

Still more good news; my boss is really trying to work with me to effect change! What a brilliant lawyer, but despite extra hours and my most concerted efforts, I find it a challenge to keep him organized! He was so very kind and putting forth effort for me today, and agreed to let me work my full-time hours over four days. Now I can have Saturdays, Sundays, and Mondays off — and for now, that means three days to spend motivating and ensuring Matt gets exercise and positive reinforcement. I am grateful for the improved turn of events, despite a waiting game on Matt's funding again.

More transitions seem to be imminent with Matthew's continuing TBI tango. You just can't make this stuff up.

The people who assumed Matt's care have pressured me, time and time again, for money. When they contracted with the agency for Matthew's care, at a significant monthly remuneration, the agency explained the first payroll would be remitted after 60 days and then every 30 days thereafter (e.g., always with one month owing, one-month payroll was a "hold out"). The agency provided them with a small advance to accommodate groceries for Matthew, but the couple was aware of the terms of the contract they signed.

When pressured, I agreed to provide the couple with $750 cash, to be reimbursed to me at the time they received their first payroll. But, when I set boundaries and advised the wife I could not provide further funds, as I simply had little in the way of savings, the wife became volatile. Interesting to note, however, is the fact that she bought two new sofas and a 62⃞ plasma TV two weeks ago. I stopped contact with her after that, and Matthew has been impeccable in his behavior here with me. I had him for 12 hrs on Saturday and again for another 12 hours on Sunday, to give the husband (Matt's primary caregiver) a break without having to pay for respite care and to save them two days of food for Matt.

I dropped Matt off promptly at 8:30 PM on Sunday, and in 15 minutes he had phoned me. Apparently, on his return to the home, the husband asked him if we had been talking about his wife. Matt said no, and why did he ask? Clearly, in Matt's 12-hour absence from the home, the couple had continued their bickering.

The husband went back upstairs. Matt told me, "Mom, I think something bad is going to happen."

I told him not to worry and signed off after saying good night. He phoned ten minutes later, hyperventilating — and telling me the couple wants him out TONIGHT and the agency was going to call me.

Matt failed to mention he had been smoking a cigarette in the open garage while naked.

I had to drive all the way back to West Abbotsford and retrieve a very medicated Mattie. On arriving, I found him standing outside in the dark. The garage door was open, but no light was engaged inside. His personal effects (clothing and toiletries and a couple of stuffed animals) had been smashed hurriedly into black garbage bags. He was standing in the driveway, in tears and smoking a cigarette, with what remained of the box of cereal I bought him last weekend sitting at his feet. They had not provided him with other groceries.

I took a deep breath. Matt fastened his seatbelt, and we drove away from the house we had both believed represented a road to his next step of progress. As Matt continued to sob and shake a leg, I gently asked, "Buddy, why naked?"

"I was naked? OMG. I was naked? Fuck. What is wrong with me?" And the sobbing caused his body to wretch. He asked me to pull over, and he got out to vomit. "Sorry, Mom. This is just so fucked up."

After a sip of water, buckling in again and feeling more settled, he continued. "When I came home, those two were yelling at each other and making a lot of noise upstairs. That's when the husband came down and accused me of talking about his wife. I didn't know what he was talking about. I wasn't here all day. You know — I was with you ALL DAY. Anyway, I knew he was mad, and I felt like he was mad at me but I didn't know why he would be mad at me. I guess when he yelled at me and told me to go to fucking bed, I got naked and went to bed. I don't remember coming out to smoke, Mom — it's like I was just there smoking and these two were going crazy on me, and I called you because they told me to, and now you're here. Is it okay if I eat some of this cereal? I wish they had let me take my cookies."

"I asked if I could take my kitten and the man yelled at me and told me that was *his* kitten, not mine. He told me I could not live there anymore, that I was too much trouble, and to call my fucking mother and get the fuck out. I'm so sorry, Mom."

I had no words. Matt could only sit in my car and cry while he ate dry Cheerios from a box. The calm confusion of unexplained trauma was all we had left, and the silence spoke volumes. I told Matthew about how tomorrow is another day, adding, "We will get through this, buddy."

It is my speculation that the aggression and continuing argument between the husband and wife triggered Matt into another dissociative state. Sadly, the "he said/she said" in this scenario is of no consequence. The homeowners were not equipped for the care of a TBI survivor and Matthew could not be a resident in a home where aggressive arguments and paranoid accusations were rampant.

He is now sleeping on an air mattress in my living room.

And just like that, I looked at adverts for a two-bedroom suite for October 1st.

PROGRESSIVE MOMENTUM TO THE LIGHT

*I*t was my suspicion that the arguing (aggression with the subtle
threat of violence, from Matt's perception) triggered him to
another dissociative state. By the time he was ready to retire for
bed (and he always slept naked), he would have been medicated.
We never determined why he sat there naked in the garage, smoking
a cigarette, but the unprofessional and shocking response from the
homeowners devastated Matthew and sent him spiraling into shame
and depression.

SEPTEMBER 17, 2011
I was up @ 5:30 this morning and made two turkey meatloaves &
coffee, along with a curry sauce for the meatloaf, cleaned all floors
& did two loads of laundry, completing all before 8 AM. Matt slept
through it all, but got up to have coffee with me and is back in
bed already! I have a busy day ahead running errands. We have rain
today, so there will be no walks through the woods & probably no
forest service road adventures. But tomorrow is another day!

SEPTEMBER 18, 2011
A few days ago, Matt said, "Mom, I really love my life; I used to
always think about what I would be doing in a few years; now I know
I might not be here in a few years and I love my life right now, this
minute. Is that wrong?" Oh my, what a profound, thought-provoking
moment.
"Buddy, it's not wrong — it's about as right as you can get.
Everybody spends more time worrying about their future than they
do enjoying the life right in front of them at this minute."
"Mom, is that what 'stop and smell the roses' means?"
"Oh buddy, that is precisely what it means. What prompted you to
think about this so seriously?"
"Well, Mom — no disrespect intended, but you are always
planning ahead, ready for anything. You're good at it, but I see how

tired you get and how you don't laugh much anymore. I don't think you are completely happy because you don't stop to smell the roses. Can we get some roses today?"

Turns out life really is all about the little moments. That's where the memories hide, and they will revisit us in the most mundane of moments in the future.

Mattie made breakfast for us on this lazy, rainy Sunday morning — some nice egg whites with a couple of free-range whole eggs, low-fat cream cheese, and some tzatziki cheese we bought from Smit's Dairy here in Chilliwack. a local dairy operation (Smit's) yesterday. It was remarkable to see him take the initiative to make breakfast, and take pride in what he had done!

I learn so much from Matt! He appreciates so many things that I completely take for granted, or fail to even notice. But yes, it is draining being a primary caregiver, his very active advocate, to be working full-time hours, exercising, cleaning, shopping, and keeping the bills paid on time.

Simply explaining the best way to dish eggs into a bowl or plate needs to be explained comprehensively (i.e., *not* from the skillet into the bowl; rather with a wide spatula with the bowl closely over the frypan!) "Children" are so prone to dumping & spilling, then beating themselves up with what they perceive as failure. SO, that prompted another lesson that every error is an opportunity to learn, to remember, and to have a goal to do it less in the future (or maybe never again)!

Interesting, when teaching a "child" to cook, there is so much to be taught... how to crack an eggshell without putting egg white draining down the side of the pan and onto the burner for one, teaching to remove any specks of blood found in the freshly cracked egg, and so much more! He did quickly learn the value of not needing to clean heated egg off a smooth-top range!

SEPTEMBER 19, 2011

Today, we will deliver a thank you basket to Matt's probation officer Peter. Matt enjoyed the adventure of multiple stops to choose local contents and then making the basket ourselves. We picked up cheese from Smit's Dairy; buttermilk cinnamon bread from another farm; bumbleberry jam from another; Okanagan wine (Shiraz) from a local winery; walnut date crackers from a local bread shop; a couple of discontinued Russ stuffed animals (Russ the Rhino and a Turtle Princess) for Peter's kids; and a lot more! Matt is so excited to deliver it this morning!

After the basket delivery, we will take a wee Jeep adventure, then it's back home to get ready to leave for the UBC Neuropsychiatric Department (which will entail a three-hour drive). I have been persistent in trying to get Matthew into that program for 9.5 years and the appointment just came thru last week. There will be a neuropsychiatric assessment over two days (today and tomorrow). I had no problems securing a day off work tomorrow.

This represents still another "win" in brain injury advocacy for us. The brain-injured are consistently denied psychiatric following ("We don't do brain injury"). Then, funding is rescinded ("We need you to be followed by a shrink"), so this is a significant victory for

Matt and for everyone in similar straits. Learning to stay one step ahead of the system is a full-time, unpaid job.

SEPTEMBER 20, 2011

Still more good news. We should know by 9 AM whether Matt has another funded care home placement. Finding myself on pins & needles, I hope I can pull myself together by the time Matt awakens again. I am all teary this morning, feeling profoundly drained — and anxious.

Today marks Day Two of Matt's neuropsych assessment with Dr. H of BC Neuropsychiatric @ UBC. Yesterday left Matt in a state of collapse and exhaustion. The round trip travel required was almost six hours. Neuropsych assessment is an invasive process and will drain individuals far more high-functioning than Matthew. He hit the wall last night.

He awakened with tears this morning because he had been incontinent again. This is the first recurrence in 1.5 years; he had no accidents from the time I brought him to Chilliwack 1.5 years ago. I surmise that discussing certain topics yesterday, AND needing to face the fact that his cognitive impairment is significant (he does not do well in testing) was a sizable trigger for Mattie.

"Do you want to talk about anything, buddy? You know you can tell me anything, right?"

He just stood there and cried, likely hiding *secrets* from his past touched upon in the assessment — secrets he held from me through the years, I suspect. Even when Matthew was convicted of juvenile violence, he refused to allow me in the Courtroom during his testimony. I know he trusts he can share anything with me, but he leans to the side of having me see the best in him.

While Matt sleeps again before we leave for the second psych assessment, I have filled the house with the smell of onions, garlic & ground turkey breast... all to be added to a mix of cauliflower and bok choy, topped with a spicy peanut sauce for dinner tonite! For me, sometimes cooking offers a way to move past some stress & sadness, and also to celebrate an appreciation for life! Besides, it is never lost on me that Mattie loves to eat.

9:30 AM, the phone rang. Matthew has another residential home care placement!

Today's testing was another traumatizing reality for Matt. For the first time in ten years of brain injury, he was forced to face his limitations, and not "do his best" and carry on. He said he could not communicate what he wanted to say without someone in there with him. "The doc is gonna think I am retarded."

"Buddy, this is TBI, and it is what it is." I reminded him of how far he had come, and how lucky he was to have survived.

"I know, Mom — and I don't want to be a complain freak, but knowing I might not be able to get much better sure makes me sad. I always thought that if I did the work, one day — like magic, everything would be alright."

"Buddy, none of us know how far we can walk until we take the first step. Remember how hard it was changing the way you ate and pushing yourself out to exercise? Did you lose that weight and feel better in a week? No, you kept doing the work, found the fun in it and trusted the process. This is the same."

"Mom, you always turn me around to thinking positive again. No matter how much I screw up, you always find something to give me hope I can be better. You always see *potential* in me, no matter how I fuck up. But sitting with a doctor is *proof* that I am broken and probably not going to get much better. Sitting with doctors always brings me back to reality — I see it in their eyes that I am just not worth the trouble."

"But, buddy, you *are* worth the effort (I like that word better than trouble), or they would not have approved the neuropsych testing. Do you know what the cost of that is? It is THOUSANDS of dollars... thousands. And hey — who was worth the trouble of finding another care home placement?"

Through tears, he smiled, "Me, I guess. I guess I am worth the trouble because you fight to make people pay attention to me. Thank you for never giving up, Mom. And I am so glad I can cry now — I still remember how, after the brain injury, I could not cry for a long time."

"Yes, buddy — I remember that day you cried for the first time after the TBI — it was 2003." I often wondered if they chose a diagnosis of sociopathy because of his inability to shed tears? I am so very grateful that the subject has not arisen for quite some time. His recent stability and improvements have been nothing short of remarkable.

SEPTEMBER 26, 2011
9 AM and this is TRANSFER DAY! Matt is calm and happy about his new opportunity. He says he has no anxiety this time and thinks that is a sign that this is the right placement at last. After the last two consecutive "caregivers" taking away all his food and even his coffee, he is going in with preliminary groceries, a new coffeemaker, and two cartons of cigarettes! He must have said "thank you" twenty times.

We saw the movie *Dolphin Tale* yesterday, and he cried like a baby! My young man is so sensitive; I am grateful for that, as it is so preferred to the alternative.

OCTOBER 2, 2011
I spent all day yesterday (Saturday) sleeping on and off the entire day. I am utterly exhausted, but today will go into the office for a few hours (at my boss' request). Matt seems to fare well at the new location, and I am keeping my fingers crossed this trend can continue.

OCTOBER 5, 2011
I have to make time for my health, starting (again) this weekend. I need to get back into the gym (I stopped again with all the emergencies surrounding Matt's advocacy & transfer) and I need to walk that Rotary Trail regularly.

I am extremely busy at work - trying to finish a lot before my boss goes to Hawaii for two weeks. Matt continues to thrive and has been enjoying what sounds like a good day program that has him learning some life skills (this being the first time he's had that in ten years of brain injury, except for what I've been able to re-teach him). He's positive, motivated & improving — and thinking about his future.

"I don't know where I want to live when I finish getting better, but I know I want to leave this area. I will never relax here. Every day I worry someone from my past is going to recognize me. Remember when someone recognized me in Burnaby before? I think my caregivers don't believe me."

I consider this to be great forward-thinking for him; he has never done that until now. At least, to my knowledge, he has never been capable until now.

OCTOBER 11, 2011
Matt continues to do well. I have great hopes for him to have a future for himself. He is more age-appropriate every day, it seems, and is staying positive. He sounds good. I haven't seen him for almost three weeks now and miss him quite a lot, but I believe the distance between us has been healthy. On Sunday, I pick him up and have him for 12 hours. I look forward to some quality time together then!

OCTOBER 22, 2011
Matt & I had another wonderful, deep conversation last night. This time, he was reciting some of his self-realized progress — including the fact that he no longer tells everyone he meets and likes that he loves them. He told me he decided it was not fair to *me* to use those words with everyone, because if he loves strangers, how does he express what he feels for me?

He added that the only people he loves are G-D, Mom, his cousin Rocky, and Peter, his probation officer. He said, "Mom, I know he is my PO, but he is really special; I love him. When my probation is over, I am going to stay in touch with him. He makes a difference in my life. I want to make him proud. He makes me want to be better — like you do." He also said his PO was the only non-blood person he trusts... and said "Maybe love means trust has to be there, too." Ya think?

Matthew's PO told me today, "Matt is a very special guy and gets my respect, attention, and friendship because he puts effort into change. When a person tries, even if they fail, they show they want something better. How can I not help? Eventually, he will succeed with bigger things, just like he is doing now. Last January, we might not have been able to see this progress... remember? This is no minor success. I don't always agree with doctors, so I might venture to say that there is hope that many of those things the doctors claim he will *not* be able to do, he will accomplish. Wait and see."

NOVEMBER 5, 2011
"Power is no blessing in itself, except when it is used to protect the innocent." Jonathan Swift said that over 300 years ago.

Gratitudes: for my son's incredible and undeniable progress... for his hard-fought funding, for as long it lasts.

Matt's placement agency is already talking about where he will go next. He has had seven perfect weeks at the new placement, which is utterly amazing. Matt asked me last night if I would be upset if he decided he wanted to live independently when this contract concludes. Wow! I am so proud that he is forward-thinking. That ability has always been limited and short-lived for him until now.

It was as though he could not see a future for himself before. He told me he wants to have a girlfriend in the future, and it would not be right for him to "make love" in my house. Bless his heart. At last, my young man is maturing. He will be 33 tomorrow and on November 14th, we remember the 10th anniversary of his traumatic brain injury. What a long, hard road, but what a wonderful outcome that so many predicted would never come to pass.

I think we might have light at the end of this tunnel, and it's not a train!

WIN SOME, AND WIN SOME MORE

Today is November 9, 2011. Wow, I had another long day at work today — another 11 hours with no lunch break. It is wearing me down fast, and it's a bit more responsibility than I signed on for. I feel like a rudderless ship in the office these days. But faced with adversity, I know it is important to remain grateful for all that IS going well. I take a moment to remind myself to be grateful that I have a job that pays a decent remuneration, and that Matthew continues to show some slight improvement with better communications and insights every single day.

NOVEMBER 24, 2011

Yesterday, during our one-hour talk during my drive home from work, Matthew told me, "Mom, I have something important to tell you." My heart momentarily sank, as this preface has always meant a confession of something less than grand. He was serious. I said "Okay."

"Mom, I have a girlfriend."

"How long?" I asked.

"For about a month!" he exclaimed.

After clarifying a little background, I was happy for him! Apparently, she also is brain-injured but high-functioning; she also wants to work part-time soon, like him. He insists she does not do drugs or drink, but she smokes cigarettes. She lives on her own in a basement suite and is higher functioning in some areas than Matt, and he is more improved in other areas than her. She is half First Nations.

He was seriously concerned with her being 20, and I told him that most relationships have the man as older, and reminded him that although chronologically he was 33, he was not 33 in other areas.

But the funny thing, with his short-term memory loss: he cannot remember her name! He calls her his *wife*! Oh my. This is a happy progression, however — and a "first" since his TBI.

Now, if I could just find another job and not find myself unemployed end of this year, life would be perfect!

NOVEMBER 27, 2011

Sunday, better known as SONday! After I clean the floors here at home, I will pick up Matt and spend a full 12 hours with him! I am so very looking forward to our visit and watching the Grey Cup together on TV! I recently realized that I have not made the time often enough over the years to watch football with Matthew. He loves it so much, so I owe it to him to learn to like it myself — or at least to give him the time to yelp and clap with excitement over pizza and wings.

DECEMBER 2, 2011

Yesterday, Matt's probation officer, Peter, took him out for a half-day. Peter needed to do some Christmas shopping and went to a jeweler to buy a ring for his wife. It was $1K. He asked if the store could give a better price; they said no.

Matt began flirting with the store manager and asked for a $200 discount for Peter, AND GOT IT! Oh my! His PO was ecstatic and said the outing was a complete hoot! He also said he has never had a client like Matt, so determined to improve his life, and who had done a 360-degree turnabout in one year's time, despite the disability of traumatic brain injury.

I continue to be amazed at Matt's incredible forward progress. Ten years ago, we were told there was a ten-year window of opportunity for his recovery, which significantly and proportionately decreases in the last five years of those ten. I've learned to denote circumstances in the course of this TBI tango into one of two categories: (1) as predicted or (2) against all odds.

This time, we speak of "against all odds." Matthew's greatest improvements have arrived in year nine, now seeming to increase in year 10.

It's a complex yet simplistic formula of empowerment + proper mentorship & guidance + good examples set consistently so that behaviors can be mimicked and conditioned + about three tonnes of love, patience & empathy daily! Voila: against all odds, as predicted!

DECEMBER 5, 2011

Today was a truly lovely and happy birthday for me today! Matt woke me up at 5:30 with a telephone call, adding enthusiastically, "I'm ready to go — you can pick me up any time!" I told him I would be there around 7:30 AM!

I arrived promptly and Matthew was standing outside waiting for me, with an ear-to-ear grin! He had presents for me (1) white roses and a balloon that says I LOVE YOU, (2) a leopard fleece bathrobe, and (3) a card he made for me himself. He made me open the presents before we even started the car to leave the group home driveway! I remarked about how much I loved the bathrobe, adding I thought it was the nicest robe I had ever had in my life! He beamed with pride and told me. "I picked it out myself; they told me you would like something more conservative, and I told them 'You don't know my mom!'"

Then, I took him for a haircut and he insisted that afterward I take care of myself and go get my hair trimmed & flat ironed. I did! He also made me go into a store to see if they had any clothing on sale, and I found a pair of black velvet trousers for \$9.99 and a lovely ruffled red shirt for \$4.99. So, thanks to my son's insistence, I now have a new outfit for my job interview on Wednesday, for only \$15 (since I already have a black jacket to wear over the top)! I would have NEVER done that for myself if he had not coaxed me into it.

After that, we shared some delicious curry, naan & rice for dinner! Then, Matthew insisted we put up a three-foot X-mas tree, which now looks lovely! Matt thanked me for giving birth to him 33 years ago and said he wants to make every birthday special for me for the rest of my life — because he wants me to know he loves me just as much as I love him. And as he does every year, he reminded me. "Mom, this is the day G-D decided you were important."

What a lovely, happy day!

ANOTHER LEAP OF FAITH

I t is hard to fathom that we are halfway through December and almost finished with 2011.

What a wonderful three days with Matt at home. He cried yesterday when I had to return him, after begging me the entire day yesterday to make the choice to leave his residential care home; he is so unhappy there. I told him to continue persevering, continuing efforts to improve and remain behaviourally stable, and he could give notice of leaving at the end of February, for a return home end of March. I *so* wanted to let him give the 30 days' notice now, but I think he needs to learn a salutary lesson — that we *all* have to experience and manage difficult and uncomfortable situations from time to time; how we do that is an indicator of our true character and spirit.

I told him that if he "acts out" as he has in the past when he wants to manipulate a situation to achieve what he wants, he could not come home. We could not start new beginnings on a faulty foundation. He replied, "Totally, Mom. I think it must be hard being my Mom. I know it is hard being me."

I am, however, going to let him transition home gradually with weekends, then extended weekends. He will feel more relaxed with that and it will be a safer transition for him. His goal is to live independently within six months to a year of returning home to live with me.

JANUARY 4, 2012
Day Two on the new job was much better than Day One. I was called in first thing this morning by one lawyer who told me not to be discouraged with the less-than-senior position I occupy there; he says they want to assure me they have big plans for me once I learn their systems... and that compensation will follow in accordance. I may have really lucked into a perfect position. Great work ethic from the staff so far, if there's politics (and I'm sure there is) — at least it is invisible, and the lawyers seem to operate with integrity. I feel very blessed to have this position, in more ways than one.

Matt tells me he has prayed more than ever for me (bless his heart), as he just wants me to have peace and happiness in my life. I am lucky to have my son improving, too, and showing promise of a future!

JANUARY 16, 2012
I am proud that Matt has been dedicated to training hard and consistently since I repurchased the gym membership for him. His doctor has classified him as Obese Level 2. He has only lost two pounds, but he has put on muscle and is quite solid, so I hope his doctor is not just relying on the scale when he attends for updates. Next, he will undergo glucose tolerance testing for diabetes; he was okay a year ago when I took him in. I truly hope he continues to be fine on that count.

JANUARY 20, 2012
I had another employment interview yesterday and left confused. I picked up on a litany of warning signs. "We are very busy; the last paralegal here did not work out; she has left a mess; there were over 100 emails unopened & unread; we expect overtime and there will be a lot of it, but we don't pay overtime. But we have wonderful parties and drink a lot."

I left wondering if that line was a "deal-breaker" for others? At least this presents the perfect definition of "not a good fit."

JANUARY 30, 2012
I moved two loads of insignificant items to the new suite; Matt was a tremendous help (actually the most help he has ever given)! On moving day, all remaining minor items can be loaded in my Jeep in about 15 minutes. I have downsized dramatically. Movers will only have to transport the queen bed, a mid-sized armoire, a small dresser, and my TV. Finding myself unemployed at the end of December has completely wiped me out. This too shall pass, however, and there will be far better days ahead. I am confident about that.

Any new jobs I apply for will receive my amended/updated resume. I have now removed "senior paralegal" from all prior jobs and used the wording "legal assistant" instead. In recent interviews, I am told I am over-qualified, so I need to represent my skills as significantly less than what they are if I am to have any hopes of working in a lesser capacity. I have decided I no longer wish to work the extended hours required of a paralegal. Losing employment this time has also devastated me emotionally.

I know a new opportunity will be around the corner; I just hope it comes my way sooner rather than later!!!

FEBRUARY 4, 2012
We have a sunny weekend in the forecast, although it is cold right now! I have another interview at 2 PM on Monday, so I remain hopeful of good news on the horizon. This is an out-of-town position, though, so if the position is offered, it will depend on whether I can muster funds to get myself up there, rent a room right away, etc. I cannot worry about that just yet; if a written offer

of employment is presented, then that will be the next obstacle to overcome. One day at a time.

FEBRUARY 6, 2012

The job search has ended. I have been offered (and have formally accepted) a position with the managing partner of the Kelowna firm, Pushor Mitchell! I drive up on February 22nd and start work on February 23rd! This is likely the best paralegal position in the Okanagan, and I am so lucky to have it. My former Chilliwack employer (and friend), FH, helped me complete my decision — and it was not lost on me he had never given me bad or unqualified advice. He was one of the few individuals I trusted implicitly. My son was also encouraging me to take the position and move to a more positive and less stressful locale! It is the chance of a lifetime for me, actually!

The firm was desperate to fill the position, as there was a sparse availability of senior paralegals in the area. Given I had no time to secure a rental before commencing employment, the administrator of the firm offered me a spare bedroom in her home until I could arrange a rental for myself.

FEBRUARY 17, 2012

Anxiety and some excitement about the unknown are building fast now. I depart for Kelowna bright and early Wednesday morning, and start work on Thursday!

Matt had some hiccups along the way, so I know he is happy for me, but it is natural he could experience some anxiety about the distance that will be between us soon. I am, however, confident this is an excellent opportunity for me. Ultimately, it will be good for Matthew to experience some distance; after all, becoming independent means standing on two feet and not using Mom as a walking cane.

FEBRUARY 19, 2012

The excitement continues to build! I have an appointment to view a rental suite as soon as I arrive in Kelowna on Wednesday, so I am keeping my fingers crossed for that. This would be temporary shared accommodation, but that is likely my best way to start, so I can familiarize myself with the area and make an educated decision for a place to call home!

Life is good, Matt is doing great, and I have a full day to share with him! We watched a great little movie together (*Real Steel*, with Hugh Jackman), and went out for a superb burger. It's chill time for the balance of our evening together.

FEBRUARY 21, 2012

Mattie and I had an outstanding full-body workout this morning! I pushed him hard; he whined all the way through until I started calling him Princess! The gym owner overheard me and almost spit out her water laughing! She says she knows how to motivate him more now! He worked like a man on a mission but was surprised that Mom can still out-lift him, out-pull him, and out-rep him on all exercises. I told him that was his wake-up call when a mom could outdo a 6-foot, three-inch, 290-pound 33-year-old man! I suspect he will set a higher standard for himself now!

My Jeep is pre-loaded and I am ready to leave for Kelowna tomorrow morning. Matt arrives at 9:30 to help me load the TV and then I am off. Hopefully, there will be no snowfall on the Coquihalla, but if so, Belinda (my Jeep) can handle pretty much anything!

I view a rental suite at 4 PM tomorrow, then start work the following day at 8 AM! Nothing like getting right into the groove!

FEBRUARY 22, 2012

I arrived in Kelowna safely! The drive took 6.5 hours. I traveled through rain, snow, hail, high winds, and sunshine along the way! What a breathtaking trek! Also saw nine eagles over the course of the entire drive, two doe, one black bear, and two wolves in a snowfield! Incredible.

I arrived exhausted, viewed the rental property, and found my way to Gertrude's place (Gertrude being the law firm administrator who head-hunted and hired me, taking no excuse of having no rental — and offering me a spare bedroom in her condo). I had a nice initial visit with her, watched some TV, and chatted incessantly! With two Gravol, I slept well.

THE POWER OF NEW BEGINNINGS

D ay One on the new job (wonderful, thus far!), Day Six of no smoking (NOT ONE!), Day Four of dieting (no cheats!), and Day Three of exercise/walking! Life begins for ME now (which will make me a better mother to Matthew in the end)!

This is the most organized firm I have ever encountered (and I've seen quite a few). It was a very good first day.

I also got word on the rental, and it will be mine from March 6th through May 31st. If the homeowner is to be in Vancouver longer, I will be able to rent the house for a longer period. In any event, by May 31, I will know my way around and have a better handle on other rentals from a financial perspective, too! For now, the house is just lovely, in a safe part of town and a mere 10-minute drive from the office.

FEBRUARY 24, 2012

Day Two on the job (so far) was even better than Day One! Being a natural cynic, based on my diverse experience in many law firms, I find the systems here to be impressive.

Each night, I look forward to speaking with Mattie by telephone. He is suffering some separation anxiety, but I keep reaffirming we will be just fine; the anxiety will pass. I told him to look up at the moon — we are under the same moon on any night. I also keep reaffirming that this was the absolute best decision and relocation for me and also for him in the end, explaining that all children must learn to run and ride bikes without their parents holding on. I think he gets it (but I am so grateful he is in excellent care and under adequate supervision).

Life continues to be good. I have not had a cigarette for a week now, I am still eating clean and my next pursuit is to work on getting more exercise in!

FEBRUARY 26, 2012

Matt's separation anxiety is improving. I gave him another analogy of a Mother Eagle and her fledgling. The Mother Eagle builds a strong nest for her offspring, away from danger, strong and sturdy. She gathers sticks and intertwines them to form a foundation. Unlined, the nest is prickly at best. Among other items, she pulls many of her own soft, small down feathers from her own body to line the nest, making it comfortable and warm for her vulnerable young. Once the fledgling(s) are bigger and stronger, they are more demanding... wanting more and more, *needing* more and more because they are maturing. Eagle Mother wisely removes the soft and warm down feathers from the nest, exposing her maturing young to the prickly twigs. They avoid the discomfort by venturing to the edge of the nest, flapping their wing. At first, they are not sufficiently strong to fly. Soon, however, the prickly twigs irritate and eventually the flapping wings give rise to flight. At first, they fail and they FALL, but Eagle Mother is there to rescue them, catching them on her back, as many times as necessary. But soon, the young Eagle flaps its wings and flies. Were it not for Eagle Mother pushing them to venture outward, sometimes with pain and discomfort, the young Eagle would never go forward, would become uselessly dependent and weak, and would ultimately fail at life.

When I shared this story with Matt, he cried. "Mom, I get it. Thank you for teaching me." And then, "Wow, I'm crying and whining at the same time, so I guess I am multi-tasking!"

MARCH 12, 2012
Mission Creek Park... three-kilometer walk with Matt yesterday, who is particularly proud to say he can no longer sit a plate on his belly!

MARCH 19, 2012
I am home with the flu today. I certainly would prefer to be at work, as daytime TV is not to be appreciated. A regimen of green tea with ginger and lemon, vitamins, and some chicken & rice soup should get me back to work in the morning.

MARCH 28, 2012
It's been a sad and lonely haul over the past week, missing my friends in the Lower Mainland and missing my son. I find Kelowna to be less than a friendly city. But, that having been realized, I am trying to remember the limbo I am in presently will end in four weeks when I move into my personal space, with my own personal effects.

I will do my best to give "K-Town" a fair shake. Certainly, the weather is significantly better than Vancouver's and the traffic is almost non-existent, by comparison, here. I spend a lot less money on gas and only need six minutes to get to the office.

I am hoping friends fall into place; I feel like an outsider here. Actually, someone at my office said someone had made a bet that I would not last two months. Another person called me the "Big City Know-It-All" (because I established a protocol that all documents, pleadings, correspondence, and reports are to be scanned and named per a designated system). Wow! Office politics and insecure women, all over again.

One day at a time. Today, I am grateful it is Wednesday! I have concluded that if there are more than three females in a law firm, there are office politics. This is a sizable firm positioned over three floors, with many staff employed here for 30-35 years. They don't like change, and they hired specifically me to effect change. Sigh.

MARCH 30, 2012
I am driving down to visit Matthew tomorrow in Surrey (and returning the same day). It will be nice to see him again after all these weeks. Plus, next weekend, I will drive down and bring him back up to Kelowna for a two-day visit over the long weekend! It will be such a pleasant drive for him to witness, as the scenery is absolutely stunning. Plus, it will be nice for him to see Kelowna, too. I am very excited about this!

MARCH 31, 2012
I just returned from my road trip to and from Surrey! Driving down was not bad, encountering only one slow snag on the Coquihalla (snow & slush), but coming back presented challenges of snow, ice, and a lot of fog from the mountains of Hope all the way to West Kelowna! The fog barrier can lurk around any curve in the road and can present as an impenetrable wall of skulking disaster. The passenger side of the Jeep windshield froze solid, as did my antenna! I made the drive there in 3.5 hours and the return drive took three hours, but I interestingly used an additional quarter tank of gas on the way back.

It was incredible seeing Mattie, and good to get my Jeep filled with more of my belongings. I also appreciated that the heavy traffic and overcrowding in the area had taken a toll on my health. I could actually *feel* the pollution when I was away from the Okanagan.

Enlightening! I am happy to be back in Kelowna. I loved seeing the bridge on my arrival and the little pocket of paradise on the other side, then just off the bridge, to see the building with my law firm's sign nicely featured in Cobalt Blue neon. I felt proud to be part of the firm. At least, I am confident that *management* is pleased to have me there.

APRIL 2, 2012
I have a short week this week and next. I will drive to Surrey early Saturday morning, loading the Jeep with more of my belonging, and bringing my son up to visit in Kelowna for two days! We are both excited about that. I know he will absolutely love the breathtaking, scenic drive to and from! I hope that seeing more of the world that is out there and "around the corner" in beautiful British Columbia will give him more of a goal to work harder at improving himself, as that is the only way he can hope to attain independence.

APRIL 7, 2012
We arrived safely in Kelowna! Matt was in absolute awe of the entire drive. He was so impressed and touched by the scenery, as I had hoped he would be (though one never knows about Matthew). On arriving in Kelowna, we had lunch at Milestones (excellent Eggs Benedict with avocado and prawns for Matthew, smoked salmon for me, with a side of fruit salad).

Then, we went go-kart riding. Matt was so excited! He made it around a solitary lap and stopped; he was done. Turns out, he was horrified. I did not know it would affect him like that. No one had ever suggested this to me.

"Mom, I almost pooped myself." Poor guy, he was terrified.

He kept saying, "Not again — not another brain injury." He also said the vibrations of the kart hurt his head; it took 30 minutes for the resulting headache to subside. He felt SO bad and apologized incessantly, but I told him not to worry. It is what it is.

He insisted, "You finish your six laps like a crazy woman." I protested, but he cried, and said "Don't let ME stop YOU from having fun, Mom — I never want that and it happens too much."

And unbeknownst to me, he requested a refund and received his money back while I finished my drive around. I would never have asked for a refund, but he impressed me, taking charge and politely communicating his crisis. He assuredly can do some things for himself, and he can, sometimes, forward-think during stress.

After the go-kart terror, Matt cried again in the car. "Oh, buddy: what's up?"

"Mom, I am 300 pounds; I am supposed to be a man, but I was so scared. I am so very sorry."

"Mattie, this has nothing to do with your manhood. I AM THE ONE WHO IS SORRY. I never imagined this would be so horrifying for you."

"I didn't either, Mom. Learn something new every day, eh?"

He's fine now, after a bubble bath in the jacuzzi.

APRIL 10, 2012
Wonderful (but exhausting) weekend with Matt. He loved Kelowna and was in awe of the trip up (via the Coquihalla) and the trip back (Highway 3, through Princeton, Oliver, Osoyoos, Keremeos, and more). We saw five RCMP speed traps (fortunately, I was not speeding at the time) and one terrible accident (a van had done a complete roll over onto its roof and down a steep incline on the highway; passengers were vacated from the scene but no tow truck had removed the vehicle yet).

We stopped to pick wild sage in Osoyoos (desert country) and took a photo of the juxtaposition of the desert region with snow-capped evergreen-covered mountains in the background. Matt said he believes this is the most beautiful country in the world, and he said this was the BEST time of his entire life. "But Mom, I don't get why we picked those dry sage plants? What was that about? We can't eat them, and they're not something to put in a vase back home."

"Buddy, I wanted you to have the experience, to make the memory. Remember when we walked in the rain that time? It's a bit like that — just a pleasant experience and a lovely memory. That's all!"

Now, if he can just address some of his obsessive-compulsive behaviors, he might have a chance at future independence, but the jury continues to be deliberating on that one. I want to be hopeful for him, but if "I read this like a file," my consensus would be that he will always require supervision.

APRIL 21, 2012

Today marks 14 consecutive days of no lies, no melodrama, and no inappropriate behaviors from Matt. I've witnessed impeccable behavior and a lot more effort ever since he returned from his trip to Kelowna. We talked a lot about how he does not like where he is living when he visited, and he returned saying that he was going to "man up" and endure this.

Now, much to my delightful surprise, he tells me today is DAY 378. What? He is marking on his calendar his goal for independence and his own relocation to Kelowna: marking 365 days from April 30th, which is the day he transfers to the new residential home care. I was astonished that he is now showing forward-thinking; one year ago, he was not capable of that, much less showing the wherewithal of monitoring a calendar countdown. I think it is an excellent goal.

He told me that for the ten years in and out of institutionalization, even with his freedom over the last two years, he has never lost that feeling of being "imprisoned" and trapped with no hope. "Mom, I was always thinking, *why try harder?* People do stuff for me and it doesn't make any difference if I work harder or not. They like me about half of the time, so that means the other half who don't like me will never want to see me do better."

Now, he says he sees Kelowna as hope; he was relaxed here and loved the countryside. He was afraid he would have to continue living for the balance of his life in a location he hates and fears, but now he has a dream — a goal. "And Mom, no disrespect intended, but I don't want to be a man on a leash anymore."

A Mother's hope springs eternal for her prodigal son, especially when he is a lot less "prodigal" these days!

APRIL 22, 2012

Mattie told me how much he missed me last night, and that I seem so far away from him now. I reminded him to go outside and look at the stars and the moon; we are under one sky looking together, and I am never far away.

Have you ever been stressed, unhappy, and filled with anxiety for so long that when it leaves you, and you find balance, happiness, and contentment, you wonder when it is all going to fade away? After 10.5 years of the hardest transitions of my life, I can now say I am happy. I am content. My friends, my son, and my employment are just a few things for which I am grateful. I love the life I have, and I am stunned every day I have this realization. But every single day, I have this heartfelt paranoia under the surface that this cannot possibly last.

Is there room for improvement? Of course, and daily I aspire to find some small way to improve and find more for which to be grateful. But I am so very blessed to be cognizant of the wonderful changes that have come my way in the past months. Perhaps I need to work more on my sense of impending doom components!

It has been a wonderful week, a great weekend, and an awe-inspiring day.

APRIL 29, 2012

Tomorrow is move-in day at last. It will be so nice to see my things again, after having them in storage for four months now. Free at last, free at last — thank G-D, free at last!!!

MAY 19, 2012

Mattie and I had a road trip to Vernon today. It was not a waste of time, but let's just say there is no reason to return. The lakes and surrounding area are absolutely beautiful — breathtaking, but it was not a place we enjoyed. We visited the Science Centre, which was a bit of a sad joke... The $15 would have been better donated to someone who needed a meal. We ventured into the planetarium exhibition and Matt developed claustrophobia and severe anxiety. He cried and could not stop; we had to leave. It was such a small, non-ventilated space that it even made me feel temporarily disoriented. I can only speculate that this environment may have triggered his feeling of experiences in nightclubs in his past. I did not ask him, in case that only triggered more anxiety. He never spoke of the depth of his panic on this occasion, and I allowed him to "let it go."

And poor Matt, after 10.5 years of brain injury, we are still learning more about what he can and cannot do. There is a lot of *cannot's* that are only being realized at this late date. His brain injury prevents effective communication on many days (talking a lot is not always communication), and his inability to focus, to be so easily distracted, to hear his racing thoughts spoken, his questions, and confusion all contribute to ineffective disclosure. Poor guy, I suspect he is not even aware of why people do not understand him more than they do. He lives in a 24-7 fog, with fleeting moments of clarity and certainty. He can still remember what it felt like to think fast, to multi-task, strategize and implement a plan, but he cannot hold names or tell you what he did two hours ago.

I felt so sad for him, so at a loss to know how to help, other than just continuing to do what I have been doing. Three steps forward, two steps back. I am caught in this web with him, as we both try to navigate our way around risk and the unknown, and toward safety.

FIGHTING TO BEGIN ANEW

I t is lonely living in an area where you have zero friends and family. I find I now dread weekends unless Matt is bussing up for a visit. Well, there's always Monday in the future! I do, at least, enjoy my work. Today is May 25, 2012.

JUNE 28, 2012

I just finished a telephone conversation with Mattie. He has been talking to his psychiatrist, his caregivers, and his funding people about his goal of being independent in one year. He just told me he wants to make the break in a year and is hoping to not need supports in place. I asked him why and he said, without hesitation: "Mom, I really needed the help and they spent a lot of money on me to help me get better. I don't want to take advantage of the government's money, cause I think there must be at least one person in BC that needs the funding more than I do now. I am ok and I know now I am going to be okay. I want to be responsible now, and I think I am being that. I know I need to get better, but in a year - I believe I will be just fine. Look how much better I got in this last year. I really AM better, right Mom?"

That was one of his rare moments of true and undeniable clarity.

He added, "When people keep giving you help and money and stuff, they always treat you like you're a victim and can't do anything for yourself. They always end up making you feel like some kind of parasite. They've always got you on a choke collar."

Wow. He actually *understood* the concept of relinquishing control to a government body that does not care. However, there's far more to the postulation than he can grasp.

JUNE 29, 2012

Well, the wait is almost over for me. Tomorrow after work, I drive 1.5 hours to Merritt to pick up Matt at the Greyhound station! SO exciting for him (and for me) that he has achieved this level of independence to travel by bus for the first time in 10.5 years — ALONE! And they said 10.5 years ago he would never be capable of learning and would never experience independence! Thank G-D for funding, rehabilitation, and the bond that a mother and son can have. Matt would have never survived or progressed this far without that magical combination.

JULY 1, 2012

Despite the unpredictable weather ahead of us today, we have plans! First, we will frost the chocolate-walnut cake we baked last night, then go to the mall (Matt wants to do a wee bit of shopping). Kelowna has a reptile sanctuary called CrocTalk, so our plan is to visit crocodiles later, and then go bowling! He has never bowled. If Matt enjoys that, we will go again tomorrow. He is going to need a good social outlet, and that could be good for him, potentially.

Later, we will take a friend and her dog to the doggie beach, then drive to a nearby mountaintop to watch fireworks from a safe distance. Neither of us fares well in crowds with our differing but similar PTSD responses. We are making a smoothie for the road, taking some crackers, a couple of water bottles, and a piece of chocolate cake! I have been trying to teach Mattie the value of being prepared with good nutrition and water when leaving the home and spending less money.

We just returned from bowling! Matt had a BLAST! He loved it, and he beat me in both games. They accommodate a discount for persons with special needs and their caregivers, which was also a pleasant bonus surprise!! So, good to know that five-pin bowling can be added to his list of activities.

JULY 9, 2012

I was sent home from work today because my illness relapsed. I was told to not come back before Friday, and they positioned a temp in my station. What a good firm.

Pneumonia has taken a toll on me. I am almost out of antibiotics and steroids now, and I seem to have relapsed already. Air quality in Kelowna is quite bad today, because of wildfires in Kamloops and winds blowing smoke from distant fires in Siberia, of all places. Certainly, this will not contribute to improving my lung dysfunction.

JULY 10, 2012

I am finally feeling better. I saw my doctor again this morning, and he suggested this could take three to six more weeks to resolve. After that, I am referred for comprehensive respiratory testing at Kelowna General Hospital. He is concerned I could have COPD. Important for the moment, however, is that the pneumonia is resolving. I am to remain home to rest for at least two more days, despite feeling better.

AUGUST 3, 2012

Well, my son arrived safe and sound by Greyhound again. I stopped at the Tim Horton's in Merritt and had an extra-large dark roast waiting for him! On exiting the bus, he introduced me to a lovely man with whom he sat on the ride up. The man actually handed me a bag with six ears of fresh-picked Chilliwack sweet corn. HOW NICE!!!

"Ma'am, you have a wonderful son here. He's so polite and a joy to talk to. You've done a good job with this young man."

Matt beamed with pride as he heard the words. As the man turned to leave, Matt shook his hand. "Thank you for the corn, sir — and for good company on the bus!"

Matt is SO happy to be here and loves my little country rental! We just returned from Dairy Queen, where he just discovered he loves a DQ cone dipped in chocolate! It was like seeing someone have ice cream for the first time! I wondered if he simply did not remember having a chocolate-dipped cone, or whether he had actually never had one in the past?

AUGUST 5, 2012

What a great day yesterday! We're both still exhausted this morning - LOL! We took "Joey" (our newly adopted dog) to the doggie beach. He had a blast! The pup is so social, with dogs and humans. He never strays far during his running about, and returns on command when you call his name. When we were ready to leave, he happily catapulted himself into the back of the Jeep! Matthew was proud!

For dinner, I cooked chicken legs, sauteed mushrooms, and fresh Chilliwack sweet corn! After dinner, my landlords invited us to their place for a bonfire (fueled by new clippings from the orchard), and for S'mores! I learned for the first time that Matthew had never *had* S'mores. Yesterday, we tested his palette with a chocolate-dipped ice cream cone, and today — S'MORES!

My landlord and his wife played guitar and sang Irish folk songs. Matt cried. He was so happy and so touched!

Great love and accomplishment require great risk.

In the past ten years, many individuals have told me to walk away from my son and the trauma of his brain injury. Countless others have told me to live my own life before I used it up. I've listened to others tell me to just let the system take care of him, all reminding me of his history, his psychiatric diagnoses, and that he physically harmed me twice, and had hurt others in the past. I chose another course, however... at great risk (and with expedited aging), but I have no regrets. The reward lies in witnessing Matt's wonderful personality, calm demeanor, and perseverance in becoming the best he can be.

AUGUST 6, 2012

Before we walked out the door to leave for the Greyhound Station, Matt asked me to take his picture one more time. He said, "Mom, I want you to remember me right now, and know just how happy and how sad I am at the same time, and that I will be waiting to see you again in 24 days. Who's counting? I AM!" He added, "And I know you'll take good care of my dog. Thanks for always loving me, Mom."

AUGUST 11, 2012

I am so content with country living. The day before yesterday, a stray mule was running down the road, then through my front yard and around back into the orchard; moments later, the mule's frustrated owner came through to catch him. Fortunately, my landlord's wife (who has three horses of her own) caught the mule, after which the owner tied him to the back of the truck and slowly guided him home again! I have missed so much with city living, all these years!

I truly enjoy having unlimited access to cherries, apricots — and apples soon! Today, I pitted about 10 quarts of cherries. This city girl's fingers are now a muddy shade of purple! I suppose next time I play in the cherry orchard, I need to don a pair of latex gloves.

I spent three hours in the quilt shop with Gertrude today, where she gifted me a beginner's quilting course. I do not feel confident to take that course and feel I am being pushed to do something I am not ready to undertake. It feels like manipulation. She wants a quilting buddy, and I have witnessed her relentless pursuit of what she wants in life.

I was up at 5:30 to walk Joey and returned to bed until 7 AM. Then, I watered the front lawn, talked to Mattie on the phone, and then pulled weeds in the backyard (which is ALL weeds). I filled a large waste container and four garden-waste bags with weeds! My landlord says he is leveling the yard and raising it by four to six inches with new soil; then we water it down well (keep it moist) and he will install sod in a couple of days. I will remove the ghastly ugly water feature in the backyard (which serves as a mosquito haven), fill the hole that will remain, and use the space for more flowers. Plans are to have the backyard in great order by the time Matthew moves up. Will be great to have our coffee and evening tea out there, listening to the birds and maybe catching the odd deer coming through the orchard!

AUGUST 14, 2012

Tomorrow, we will attend the annual meeting with the Acquired Brain Injury Program, the agency with my son's current Surrey contract, his caregivers, respite worker, and me. Matt will tell them tomorrow he is ready to move on... that it is time for him to leave the Lower Mainland and live by choice where he wants to be. Tonight on the phone, Matt said to me, "Mom, you just let me do the talking tomorrow. I've got this. I am really happy to show everybody I can make my own decisions and speak for myself now." WOW... He has utterly transformed in these past five months.

AUGUST 22, 2012

Matt continues to do remarkably well. The annual meeting with the Acquired Brain Injury Program was a horrible insult to his improvements, however. There has been a longstanding history of the ABI Program resenting my involvement as his Committee. Today, they wanted only to fight with me. Despite historical recitals on record and protocols in place for more than a decade of TBI, confirming he could not and would not enter the City of Vancouver or its proximate suburbs unless it was for a medical emergency, the protocols have been ignored. In earlier years, post-TBI, several day workers had violated protocol and taken him into Vancouver with complicated results. The ABI Program now wanted to place him in a Burnaby group home, Burnaby representing a trigger zone positioned too close to Vancouver and with risks of recognition by those from his gangland past. Years ago, in or about 2005, Matthew had been followed home by a former associate who recognized him, after a care aide took him to the Army-Navy store on East Hastings Street in Vancouver — a mere half-block from where he survived his brain injury. The ABI Program is privy to that information, as the matter was carefully documented. At that time, we moved from our then Burnaby location via Police escort. Yet, here we are — fighting over protocols in place to ensure Matthew's safety and the safety of any would-be caregiver for him.

I told them he would not be going to a group home in Burnaby and they dismissed all his hard work simply to fight with me. Once, they told him "Be quiet — you can't understand these things."

Matt responded, gently but firmly, "No disrespect intended, the problem is that I DO understand." I was proud of him.

He also told them, "I am moving to the Okanagan whether I live with my Mom or not. But I think it is better to start off with my Mom and my dog and wait for a group home spot *that way*. Can you understand *that?*"

He continued (I sat and listened). "I know you can't stop my decision because I am not retarded. I *do* understand what's going on. If I mess up, it's on me — not on anyone else, and I will get what I deserve." But he added, calmly, "What I deserve is my FREEDOM. I worked hard for it and you haven't told me once how good I am doing. But even if you don't want to admit it, I know I am doing really, really well."

A year ago, this kind of upset would have thrown him an emotional curveball. Heck, even six months ago, he could not have achieved this, but he has excelled today. He seems more determined than ever to improve and continue doing the right thing.

The meeting did not endear my presence with the ABI Program, but it pleased me that Matthew made efforts to communicate his wishes and hopes.

AUGUST 29, 2012
Well, one more coffee and shower-up so I can attend to litigating against irresponsible drivers some more! I am grateful to love the work I do (especially when office politics can be ignored). Matt arrives tomorrow, which is outstanding. I won't have to walk the dog by myself at 5:30 AM! I predict a great day ahead!

AUGUST 31, 2012
A store clerk today was rude to Matt, noticing his disability and telling him, "Let your mom do that. You won't understand. Let the adults do this." I have to say, Matt has come SUCH a long way in his personal growth. Until now, he would have been angry and would have retorted inappropriately. This time, he cried in the car and said that really hurt his feelings... she really was a bitch... I told him I was proud of him for not being angry, and he said I had taught him to not channel hurt into anger, to feel the hurt because sometimes

it was good. I had forgotten teaching him that, back when he was being so tough and full of himself... He is so very humble now; it is so refreshing.

SEPTEMBER 1, 2012
Incredibly productive day with Mattie so far! We had breakfast at Chances Casino (two eggs, brown toast, two sausages, hash browns & coffee for $5) — and Matt played his first casino machines. He spent $10, won $3.25, and commented that it was a waste of money, but interesting! Then, we picked up all supplies for the next round of renovation projects at the house, came home, and together planted more flowers and two evergreens in the front yard... We walked Joey together and now have some downtime before going to the hockey game at 7 PM! What a great day!

SEPTEMBER 6, 2012
Things continue to be great with Matt at home; he has fared well alone at home while I was at work. I check in by telephone often, typically every hour. He is keeping the house clean, and walking his dog a lot (and has tried running again)... Tonight, I am taking him to the Kelowna Community Theatre for a battle of the bands, organized as a fundraiser for a local musician who recently suffered a brain injury. Matt could never attend such a function in the Lower Mainland (for fear of being recognized), but here in Kelowna, he can try some fresh adventures. He is so very excited! I will be sad to see him leave on Sunday morning, but he will return to Kelowna on September 27th!

We went to the battle of the bands; Mattie was SO excited; he said it was the happiest he'd felt since his brain injury. We sat down inside to hear some incredible music, but he could not tolerate the sound levels. In the past two months, he's developed a hypersensitivity in his only operative ear. He was incredibly disappointed to have to leave; he even tried putting toilet paper in his one good ear, but it was to no avail. The music volume triggered a migraine, and we had to leave. I will take him to the doctor after work tomorrow to get him on a waitlist for a hearing specialist. Poor guy. But he was so happy to venture inside a concert theatre, as he has never had that chance since 2001, before his TBI.

I will buy some foam earplugs for him and hope that will make the hockey outing we have planned for Saturday night more manageable. He is excited to attend a hockey game — something he has not done since he was a child.

SEPTEMBER 8, 2012
Matt had an absolute BLAST at the hockey game last night; his new foam earplugs helped a lot with the loud sounds. He was just fine. He also went out on his own at each intermission for a 1/2 smoke and to go to the washroom. Friends of mine asked if he could navigate his way back and he did well. I told them he had to learn to do this if he was to become independent, and I was pleased to see he passed with flying colors! The game was a 2-2 tie and went into a shoot-off, which Victoria won. Kelowna played well, however; we have a good

team. I look forward to the next game and only wish Mattie could be there. But he will be back in 2.5 weeks.

Mattie made breakfast for us this morning — without prompting! Seven free-range eggs and half a brick of low-fat cream cheese with some yellow peppers and onions! Good job, Matt!! (Why seven eggs? One was for Joey, the dog - and he reminded me "Seven is my lucky number")! He decided that our Sunday morning tradition will now be for him to prepare breakfast, with the caveat that Joey always gets scrambled eggs!

Thursday morning surprise: Matt was very responsible and took the garbage cans to the curb! "Good job, buddy! Thanks for that!"

"Mom, this is my home too and I feel proud to make it better!" Ahhh, the little appreciations we take for granted... His freedoms have been so very removed from him because of the brain injury and now he truly seems to appreciate so many of the "little things" that comprise "normal" life.

Matt had just finished getting dressed this morning and Joey barked an odd bark; I knew something was in the front yard, but assumed there was a fox or a coyote (and hopefully not a bear). We went outside and our landlord's son, Chad, had brought his horse down for a visit! How incredible! This would never happen in the city! I truly love country living! Matt loved spending time with the friendly and calm 29-year-old mare! She also trimmed some of the grass in the front yard!

SEPTEMBER 10, 2012
Well, formal notice has now been delivered to Matt's agency and the funding providers in the soon-to-be-former health authority! He will travel to start his new permanent life in the Okanagan on December 13th. That will put him here in time for Christmas and new year's holidays and will also provide his former caregivers and the agency with time to see Matt off as they begin their own holidays. Giving notice this early *also* permits the agency (and the slow-moving funding authority) to line up the next contract for the residential caregivers that Matt has worked with these past few months. It's a very exciting turn of events, but it has not come to fruition without a lot of organized effort (over 11 years, but with very careful consideration and strategy over the past 60 days!). Congratulations are in order for Matt's diligent efforts and motivation to improve and move forward.

I woke up missing Matt so much; it was really nice having him here and having that first cup of coffee & breakfast together. Joey misses him too, and seems depressed without Mattie here, poor pup.

SEPTEMBER 12, 2012
Today was a productive day. I cleaned all floors in the house and washed bed linens, throw rugs, and dirty clothes. I took Joey to the groomer, washed the Jeep — inside and out; put out more grass seed in the areas where it didn't germinate in the yard before; watered the back yard; washed down the patio; pulled weeds... NOW, I will turn on the TV and paint one focal wall in my living room dark grey (I want my new white mantle to "pop"; the newly painted pale grey doesn't offer enough decorative contrast with the white mantle)...

Then, tomorrow is another day (mowing the lawn and painting the kitchen)!

By the time Matt arrives again, I will surprise him with the progress!

The power of new beginnings. We step outside our comfort zone into what we hope will provide more comfort because *sometimes*, obstacles are put in our way to see if what we want is really worth fighting for.

While I cannot deny my anxiety over Matthew's decisions, the entire purpose of working this hard with him was to let him achieve control over his life decisions. How do we *refuse* the opportunity when the hope of independence was the focus of all rehabilitative efforts?

CHANGE - CONSISTENTLY FLOWING

W ell, once daylight breaks, I will take Joey for his morning walk — then hit the highway. I picked up a one-ton cube van (truck) last night from Rent-A-Wreck, and I am off to Surrey for probably the last time ... Matt is so excited you would think he was a little boy waiting for Santa. He told me moving up here was not a reality until he was packing his stuff. He says now, with a room full of items to go on the truck (yikes — a room full?), he knows this is not a dream! Nice!

OCTOBER 1, 2012

I just spoke with my young man during my lunch break. I left my cell phone at home with him so I could check in to make sure he was okay. He has slept a lot this morning, still completely exhausted. But he was quick to tell me he woke up, had a bath, ate his lunch that I made this morning, folded the clothing from the dryer, and transferred the clothes in the washer into the dryer (I didn't even ASK him to do that; he recognized it needed to be done and, like an adult, just DID it!)... When I phoned this time, he was out walking his dog and told me Rosie (one of our landlord's wonderful dogs (who we now refer to as Joey's girlfriend!) had joined them for the walk. Matt cried (again) saying how happy he was.

"Mom, thank you for letting me live with you again. I love you." He added he was getting happier and happier and he didn't think that was possible.

I know some who view this picture in my book will find it peculiar that I would include such a seemingly inconsequential photograph. But this photo depicts significant progress in Matt's cognitive abilities. He WANTED to see if he could determine how to close the latch on the moving truck, told me not to show him, and he figured it out all on his own. I was as proud of him as he was of himself. The fact that he regularly pushes past his apathy and exhaustion is also impressive. All this from a young man who was thought to be incapable of walking or learning ever again, just 11 years ago.

Matt, closing the door to his moving truck with pride!

We just finished an exhausting trek across the Coquihalla Highway and unloaded his personal effects and furniture at our destination in Kelowna. He climbed right up there to pull down the door (stopped ME from doing it, as he wanted to do it himself)! What amazing progress on his motivation levels!

I witnessed *some* reasoning that explained why Matthew had been unhappy in his Surrey care home placement. He was (undeniably) treated with kindness, but he was not permitted to attempt physical improvements — to do *more*. He was assumed to be developmentally delayed and incapable. Certainly, his attitude and apathy through the years contributed to those misperceptions.

His caregiver at the residential placement in Surrey stopped him from trying to carry his mattress to the truck, and insulted Matt, saying in a very negative tone, "You know you can't do that — get out of the way" (right in front of me). Matt is STILL sad (three days after the fact) over that, as he was *trying his best* to do something he rarely did and was insulted by someone he had trusted and adored for seven months. He was moving outside his comfort zone.

Poor Matt... learning another sad reality of life, that most "caregivers" are simply in it for a paycheck; niceties often fall by the wayside when you decide to move on.

OCTOBER 5, 2012
Matt's first independent program outing (to a cognitive improvement group) via HandyDart & back was a complete success! He said there is NO COMPARISON to the quality of people here in the program (as compared to how it was in Surrey). He phoned me right away, as he promised he would, to let me know he was boarding the HandyDart bus to return home and called again when he arrived home. What an outstanding success on his first solo outing. Wow, I have such hope I could cry!

I had countless concerns about bringing him up here, not knowing if it was the right thing to do, wanting to honor the promise of letting him make some life decisions for himself *if* he did the work. He did the work. Now, every day, his improvements in motivation, memory, and cognition are so clear that it feels like a miracle.

I spoke with one doctor who said that living in the Lower Mainland was triggering and reinforcing his PTSD daily and that was holding him back from further advancement. As he relaxes more and becomes more adjusted to his new environment, I see him blossoming. One day at a time, but so far, we are truly enjoying these positive improvements!

OCTOBER 6, 2012

More insights from Matt. When we reported to BrainTrust for the initial meeting this week, their staff asked me if Matt would benefit from a substance abuse program. I deferred to let Matt answer that (trying to guide him toward independence). He thought about it and replied, "Well, right now, I think it might not be good for me. I used to have a problem with alcohol, but I don't even think about that now. I used to smoke weed and I miss it and I still would like it, but I don't like what it did to my life; it messed me up. So if I go to one of these groups and hear other people talking about *their* problems with weed and drugs, I think it will make my mind go to thinking about it and that's not good. I kinda think about what I hear. So if I have problems, it might help me — but right now, staying with positive people who don't drink and do drugs is my best program."

WOW. Good answer. I was amazed.

OCTOBER 8, 2012

Matt's self-disciplined conditioning efforts have been impressive. Every night, at about 8 PM, he gets his meds laid out for the next day (a triple tray dish for morning, one for 5 PM, and one for bedtime meds). He sets up the coffeepot for the next morning, so all he has to do is push the button, and *voila*! We have coffee without thinking in the morning! He brushes his teeth without prompting and puts out his clothes for the next day. I am so impressed that he does all this on his own. It's a first. It is also evidence that all the lessons have paid off. He was paying attention.

OCTOBER 10, 2012

Matt spent most of the day resting yesterday; I recognized it as a slight depression.

When I finally coaxed him to talk about it openly with me last night, he said he was just letting go of 11 years of stress. He says he was thinking about all the people who were paid to help him and how everyone was just after a paycheck. I told him that was typically part of funded "caregiving." He said he KNOWS everyone was trying to hold him back, and he believes it was to just keep the paycheck coming. "But Mom, I was a handful, too. I wouldn't have wanted to put up with my shit if I was a caregiver."

He has astounded me with his insights, despite his clear disabilities.

For the past year and a half, he has not been permitted food in his suite (nothing; they delivered a meal of THEIR choosing, three times per day) and they did not let him learn to cook, despite his many requests to learn. Matt has been using the range in our home for three days now; he makes breakfast for us each morning and makes tea every night, without supervision (but granted, I am only a room away!). He has performed perfectly and has shown he is capable of so much more than the "caregivers" ever let him try.

I am grateful he is with me here, for whatever period it is. I think I can bring him forward more than most have in the past and prepare him for his next hopeful group home placement here in Kelowna.

OCTOBER 13, 2012

I went for lunch alone at my favorite little sushi place yesterday. I walked in and the owners gave me their usual warm greetings & smiles. Nice. I placed my usual order and sat in my usual seat, my back to the door. I was the first lunch customer of the day.

I could hear a large group arrive, and they sat down at a reserved table. Recognizing one voice, I turned to see this was my ENTIRE 3rd-floor section of support staff, including my immediate co-worker, and the two personal injury paralegals from the 4th floor. I was the *only* person not included in the lunch. I was stunned and so deeply hurt.

I took my order as takeout and left. Instead of letting myself channel this into anger (my first inclination), I considered what I invariably teach my son: feel the pain and work through it, don't mask it with anger, ill will, and inappropriate behavior. After all, anger is merely depression in hiding. So, I cried like a 14-year-old for the next two hours and had difficulties focusing on my work.

Now, I don't even know how to walk into that office with any semblance of pride. What do I feel? I realize I am not liked by the support staff here, only by management and lawyers. I have overheard my coworkers gossip, more than once, that I make their jobs more difficult because of the changes being implemented. Of course, it is a change being directed and designed by me, but at the request of the managing partner.

I realize I am there to work, not to have a social outing... and my boss tells me every week how pleased he is with my abilities and loyalty. He called me his "right hand" just yesterday and told the personnel manager, "I never knew it could be like this."

How does one deal with bullying at this level, at this age? I simply do not have any answers. I continue to be stunned and devastated. Yet, it is an all-too-repetitive issue with women in law firm employ.

OCTOBER 15, 2012

Well, another enlightening weekend with Matt. So much insight forthcoming from him, so many improvements. He is truly tired these days and is sleeping an unusual amount... but he even told me he is letting go of a lot of stress; he says he is so happy to sleep.

He continues to be so responsible in the home, so positive and so helpful. He is so visibly cognizant of how much I do (and have done) for him, too, it truly amazes me. I am so very grateful — and we are both so very lucky.

We went to Montana's for ribs on Saturday (the first time at Montana's, for both of us) and he said he liked it even more than sushi. "Is this healthy?" I laughed so hard I almost had to get up from the table! He looked at me curiously, and said, "Guess not, eh?!"

I am thrilled to have him living at home again. And, of all the times since his brain injury, this is the longest term he has spent with no serious malfunctions surfacing. The worst thing he has done was to call his cousin long-distance three to four times in one day; and after I talked to him about the cost of long-distance and how that money had to come from somewhere, that being our coffee and food outings, I don't think he phoned again! He says he wants to learn as fast as his dog does!

OCTOBER 22, 2012

I have been so busy of late, but have nothing negative to report! Matt continues to show significant improvements every day. He is now studying his book to prepare for taking the test for his learner's permit, as it is his goal to apply for his driver's license for the first time.

Matt continues to fare just fine alone in the home and has proven to be exceptionally responsible with his dog. He has traveled to and from his programs via Handy Dart (alone), and has taken his meds diligently (supervised by me from afar, though I don't let him know I am watching to see how he does)... and he has kept the house impeccably clean (floors, bathroom, laundry, bed made). He is also learning to cook and is proving quite capable and responsible for that.

All this from someone that the Fraser Health Authority's Acquired Brain Injury Program said (just 30 days ago) would always need 24-7 supervision. I won't dance to an "I TOLD YOU SO" dance just yet, but I am in rehearsal!

They also said he could not be trusted with food in the home as he was a compulsive eater (they never let him have anything but milk in his suite for 1.5 years). Our fridge and cabinets are packed with foods of all kinds and he has not compulsively eaten. He has been responsible in every sense.

OCTOBER 25, 2012

Trouble in paradise. Today, I arrived home to find Matthew literally passed out, the door to the house wide open. Before I could even check to see if he was okay, my landlord was at my door asking to have a chat.

It turns out that three different neighbors complained today that Matthew had been knocking on their doors, seeking marijuana. He visited the lesbian couple two doors down so much that they became uncomfortable and asked my landlord to ensure Matthew never returned. In fact, they had become so uncomfortable they told my landlord they felt Matt was creepy and because he was so big and had a brain injury; they were afraid of him. It's not the first time I have heard women speak of Matthew in this manner, although it has been years of freedom from that concern.

I had no words to express my shame, and my apology felt meaningless. Assuring my landlord that I would handle this, he asked, "How? I think it makes sense for you two to find another place to live, don't you?"

I told him I understood and would seek an alternative rental right away. When my landlord left, I vomited.

Matt awoke about an hour later, feigning a "Welcome home, Mama Bear — are you okay? What's wrong?" We discussed the need to find another place to live, and the issues that cannabis presented for him, as no group home environment would permit residence if he was using drugs.

Of course, he cried and promised to be better. He wanted to visit my landlord to apologize, and I told him that was probably not good timing. He said he was feeling like he was afraid to fail and just wanted to sleep, and he knew the lesbians down the street smoked weed. I did not bother to ask how he knew that, but it was clear he had visited before and had neglected to share that with me. His olfactory senses are likely as good as those of a K9 unit.

I spent the next two hours online researching available rentals. I have an appointment to view one, a ground floor suite in a home on acreage, tomorrow.

OCTOBER 27, 2012

What a whirlwind of packing, cleaning, and organizing. We move to a new rental on October 31st. The owners are both retired, and the wife is a former neurological registered nurse, so disclosure of Matt's brain injury was not an issue. We omitted any discussions of marijuana issues, as that was a *need-to-know basis* and they did not need to know. In this location, there would be no issues with marijuana, as Matthew would have no means of solicitation, thankfully.

Ahh, we do what we have to do to get done what needs to be done — repeatedly!

I hope that the new location, out of harm's way with no neighbors for miles, will be a positive for Matthew. At least, he cannot seek marijuana from neighbors (as there are none).

Onward and upward. We hiccup and take a sip of water or hold our breath in response. Brain injury tango is no different.

NOVEMBER 2, 2012

Matt's intake appointment with Interior Health Acquired Brain Injury Program just got delayed by another 45 minutes! Poor guy, his anxiety is steadily climbing, evident in his leg-shaking and eyes darting about the room. I always tell him we must find OPPORTUNITY in everything. Earlier this morning, he told me, "I guess this is my opportunity to be patient!" I told him good things come to those who wait, and he replied, without blinking an eye, "Okay, then; I think a lot of good stuff must be about to happen!"

I had a telephone conversation with a friend from Chilliwack tonight. She told me, "Matt sure has come a long way. I know how proud you must be of him... I like his way of thinking, and I always have. It's easy to see why you are so dedicated to him."

Of course, I did not share that we lost a good rental because of his side-stepping.

I told her he had done so well in the especially long meeting today. He really is different, now that he is out of his PTSD zone in the Lower Mainland. All those years, I told the "caregivers" that his PTSD held him back and prevented him from learning, from focusing, from even trying, and they all ignored me as though I had two heads and should be invisible. This woman today acknowledged that PTSD would have assuredly prevented him from moving forward and more. She asked questions in this interview that NO ONE in 11 years of brain injury ever asked. I was very impressed, relieved — and filled with immense hope for his future. While I realize that, ultimately, it is all up to him to push himself to achieve and accept the opportunity for real help, I am hopeful he will seize this opportunity.

NOVEMBER 3, 2012

Well, I am determined to make this a positive day, despite how it has begun. (1) 2nd night in a row I have had "nightmares" about returning to work and (2) Matt woke me at 4:30 to tell me there was water all over the floor of the laundry room... The owners brought in a lovely new washer & dryer yesterday, but it would seem the hoses were faulty. Interesting that no one tested that after installation.

Now all our towels are wet and dirty and inside the washer that cannot be used. I had to disengage the water supply to stop the water from pooling on the floor.

Employment nightmares, however, are probably a subliminal message of how unhappy I am with the continuing, imminent office politics, and likely another subconscious response to my worry about Matthew in the future.

Matt has been exhausted, and ashamed for ruining his long run of progress. I have tried to redirect that, unsure of how far to take the "don't worry — let's just move forward" and how far to go into discussions of marijuana and the issues it has always precipitated for him.

Me, just now — talking, talking, talking (to Matt), with Matt giving no response. I look and see he is sleeping!

"You fell asleep while I was talking, buddy!"

Without missing a beat, that quick wit surfaced, "Well, at least I didn't interrupt you!"

NOVEMBER 6, 2012

After his first cup of coffee, on this, his 34th birthday today, Matt leans back and says, "Mom, I'm so happy to be alive!"

NOVEMBER 9, 2012

Martin Luther King once said, "I have a dream"... Well, I sure HAD a dream — wow. I dreamed Joey (our dog) ate a spider in the garden, started breathing heavily, his face swelled and turned into a pig's head — snout and all... Then he laid down and died. Two Mexican workers (what?) dug a grave and buried Joey, as we didn't want Matt to come home and see he was dead. I cried for Joey and cried for Matt and told him Joey was the best dog anyone could ever have. My mother was there (What? We have been estranged for 32 years), and said "How about Dutchess [my childhood pet, a Boxer]? He wasn't better than Dutchess." I retorted with "He was twice the dog Dutchess was" (another what? As I would never have challenged anything my mother said)... Then, in my dream, Matt came home and asked where Joey was. I was about to tell him the truth gently, but my husband (what? haven't been married for 32 years), who was Barack Obama (What? I have never liked Barack Obama) told Matt Joey went walkabout. My last thoughts in the dream sequence were, "Just like a politician — covering the truth and keeping someone ignorant."

And I reviewed what I had for dinner prior to that dream!

NOVEMBER 13, 2012

Good day, today. Office politics seem to be resolving and settling down. My brutal co-worker is to have her employment terminated this week and there is a new hire already approved and in the works.

Matt continues to show various slight improvements daily. I note he is particularly tired, and I am wondering whether it is (1) the new environment and adjustments and the letting go of 11 years of PTSD triggers or (2) all that with perhaps not needing the same level of medication he did before; now that the PTSD triggers are gone, is his current level of medication too high? He is asleep by 8:30 or 9 PM every night and nodding out by 7 o'clock. Of course, my first suspicion is whether he has somehow resorted to cannabis again. I am hopeful; I am proud — but reality dictates a history that cannot be ignored.

Happily, his tox screen results just returned negative; he is totally clean (no marijuana), so that is wonderful. I will speak with his doctor on Monday when he has his next appointment.

Kelowna has been really hard on me. Now, with almost nine months in (like a pregnancy, eh?), I can still say I find Jon & Jane Q. Public superficial and insincere — more "uppity and entitled" here than in Vancouver.

NOVEMBER 25, 2012

Today marks Day Two on my Synthroid (thyroid medication). HOLY CROW! I cannot BELIEVE the difference in how I feel. Even Matt said, "Mom, it's like you got younger overnight." My energy levels are off the scale; I have not felt this good in at least four years. I am so glad I made the time for myself and asked for a full blood workup a few weeks ago.

NOVEMBER 30, 2012

Wow, another very productive day, but I still haven't finished organizing things. Tomorrow, I should be able to complete most of the balance. Today, I hung curtain rods and drapes and assembled my log bed (I am now the proud owner of my first socket set!)... The place is really coming together now, although I truly miss the little house on the orchard property.

I returned to the former house and got all floors mopped, fridge cleaned, oven cleaned, and bathroom spic & span. I will return the keys to those landlords and get on with my day.

Matt was incredible help today; he pushed himself to exhaustion, and I was proud of him. He went to bed at 9:30; I'm sure he will be pooped tomorrow.

DECEMBER 5, 2012
Today marked perhaps the nicest birthday I can remember. Matt was so loving and attentive; he made two cards for me, made me coffee this morning, and sent me four happy birthday emails. He also did most of the dinner cooking tonite!

At work, my boss and the firm partners gave me a gift card for Orchard Park Mall, my new coworker came into work last night, just to put a surprise card and a rose in a lovely vase on my desk to surprise me (WOW), another coworker brought me homemade cranberry shortbread... and about 12 people in the firm wished me Happy Birthday. Three staff (none of the paralegals from the personal injury law group, however) took me out to lunch and tried to buy my lunch for me, but the owner of the Japanese restaurant treated me to a free birthday lunch!

DECEMBER 10, 2012
Poor Matt, sick again. He has really had a time of it; he's been sick at least one day per week for three consecutive weeks now. It never lasts long, but it is disconcerting. Poor guy.

DECEMBER 9, 2012
We woke up to snow pouring down, so we went into the hot tub (yes, there is a hot tub for use here and Matt is in heaven with that) at 9:30 this morning with the snow coming down! It was outstanding! Joey played in the snow while we enjoyed the hot water — and Joey's new friend, Levi (a lovely fluffy white Samoyed) came bouncing down and they played in the snow. What a lovely day off!

One of my friends gave us her old seven-foot tree yesterday. When she visited, she brought her son and grandson with her. The son said, "Damn, to live this far out, it'd have to be a really nice place — and it is!"

Yes, we are a 30-minute drive to the "city," and folks in Kelowna think that is a long drive! I remember living in Surrey and driving 1.5 hours to Chilliwack many times (to go to work, one-way)! I love living in the wilderness, and Matt is just thrilled with it!

So nice to be where we are right now; we are truly lucky.

DECEMBER 17, 2012
So now the begging begins with this health authority, for funding for Matt and hopefully placement into a small group home for high-functioning brain injury survivors. Even the psychiatrist agrees Matt is too dependent on me right now and this may deter him from moving forward as much as he might be capable. Matt also agrees, so it is wonderful to all agree. Fingers crossed... Our meeting with the health authority's Acquired Brain Injury Program is on Wednesday.

Being a primary caregiver and the sole parent to a 34-year-old, 6⫽3⫽ 290-pound man with a brain injury has its trials; our days are seldom drama-free. But there are days of clarity when everything has been perfect, and I realize how very far my son has come, and how very proud I am of him. Today, he did all the laundry and vacuumed the entire house. He then walked two miles down the road to meet me partway when I came home from work to pick him up and take him to see his psychiatrist. The doctor told him he was doing VERY well, that he was now showing more insight and awareness, and thus he can progress further still.

DECEMBER 18, 2012

Matt says almost every day that he is a better person for having had the brain injury. He also never complains about his double vision or lack of peripheral vision, or full deafness in one ear. His TMJ issues persist, though he does not complain about that, either. "I'm sorry about my jaw clicking" is as close as he gets to a complaint, and that is because he is very embarrassed by it in public. He is also self-conscious about the appearance of his lazy eye and still tries to wear sunglasses when he visits anyone or any place, whether outdoors or indoors. He often mentions that he just wants to be seen as a normal man for a change.

I think he has reacted to the horrific in an ultimately positive manner (it took 11 years, but that's not the point)!

Hope springs eternal. I am grateful not to have lost mine.

THE AUDACITY OF IGNORANCE

W ow! 1:30 AM. I just finished another five hours of holiday baking. Matt stuck it out with me, helping & learning, for 3.5 of those hours — which was simply remarkable motivation. We made five different savory tarts... with more to follow on Thursday. Tonite, we created (1) portobello mushroom, brisket, black olives & gorgonzola with pecans & cranberry; (2) sausage & cheddar; (3) walnut, blue cheese & pear with thyme; and (4) creamy swiss cheese with dill and almonds. Yes, some weird flavors, but they all worked! I am exhausted but grateful for another simply wonderful day!

DECEMBER 20, 2012
    Baking concluded! We will only cook for Christmas day, and then we are strictly on egg whites, turkey & chicken breast, and a lot of fibrous veggies with gallons of water again! We sure have made some WONDERFUL memories for Matt to have the balance of his life; he is so very happy — and says so every day!

DECEMBER 22, 2012
    "Mom, that sure is an ugly horse, eh?" Matt's words after being told he just saw a bull moose on the property where we live!

Matt's idea of an
"ugly horse!"

We have over 12 inches of snow on the ground, despite seeing a sunny day today! It's a winter wonderland for real, up here! People love riding snowmobiles and Mattie remarked, "It's the sound of fun!" We also enjoy seeing the wildlife prints every morning from deer and coyotes. We've seen no evidence of cougars or bears yet, which is a positive, although we've been told that they exist in the area!

Matt chose tree decorations and decorated the tree himself; he was very proud! He opted for lots of colorful, glittery butterflies and dragonflies in the mix!

DECEMBER 24, 2012

Matt asked if we could open one present this morning. My resounding reply was an emphatic, "NO!!"

DECEMBER 28, 2012

I had to rush home from work yesterday to deal with a serious situation. Yesterday (late morning), my new landlord SMOKED A JOINT with Matthew. Matt vomited, passed out in a chair at my landlord's shop, and could not be awakened. The landlord's wife is a nurse and said he was showing "neurological signs" (twitching of face and hands). Then the landlord transported Matt up to our side of the property via snowmobile, as Matt could not walk. When I got home, Matt was passed out in the center of his bed (not sleeping, but unconscious). I have always suspected that marijuana was triggering seizures and changes in his brain. *Neurological signs* are residuals from seizures.

NOW, I have to take ANOTHER day off work (losing money here) to get Matt tox-screened (drug test) to find out exactly what went into his system, so I have it documented.

And disappointingly, my landlord knows full well that Matthew is on serious medication and cannot entertain the use of illicit drugs. His wife is even more aware.

We attended with Matt's family physician this morning and received a confirming opinion that Matt was unconscious yesterday, likely because of a seizure. He has minor neurological signs continuing this morning, but he is slowly improving. He has regressed cognitively and significantly. They performed a tox screen for marijuana, amphetamines, barbiturates, opiates, cocaine, and benzodiazepines. We will know late afternoon today or Monday morning whether it was "just" marijuana or the illicit substance was laced with something else.

Matt should be placed into a funded group home in two to four months, so when he is placed, I will make an educated decision on my move from this location. I seriously doubt this landlord will interact with Matt ever again. Everything is formally documented now, so I've covered all bases. There's a logic in conferring with a lawyer on all this. I should not be jumping into another immediate, fast-tracked move again. I feel it best to let this sit for now as an educational awareness lesson. I need advice.

Matt is slowly on the mend, thankfully. It's 8:09 PM now. He spent all morning vomiting, but now is keeping food down and improving cognitively. I still see signs of a very significant setback. I am trying to view this as another learning opportunity — a BIG FAT learning opportunity... and a chance to feel gratitude for the situation not being worse than it was.

I received an apology from my landlord. Although it was a wholly inappropriate thing to give cannabis to someone with a brain injury, I truly don't think he had any idea how serious it was going to be for Matt. I surmise he's had a learning opportunity, too.

I believe in moving forward and being grateful for recovery.

Thanks to the Universe for a bit of good news in the mix. I received a call from the health authority today, advising that Matt may have funded residential care in three months! Great news for BOTH of us (especially Matt)!

DECEMBER 29, 2012
Matthew seems to be gradually improving, still; he has cognitively digressed, however, with short-term memory, speech, and communication skills diminished significantly. He slept for three hours this afternoon. Now, I am filling him with more water (to flush his system) and large quantities of odorless garlic capsules (to further flush his system). I have also administered a B12 injection.

Good grief, I am drained. Alas, this is TBI and all the trials and tribulations that go with it. Five steps forward, three steps back. Can't dance that one to music; it sounds like a bad country tune!

JANUARY 4, 2013
Amid counting gratitudes, and indeed I have many, I cannot help but continue to turn my mind to my landlord's wrongdoing in smoking marijuana with my son. I cannot get past it, despite trying to do so. It has adversely affected the professional relationship that ought to exist and the more time that passes, the more this gross breach of trust outrages me. I am calm, but I am internally livid. The audacity of such ignorance boggles my mind.

Matthew is in good spirits, but his cognitive levels continue to be problematic. He is cognizant of the decline. I hope he returns to his former level, but it is too soon to speculate.

JANUARY 5, 2013
Today was a good day. Matt did well. He attended his cognitive rehab program at BrainTrust after weight training at the gym with Cindy, the RN I hired to work with him for four hours on Fridays. I drive him to her house each morning on my way to work. Funding was also just approved for Wendy to work with Matt three hours per day, two days per week, starting next week. We are off to another outstanding start, taking a deep breath and moving forward again.

And I count my blessings for a good day at work today, too. My boss told me (out of the blue), "In all my 32-year career, I have never had the quality staff I have now. I'm thrilled with the way we work together." WOW.

JANUARY 8, 2013
Life is all about choices. I don't want to focus on the melodrama from the now-paranoid landlord that forced me to stay home from work today, but with all things as an opportunity, today became an impetus for educated decision-making.

Matthew had nightmares during his afternoon nap and woke up screaming, but I am grateful he is faring better now. Love can bridge an enormous gap, more often than not. "I am so sorry to cause this trouble, Mom. I was getting smarter, but now I am retarded again. Those people with the brain injury association might be right — maybe I *can't* make good decisions all the time, and sometimes one little decision makes a monster of a disaster. I am so sorry, Mom."

With the continuing discomfort and distrust of our presence on this property, and after careful consideration and discussion, Matthew and I are opting to move again. The breach of trust that occurred here just can't be overlooked, and neither can I ignore the fact that these are property owners in their 60s — they KNOW better. The lawyer suggested to me that because I now know that the property owner smokes marijuana and the drugs are on the property, to remain there would place Matthew (and others) at risk; assuredly, with his compulsions for marijuana, we cannot stay — and we can't "move forward" from something that has born such consequences. I have secured another rental in West Kelowna for mid-month.

The audacity of ignorance creates its own karma. The property owner has lost a tenant again. But if I remained, it would be my audacity of ignorance with consequences to follow.

THE CONSEQUENCES OF RELENTLESS ADVOCACY

W ell crap. Never one to give in to exhaustion for long, I may have pushed too much. The doctor told me I had a stroke Saturday night. Now, I have instructions to be off work at least for this week. I am in Kelowna General Hospital's stroke clinic Thursday morning at 8 AM for an EEG and CT of the brain. If I have any further symptoms, I am to transfer by ambulance to the hospital.

This is not exactly the holiday from work I would have imagined, but it represents a very serious wake-up call of the timely need for Matthew to have professionally supervised care. If anything happens to me, the response for him will be catastrophic.

JANUARY 17, 2013

Just got back from the KGH stroke clinic. I will return for an ultrasound of the heart and carotid artery, a CT of the brain, and an EEG tomorrow.

The neurologist says I definitely had an event warranting concern, and that I was at high risk for another if I did not follow secondary protocols (being attentive to my nutrition, being consistent with exercise in moderation, and with the medication prescribed). My blood pressure was 180/100, so that is also a less than promising sign.

I truly hope to return to work on Monday morning. I dislike being at home like this, sedentary and not using my mind.

JANUARY 18, 2013

After I drop Matt off with his life skills worker, I will report to the hospital for further testing. After that, I will see my GP for a blood pressure medication prescription. Yesterday, the neurologist alluded to me being off work another week. Ugh. I actually *miss* work. I suppose it is better to be rested and let medication run its course, so I can *remain* at work.

They have ordered me off work for another week; blood pressure meds are to be started and monitored, and I am then back to see my

GP on Wednesday for the results of the CT and carotid ultrasound. Appointments for EEG and echo-cardiogram will be forthcoming, and I will attend for further bloodwork, as well. Having access to comprehensive medical care is something I appreciate.

JANUARY 25, 2013

I am back to work on Monday; will be happy to be there. Matt has proven very helpful in the house since I became ill. He actually finished shoveling our driveway today (while he smoked half a cigarette; go figure).

JANUARY 27, 2013

It's been a genuine relief to see Matthew improving cognitively over the past three days. He is still not back to *baseline*, but he is doing well. I am so thankful he remains kind, calm, and gentle. The cannabis-induced seizure really damaged him. We've seen 4.5 weeks pass, and he is just not who he was before the seizure. I am trying to keep him focusing on the positives and grateful for all that *is* going right.

FEBRUARY 20, 2013

There's still no word on residential placement for Mattie, but the great news is that he is now visiting a group home for severely brain-injured adults, four days per week. He reports he loves going and looks forward to being there the next day! Feeling helpful, welcomed, and liked makes him appreciate his life even more because he is the highest functioning client there.

"Mom, all the women have crushes on me, and that makes me feel honored. When I'm there, I know I'm a hunk. Plus, everybody *likes* that I want to help, instead of telling me to sit down and let the adults handle things."

Ahhh, that distinct need for all of us to feel valued and appreciated.

He arrives home around 6 PM, so this also gives me 1.5 hours alone, which is a good reprieve for me — a compromised respite of sorts.

MARCH 4, 2013

It's hard to believe I've been in Kelowna for almost two weeks now! Time has flown. I am now moved into my three-month temporary sublet, a lovely house on a quiet cul-de-sac (the owner is away for work in Vancouver for three months). I will begin the search for a place to call my own, soon!

MARCH 7, 2013

TGIF... not because I want to rush my days away, but because work drama has reared its ugly head again, and I am bothered by the childish irresponsibility of it all. At least, my co-worker arrives late every morning and takes extended lunches, so I don't have to endure her disdainful, entitled, self-absorbed attitude for the full day. I will leave early today to go to the hospital for my long-awaited echo-cardiogram. After that, I should have an updated status report of what's going on with my heart. I have been having daily arrhythmia (fluttering) for a while now).

I look forward to the weekend with Matt and have lots of walking in our tentative plans.

MARCH 10, 2013

We had an outstanding walk through the bird sanctuary across from our home this morning. Matt really persevered and chose a rather steep path! He almost could not navigate the incline, but he did not give up! I was proud of him, and now, we both have sore calves, quads, hamstrings & glutes! He says he can't wait to go again, right before dinner! "That's music to my ears, buddy — you are taking care of your health!"

"Mom, I am taking care of *your* health! If I push myself, you will push yourself, too!"

MARCH 22, 2013

I have tickets for tomorrow night's Kelowna Rockets hockey playoffs! We've developed a love of hockey in the past year! Matt is excited!

MARCH 23, 2013

After taking a walk along the beach on the West Side today, we went for a drive. Matt looked at the top of a mountain and asked, "What's that? A jail?" I told him I didn't know, but it looked like a monastery to me.

"What's a monastery?"

I explained and asked if he wanted to figure out how to get up there. Without a moment's hesitation, he was primed for the adventure! We took a lot of wrong turns and saw half of G-D's creation on that side of West Kelowna, along with some crazy beautiful views (and homes). We finally found our destination (after 45 minutes of guesswork driving). Turns out, we found the Mission Hill Estate Winery! We got out and walked around the grounds, which were immaculately groomed and breathtaking. We were there for the bell chime at 2 PM.

Matt is now back home, exhausted, asleep, and snoring! What a beautiful outing — simple, low-cost, and a memory for a lifetime!

MARCH 26, 2013

After making me a cup of coffee this morning, Mattie asked, "What's for brekkie this morning?"

"Healthy!"

"Okay." He returned to the living room to turn on the morning news and I delivered cooked large-flake oats (porridge), with fresh Fuji apples, dried cranberries, a few raw cashews, and some almonds, with cinnamon and Stevia.

He could not stop raving about the flavor! "This *cannot* be good for me! It's too good!"

MARCH 30, 2013

Matt: "Can we get a snack?"

Me: "OK, what would you rather have — a cookie or frybread?"

Matt: "Wow, only one piece of frybread? How can anybody eat only one? I guess if it has to be one, I will go with the cookie. No second piece of frybread might make me sad!"

We heard from the health authority today and have fingers crossed again. Apparently, there has been a group home with an opening for a few weeks. We toured the home and are hopeful. Now, the "concerted beg for funding" begins again.

APRIL 7, 2013

Still no word from the health authority regarding the group home placement. Mattie keeps saying, "Patience is a virtue!"

Today, I finally started a nutrition and exercise plan. I just got sick and tired of feeling sick and tired. Besides, if I ever want to see myself away from these horribly costly meds, I need to smarten up and do something about my health right now. If I leave my current employment, I have to face the reality of having no extended health benefits. If I had to pay for my medication, the cost would be over $1,100 every second month.

APRIL 10, 2013

Matt woke me up at 5 AM again, trying to sneak out for a smoke. I am exhausted, and he knows our agreed protocol with smoking. I cannot help but be irritated, but I am trying diligently to turn it all around and be positive, eat clean and work toward getting *my* health back in order. If I collapse, I won't be of any use to Matthew.

We still have to be attentive to Matthew's health issues, so I will leave work early today to take him to his doctor to query foot pain that has been longstanding and getting worse. It had to be excruciating for him to say anything, as it is atypical for him to complain — unless it is about weak cigarettes.

He cried on the way to the doctor. "Mom, what if this is G-D punishing me, even though I am a good man now?"

"Buddy, this has nothing to do with G-D; this is TBI."

"Mom, I will pray for you so G-D doesn't get mad at you, too."

Matt's diagnosis? Plantar fasciitis, right foot. Heel arch supports are to be purchased, some stretching exercises implemented, and regular ice applied to the affected area. I never figured Matt could be so happy to hear that his limping doesn't mean he's dying. Poor guy.

I often reminisce about the events of our day. I was disappointed in myself for becoming irritated with him for waking me up this morning, trying to sneak out for a cigarette. He accepted my reprimand rather than communicate to me how stressed he was and how much pain he was in. I know Matthew has a low pain tolerance and had I realized he needs the "tranquilizing effect" of tobacco to deal with his stress, I suspect I would have been more understanding and compromising.

Matthew is afraid of complaining, so he doesn't. A complaint finds him judged and results in him being accused of being ungrateful to be there. Complaint sees him being told he is attention-seeking, and in a group home, he finds himself told to go to his room because someone is busy and can't deal with him right now.

The organic brain injury constrains his ability to communicate effectively, but also the historical disciplinary response from a litany of less-than-optimal group home management scenarios has created a barrier to communications.

At the end of our day, I apologized to Mattie. Earlier, he'd told me he did not sleep through the night because he was so worried about the pain. He laid there, tossing and turning with his racing thoughts. He truly feared he might be dying. "Mom, I really tried to be silent and not wake you up. I am the one who should be sorry."

Heck, he could have opened his bedroom window and had a smoke right there (that is something he did for years post-TBI — in my home and in care homes), but he didn't. He waited to do the right thing in the best way he knew how. How sad, and a little tragic for *both* of us.

APRIL 11, 2013

Someone in my office told me yesterday I should wait to start a diet (clean eating) until Matthew's placement is approved — this coming from a woman at least 100 pounds overweight. I told her I'm now four days in, and yes, with a headache and feeling somewhat grumpy with sugar withdrawal, but with health concerns, there is one day or DAY ONE, and no time like the present. This way, I have a head start on the time when Matt gets his placement and I am more relaxed and more motivated. Green beans, tuna & brown rice just don't fill the void like poutine - true, but they also don't extend my belly and widen my arse either!

Earlier this week, my Boss brought me back a box of milk chocolate-covered macadamia nuts from Maui. The unopened box is still in the trunk of my car!

The steady and surly saga of ridiculous office politics continues. I am taking tomorrow off work because of it. Flex-time is available because I put in over 10 hours of overtime this week. Gym training is ahead and I will take a couple of walks tomorrow, hoping to get my head screwed back on straight for Monday.

APRIL 12, 2013

With the struggles (and victories) of TBI, we learn to take each day as it comes. Most days, we can dig deep to find positives on which to focus, despite the side-steps of the moment. Today marks a double victory, however!

1. Matthew's funding for residential care placement has been approved! Now we await the contract, and he should be able to enter on May 1st!

2. Taking the day off work was a plus. My irreverent co-worker was reprimanded, and I am to be moved to a private office. I will visit my office on Sunday and discreetly transfer all files and binders, and clean and organize my desk. Quiet transition, hoping to avoid the melodrama certain to flow from the disgruntled two personal injury paralegals on the 4th floor.

APRIL 13, 2013

How ironic! Just yesterday, Matt told me he didn't correct someone at his day program because it was better to let him think he was right and feel good about himself. WOW. There's no disputing that I learn from my son every day. Despite feeling I want to "go on strike" from time to time, I value seeing the insights he has developed because of living with his own consequences.

> "If you have to choose between being kind and being right, choose to be kind and you will always be right."

Things are really coming together now. Matthew can move his bed into the group home on the evening of Friday, April 26th. I will drive him over with his clothing, family photos, stereo & computer on Saturday. Here's to hoping the honeymoon phase can expand into a good fit with this group home. I am grateful for the reprieve and the hopeful opportunity for Matthew to learn and achieve the next steps toward his personal goals.

Right now, I cannot share this incredible turn of events with him! That will have to wait until Friday evening when we move his bed into the home. He has a neuropsychiatric assessment during the day that same Friday. If I tell him of the move-in date before the assessment, I know he will be too excited and over-stimulated to relax for the grueling seven-hour assessment.

What wonderful opportunities for him... a new baseline of neuropsych assessment, so we can truly see how far he might improve from here, and also compare with prior neuropsych results to determine progress or decline. The chance to live in a group home with peers again is timely, too. It is important that he develop a lesser dependence on me.

AND, I feel a wee bit guilty saying it, but this will be the first time I can relax and have an adult life since his TBI... I am so glad to have fought the good fight for him, and I don't regret the sacrifices made. But I am looking forward to having a glass of wine in my home if I want, to having friends over for dinner again, and to having friends and family here to visit! I also look forward to being able to keep knives in my kitchen again.

MAY 25, 2013

Time at the group home has fared well. There have been minor behavioral hiccups, with Matt pressing boundaries in the beginning. But all seems to be stabilized now.

Matt stayed over last night. After coffee & breakfast, we had a little walk through the paths in the bird sanctuary across the street! Made Matt take a route where there was NO path, but he giggled all the way, calling it SO much fun! I pointed out nature's art, such as fallen trees, a decaying tree stump (with a rock at the center, and fascinating roots entwined, which had grown around the rock). We saw wild roses, red-winged blackbirds, magpies, an eagle... and bless his heart, he told me I am the most interesting person he knows. Poor guy doesn't get out much!

He always laughs at me when I point out the beauty in rocks. As with any other such occasion, today he chuckled another, "Rock on, Mom!"

What a beautiful bonding opportunity. We will rest and do another walk around Shannon Lake later!

Sometimes, the consequences of relentless advocacy take a toll on our health... but sometimes, the wake-up call is all we need to see ourselves back to the victories of relentless advocacy. We give our heads a shake, take a deep breath and give some gratitude to G-D for the reprieve.

ANOTHER STEP IN THE DANCE

Mattie moved into the Kelowna group home end of April. It made for an exhausting morning, but we got managed! I returned home and slept the entire balance of the afternoon and through the night. I haven't done that for a long time. Sunday, I was literally, physically sick (exhaustion I think)... and was in bed all day. I did not leave for anything.

Matt is extremely homesick, but faring well. There will be significant adjustments for him, but I predict he will be just fine.

I miss him, too — this will be an interesting transition for both of us!!

MAY 4, 2013

What a fabulous day today. We had a stress-free outing after I picked up Matt at 11:30. I love we can now be just *family*. I no longer have to be a case manager, disciplinarian, teacher, chief cook, and bottle washer! We had coffee, then went for a drive to Peachland, and walked along Lake Okanagan there in the 22-degree sunshine. On the way back, we stopped at The Kekuli Cafe in West Kelowna for an Indian taco (chili for me, pulled pork for Matt), then went back to my place and just talked! I baked a huge carrot cake with orange creme-cheese frosting for the group home, which was a great hit with all (and made Matt feel so proud). He is SO happy and adjusting so very well to his new environment. I am so pleased to see that.

MAY 6, 2013

I almost have the guest bedroom organization finished. Matt took all the furniture for his new placement, so I had to shop for a bed, end tables, shelves, and a desk. I secured a decent bed & desk over the weekend, picked up a shelf after work today, and will pick up tables after work tomorrow! I am almost ready for visitors now!

Mattie telephoned to leave a message for me at 4 PM. "Mom, don't worry — it's NOT bad news!" He merely called to let me know he could not phone at the usual time, as they were going bowling.

I am thrilled that he is transitioning so well and has these incredible opportunities to socialize in safety with supervision!

MAY 11, 2013
Two weeks in today. Matt is settling in nicely at the Kelowna group home. He tells me every evening, in our one conversation by telephone daily, that it is so much better than what he had before and he loves it there. He said the same thing about the early days with his last Surrey placement, however, so this is part and parcel of *the honeymoon phase*. Everyone, including Matthew, is on their best behavior initially.

I am very fortunate that he has this opportunity, the funding for it, and the ability to live peacefully. He is safe and supervised again, and it can be "Mother's Day" every day of my life now!

MAY 18, 2013
When I think about the happiest, most memorable moments of my life — it is not in remembering large purchases or great promotions... but rather of the small moments of appreciating life, having those profound epiphanies of knowing just how lucky I am (or was)... The memories of so many minor victories with my son, quiet explorations in nature, and learning that humankind can have so much in common and at the time be so diverse!

I find myself overwhelmed with having less "overwhelm" now! I believe my body (and mind) have been in a continual cortisol rush since Matt was about 11 years of age.

I decided a housecleaning blitz was in order for today! I was up at 5:30; watched the news & had one cup of black coffee. I rearranged the furniture in the guest bedroom, moved two mirrors and two end tables from the living room to the guest bedroom; mopped & waxed hardwood floors; mopped tile floors; cleaned both bathrooms; washed two loads of laundry; disposed of the dead flowers in pots on my balcony (gardening is not working for me right now; time to pursue that another time). I had my bath and styled my hair (all done by 9:44 AM)! Finally, I am ready to pick up Matt at 11 AM for two days of fun!

It's 3:41 PM as I write this — typically a time spent with my son, but it turned out to be a short-lived visit with him today. Turns out, he smoked weed yesterday... so I had to deny him the movie, the walk, and the overnight stay we had planned. I set boundaries and conditions before, including "if he smokes marijuana, he cannot have time with me." Consequences for him, and consequences for *me*, as I face having to keep my word. Ahh, the struggles of brain injury... and the worst part is, he has received a warning from the group home already, that they cannot permit him to live there if he brings drugs to their premises again. How did he come to have the marijuana? He went to group therapy yesterday, and another participant passed him a joint under the table. No more group therapy now, either. Holy crow.

Random Thought: I remember when I had rare moments of realized happiness, and every time one popped through — I was afraid something bad was going to transpire and ruin it. WOW. I am now trying to focus on the good that is there every single day. Truly, we all need to be happy *in the moment*, but I honestly don't know how I am going to muster rescue for another potential decompensation from Matt. This vicious cycle has really taken a toll on me.

MAY 25, 2013

Funny, Matt suggested I buy myself some more clothes (mine are just fine, but I do wear the same five outfits repeatedly to the office). He seems to think other people would notice if I arrived in new attire, and would be impressed, and I told him, "Buddy, I really don't care what other people think, so long as I, myself, know I look appropriate & professional!" Caring less about things that ultimately do not matter is a wonderful release of unnecessary drama & anxiety! But, bottom line, Matt does not know that I cannot afford new clothing and the necessity that remaining frugal is for me. It is a burden of knowledge he should not have to bear. I never know when I am going to be facing financial hardship in order to advocate for him again, and experience has taught me it happens far too regularly. Alas, this is my life: my choice. Despite the challenges and complexities ongoing, I love my son with all my heart. No one else is going to advocate for him OR love him, and he did not ask to be born. I will never abandon him; the pain of that first-hand experience is nothing I want my son to suffer. He has enough to endure and overcome as it is.

JUNE 7, 2013

Incredible news for Matt! In 12 years of brain injury, he has had 24-7 double vision, no depth perception, and no peripheral vision (for which he never complains). Ten years ago, he underwent four surgeries with a neuro-ophthalmologist, but to no avail. They said it was as good as it could get and could not be improved. Since 2001, he has been self-conscious about the appearance of his lazy eye and tries to wear sunglasses when he ventures out, whether outdoors or indoors. He sometimes wears sunglasses inside the home. He often speaks about how he just wants to be seen as a normal man for a change.

Yesterday, he was placed on a waitlist for another eye surgery. He was told that in the past decade, they've come a long way with progressive surgical procedures. The ophthalmologist believes Matt's vision can be largely corrected, or at least improved, and the further good news is that they will cover the procedure under the Medical Services Plan. I only hope that the surgeon has not given him false hopes.

NAVIGATING LIFE BETWEEN HUMOR AND STRESS

I t's the first week of October 2013 — and Mattie's weight continues to drop with consistency, with improved nutrition and more walking. He was at an all-time high of 368 lbs 1.5 years ago and is now at 272. People are noticing how much his face has leaned out, his "man-breasts" are smaller and his back has leaned out immensely. I am so pleased (and relieved) to see this happening to him! His goal weight is 220 pounds. At 6⁄3⁄, that would be an optimal weight for him!

He is flirting more with the ladies since his new weight loss, too! We went to get gas yesterday, and I thought, "Wow, he sure is taking a long time; maybe he went to the bathroom." He came out with this ear-to-ear grin and said, "She's so nice! Since I lost weight, I get more attention when I flirt!"

OCTOBER 12, 2013
I took Mattie out for dinner after work last night. He chose a healthier alternative, which was amazing (salad with a chicken quesadilla)!

He also was sporting a black dress shirt he could not wear for six years! He is now down from 346 pounds to 272, and quite motivated to keep going. I am incredibly proud.

He has so much more pride in himself now; it has been quite the journey. He continues to make regular and consistent positive changes.

OCTOBER 26, 2013
Matt and I tell one another, "I love you" several times a day, every single day. We've talked about it many times, especially when people in the community criticize us for doing so. We both agreed that nothing in life is promised; life can change in a split second, and unexpected tragedies can occur to good people, with no warning. We never want to risk being in the position of not knowing when we

last heard the other say "I love you." **Another tomorrow is never guaranteed.**

NOVEMBER 1, 2013

I had a cardiac assessment yesterday; an angiogram today; and new medication was added to the mix. Apparently, I now warrant a beta-blocker. The cardiologist says I may need a stent inserted in the future. My heart is not pumping sufficient blood supply in one ventricle... Hopefully, a gradual increase in exercise will help. This is not information I will share with Matthew, however.

Yesterday's email exchange with my son:

"HAPPY VALENTINE's DAY, MOM!"

"Valentine's Day? Sweetie, it's November."

"What holiday is it today? *Novembrance* Day?"

"Not a holiday today, buddy. Maybe it is SOMEWHERE in the world, though! Funny, you always ask me when is Halloween on Valentine's Day, and you always tell me you want to dress up as a woman on Halloween!"

Matt: "Oh, did I miss Halloween again? THAT's what the holiday was, but it was YESTERDAY! I don't get you a present for this one, either, eh?"

"No buddy, no presents for Halloween OR Valentine's Day, and this is neither!"

Neither of us mentioned his birthday approaching on November 6th.

NOVEMBER 3, 2013

Yesterday, Matt said to me, "Mom, isn't prayer meditation and vice versa? I pray and meditate all the time; it keeps me out of trouble."

Interesting perspective.

Speaking of "trouble," Matt was accused of smoking weed last week. The homeowner found a half-smoked joint in the area where Matt smokes outdoors. Of course, given Matt's history, Matt was blamed. Matt insisted he had NOT smoked weed and challenged them to send him for a tox screen. The rather surly group homeowner left that up to me, and I was all over it. Two days later, test results returned, confirming Matt is CLEAN!

He took the test results printout to the group homeowner with a big smile, and said (this surprised me), "I'm clean! I know you had to blame someone and I understand why you blamed me!" He received an immediate (and appropriate) apology from the homeowner. Now, based on my suggestion, the group home is keeping strips for instant "at home" testing! Whew — another disaster averted. But I know it is subject to change without notice.

Someone in my office recently asked me why we moved from Vancouver to the Okanagan, especially since the income level is so much higher in Vancouver (and one can actually live for less there if you don't need a downtown condo). I couldn't help but wonder if this was another woman who resented my appearance at the firm. I moved us here 100 percent so that Matt could have better-quality medical care. Many in the system scoffed that 22 months ago and someone in the healthcare system actually told me, in writing, that I was making a mistake and Matt would never be allowed funding in the Okanagan again (i.e., there was no turning back). Just short of two years later, Matt is doing better than he has in his life, and has been stable for the full duration. He has a team of incredible doctors and the best residential care he has ever known. I have no regrets about having jumped off that cliff. Today, I am feeling so very grateful for the third chance (Matt's words) he has been given. We are so very blessed. I hope I never lose sight of that. With TBI, absolutely nothing should be taken for granted.

NOVEMBER 6, 2013

Matthew just sent me an email. "MY CUZ ROCKY CALLED, THEN HIS DAD!! PLUS I AM GOING FOR LUNCH WITH PAULINE & LOUIE! I'M LOVING MY LIFE!"

Friends, Louis & Pauline, took Matthew for a birthday sushi lunch today (while I was at work). Pauline's Facebook message to me was: "Louis & I had a great time with Matt at lunch, Sarah. Such a handsome dude and he has such great manners... You've taught him well, and he highly respects you! Sorry about all the sweets we fed him today, but what the heck, it's his birthday!"

In November 2001, Dr. T, Matt's neurosurgeon, advised he likely has a life expectancy of around age 35. Well, today he is 35 — and going strong, healthy as a horse (big as one, too), and he's continuing to show signs of cognitive and behavioral improvements. His family doctor thinks his life expectancy is not as shortened as they predicted in 2001! Miracles happen every day, and in Mattie's words, he's *a walking miracle*, still.

NOVEMBER 8, 2013

Happy Friday all. Happy there's a long weekend ahead, and I also took 2 vacation days after that. Off for five days; will spend four of them with Matt here at home, as the group home is taking in a new resident who is reported to be "trouble." Good for Matt to be away and try & let the new chap get settled & acclimated to some of the house rules. He can relate, as he had to go through this transition recently himself.

NOVEMBER 9, 2013

I turned on the heat this morning since I could see my breath in the house this morning! Matt never once complained, but he SO raved at the warmth passing through the vents! I continue to be amazed that he really never complains.

He smiled proudly, exiting the bathroom, and said, "I love my new haircut! Thanks for helping me feel proud of myself, Mom."

I have always found it fascinating that Matt has never once expressed shame or embarrassment about the scars on his head from brain surgery. He often says, "It's proof it's not a mistake that I am still alive!"

Then, more observations in gratitude from him followed. "Mom, I'm a boobless wonder now!"

"Pardon?"

"I'm losing my boobies; I think I have pecs coming in!"

Yep, if he wore a bra, he'd now have gone from a DD to a B cup. Phenomenal weight loss achievement! I am all too happy to buy him new clothing (no more triple XLs now; even a double XL is loose on his new physique)!

NOVEMBER 11, 2013
We were just sitting out on the deck... Matt asked, "Mom, what's that red thing moving up there on the mountain?" I looked up and would have LOVED to have had a pair of binoculars. It was definitely a red-brown bear, as it moved way too quickly to be human. "Mom, are you sure that's not a Sasquatch? What if it was?"

NOVEMBER 12, 2013
More amazing insight from my son... I am off today and tomorrow (two vacation days), and despite that, my co-worker is pushing my buttons via email while I am away. Of course, out of professionalism, I ignore it all and do not respond, other than to forward the confrontational emails to my boss and our human resources manager.

Matt cried, stunned by the immaturity that could continue in such a large firm. He said, "Mom, I don't know how you are still such a nice person. You gave her the olive branch (his words) so many times before, after she started problems... but she still keeps picking on you." I told him sometimes it is difficult to keep turning the other cheek. What I did not tell him, however, were my thoughts that eventually, one feels the world is a terrible place and bitterness does set in.

Then, Mattie remarked, "Mom, I guess a lot of the world *is* a terrible place, but it is up to us to find what's not terrible. We make our own life, and even though I am so mad, I don't know what to ask from G-D right now. I know G-D understands and everything is going to work out, though." WOW.

NOVEMBER 16, 2013
I apologized to Matt this morning for being a little short with him... He said, "That's okay, you're only 5′6″; you ARE short, plus right now you have mad-sad disease! I understand!"

MAD-SAD DISEASE? Well, if that's not an adept description!

DECEMBER 5, 2013
Mattie decided to "dress up" for me on my birthday today and told me he wanted to respect the day I was born by looking the best he could. He said I raised him that way! Bless his heart and his true depth of caring!

It's my final year to say I'm in my 50s! Crazy to think I will be 60 next year... but my brain still thinks I'm frozen at 36 (heck, even my profile pic on Facebook has me at 47)! I can say that my life is abundantly better this year than it was this time last year! I can say that I am healthier this year than I was this time last year!

I can say that Matt is incredibly stable again, and I love the little home I am in now. Plus, I have a new job to begin on January 2nd! Superficial people are removed from my life, and what's left is gratitude and happiness for everything and everyone remaining!

DECEMBER 12, 2013

Office politics has become unbearable now. Today, I resigned and provided three weeks' notice. I have accepted another job to begin January 2nd, which will mean no benefits for three months, no vacation for a year, and a $10K per annum pay cut – with no guarantees it will be paradise.

This morning, my boss at the existing job offered me a position on an independent contractor basis. He would pay me the hourly equivalent of what I make now, including a portion for vacation pay, and set me up with a new computer, printer, double screen, phone line, and stationery supplies at home. I can come into the firm at will to give instructions to administration to scan my materials and forward those to me by email, and then work electronically from that at home. My schedule would be entirely flexible, at my discretion.

What to do... This is tempting, particularly as I am jumping off a bridge into dark waters with the other firm. Comments from the interview keep ringing in my ears, such as "This is not rocket science." I know I will not be considered or respected as a paralegal; rather, I will be more of a legal secretary in the Old Boys' Club.

I had to consider the fallout that would be imminent from the jealous women in the firm, and consider the chance that having an assistant scan material for me could set me up for sabotage. This was not something I could state to the personnel manager or to the managing partner for whom I worked. I was left feeling that change was required, and I declined the generous offer.

DECEMBER 13, 2013

Well, the wisdom of Yoda rings true again: no good deed goes unpunished! If I had been dishonest in the workplace, pretending I will kowtow, and not leave the firm, I would have had a significant year-end bonus. Now, I will receive absolutely no bonus for the past year of hard work, service, and endurance of bullying. I just lost $2,000 by being honest. Bah humbug. I still prefer to be the better person... but it means there will be no Christmas baking... *nada*. Oh well. I gave formal resignation with three weeks' notice to my firm today. I should have just given the requisite two weeks, I suppose, but I didn't think that fair to my employer. Alternatively, I could have collected my bonus and resigned on the last day before the holiday break, but that would not have been honorable. Honor cost me a four-figure bonus, though.

Even Matt told me he was proud of me for being the better person, and he reminded me we don't need Christmas baking and gifts. We have each other! It is still so disappointing, though I do my best to remain upbeat and not show signs of my "mad-sad" disease.

DECEMBER 15, 2013

There were more issues with Matthew seeking and smoking marijuana on the group home property. No one seems to have any idea where he got it, either, but they have warned him again that he will be asked to leave if he brings drugs on the premises.

I cannot help but wonder if the alcohol on the premises, and seeing staff drinking, are triggering Matthew to other behaviors. They also allow 2% beer on the premises, for all the male clients there on psychotropic drugs. We cannot forget the results of that in a Langley group home, all of which resulted in Matthew's decompensation and another term of incarceration for violence.

Perhaps I am just too conditioned to structure and an abundance of caution with brain injury. I feel I am seeing a double standard in this group home, a complacency of sorts that may well lead to disaster. I have not voiced my thoughts to anyone, however, particularly not Matthew, and certainly not with the health authority.

We are in a very precarious position, *needing* group home supervision for him. It becomes harder and harder for me to let him come home to live again.

DECEMBER 25, 2013
What a wonderful Christmas morning we have had! Even though I am not one to celebrate the season, I am left touched by what my son wrote to me on a card, adding that it took him one hour to write it with help from staff.

"You are everything; even though I know money cannot buy love, you've shown me unconditional love all my life and made a lot of sacrifices for me. I cannot understand why I do the things that I do sometimes and I feel worse than you can possibly know about that. I know I can't undo what I've done, but I know I can try to change it. I just keep needing your love and support. My injury is no excuse for my actions, but I'm not quite sure how to correct them. I understand that trust is earned, and yours is broken. I truly hope we can heal and move past this! I also understand I need to accept the consequences of what I have done. Mom, I need you in my life. I LOVE YOU and MERRY CHRISTMAS 2013!"

DECEMBER 31, 2013
I don't enjoy feeling pressured to give gifts at Christmas time, so I give almost nothing during this fiscal-year-end holiday. I just say, however, that it was so wonderful to give New Year's presents to all the residents and staff of Matt's group home, and to see the beautiful smiles it brought to everyone, especially my Mattie!! We gave one young man a Playboy magazine — the Kate Moss special, and he was giggling for an hour afterward; Matt chose a cigarette case for another man since he always remarked about how much he liked Matt's cigarette case. We gave Matt's favorite staff, who we knew would work today, a basket that included wine, cheese, dragon fruit, homemade frybread, and cookies. Everyone else received a box of Purdy's chocolates. We made sure there was a HUGE basket

for the owner, his daughter, and their Auntie Cheryl, that basket weighing 42 pounds — with wine, cheeses, dragon fruit, mangos, cactus pears, crackers, cookies, and homemade fry bread! THAT made for a wonderful day.

The lesson was not lost on Matthew, either. "Mom, *nothing* beats giving something to people who don't expect it! Thank you for making the sacrifice!"

"Sacrifice, buddy?"

"Mom, you just quit your job and you will make less money for the next one, probably. You sacrificed your savings so I could feel happy to give presents to my group home. So yes, thanks for making the sacrifice."

Wow.

JANUARY 5, 2014
Well, after spending an unanticipated $500 on my car in the past week, the budget is now toasted. I am just grateful I still had this in my account! Today will include a pleasant walk with Matt and a trip to the gym to see what he needs to do to reinstate his membership (for free). I have been utterly exhausted over the past two days, but then again — life has been a bit of a rollercoaster. Perhaps it's just a discharge of stress hormones from now being away from the stress of my former job. I do, however, miss the rapport I had with my boss.

FEBRUARY 4, 2014
Implementing tough love surely can make the heartache... and the child never knows you suffer for their betterment. Below is my letter to his psychiatrist.

Dear Dr. D:

RE: Matthew
I write regarding matters of recent disconcerting development with Matt.

It would seem that his "sex drive" has increased significantly — with the frequent viewing of pornography on the internet and a recent incident that could have gone awry at the Group Home.

Accordingly, Matt's computer has been removed — as the pornographic sites are filled with viruses and result invariably in computer damage, costing significant amounts of money for repairs.

Matt has begun to speak more frequently of his sexual frustration as well, and recently permitted a female resident at the Group Home to engage in fellatio with him (it was her invitation, and given his impulsivity and sex drive, he entered into the inappropriate conduct). The Group Home managed matters exceptionally well and has instituted still further precautions to guard against this occurring again. Of course, concerns about STD transmissions and pregnancy are also of dire concern. While Matt, and any female resident of the Home, are of consenting adult age – they are not, however, mentally competent to make such decisions responsibly.

Of further concern, in conjunction with this same timeframe, Matt has paid less attention to grooming, maintaining a clean and tidy room, and has refused often to go for walks with staff (it is his only form of exercise, which is quite necessary for him of course). He has also resorted to small mistruths ("white lies") over the past week on a daily basis.

In the past, these indicators in consecutive occurrences would indicate a "hiccup" or potential decompensation around the corner. While I am hopeful he is NOT headed for *decompensation*, I do have serious concerns for his continuing stability, no matter how "minor" the events.

When you see him next, could you please engage in some conversation with him in this regard?

Thank you, Dr. D.

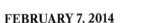

FEBRUARY 7, 2014
Well, wonderful. I am feeling my days could be numbered at the new job. The receptionist is an idiot and is gossiping and alienating me already. Is this small-town mentality reflecting what occurs in *all* law firms here when outsiders come in? The altered response started with her not showing or phoning for a sofa I was selling two weeks ago; I even held it for her for a week and lowered the already great price of $100 to $75. Matt and I stayed home all day two Saturdays ago, waiting for her, and she did not show and did not call. I never heard from her on Sunday, either, and received no apology on Monday in the office — just a comment that they still wanted it. The first email from the advert was the one I sold it to. It sold quickly. She did not speak to me for a week after that, then started gossiping about what a bitch I am (behind my back) and today invited everyone else in the office to lunch except me. Great. It's far too soon to experience this cruel response in Kelowna, already.

I have racked my brain trying to take any ownership that anything here could be my fault, but I swear, I do not see myself at fault in any way; I even tried to be kind and communicative (as any professional would) but no. No good deed goes unpunished.

FEBRUARY 10, 2014
Today is BC Family Day — another holiday on our "priority list" of holidays! I'm looking forward to taking Mattie to a movie!

FEBRUARY 11, 2014
If I am successful in getting into seniors' housing, I am considering a career change. If I cannot find *part-time* work in law, I am seriously considering leaving it. I love it, but I suffer fools (insecure women and their infernal politics) less well every day, and I never did very well with it to begin with.

FEBRUARY 13, 2014
Decisions, decisions. There comes a time in one's life (not ironically, around my age) that we determine what has been most important to us in our lifetime, and what we want to do with the

limited years we have left. I awakened with clarity of mind this morning, and here's what I believe to be true for me:

1. I want to live with, and need, less (less is more).

2. I need to get myself into senior housing, for the lowered cost of residence and community with persons my age and older. For those older, I might be of some value, and they might share stories & experiences and teach me some of those things I have not yet learned and experienced.

3. Once into senior housing, the plan is to work another year in law, two if I can endure it, then find a part-time job doing something I truly enjoy, something that truly gives my life depth and meaning, whether it is working with the disabled in some capacity, with a thrift shop for the homeless, or whatever other opportunity might come my way.

4. I considered returning to Vancouver, as my income would increase immediately by at least $35K per annum (yes, crazy, eh?) and I could live for the same cost of living required in Kelowna (again, crazy). I could afford to fly up to see Matt twice a month. But, the fact remains that he is my "why" — my primary reason for living all these years and profoundly the most important aspect of my life. I do not want to be away from him. I do not want to die so far away from him when my time comes.

So, now that I have determined work in law is now temporary, I hope I can better survive the shallow, chest-beating individuals that invariably encompass this line of work.

I want to enjoy life, to see the beauty that surrounds us, to feel the breeze, to walk through the wilderness, to take a picnic lunch to a mountaintop and enjoy — and not be criticized for my age, the label on my clothing, where I park my car, or what kind of car I drive. Enough is enough.

ONE TO TWO YEARS MAX, and I am done with working in law.

FEBRUARY 17, 2014

Yesterday, Matt and I were planning to go for a walk and to a movie; instead, I ended up hitting a rock in the road and ripping the rim of my tire. With the better portion of the day spent waiting for Canadian Tire to get me in and replace it, I apologized to Matt and he, without a second thought, told me: "Mom, I am just so happy for every minute I get to spend with you. I don't care what we're doing or where we are. Canadian Tire is as good a place as any to be with my Mom!" Wow.

FEBRUARY 21, 2014

Matt told me last night he wanted to celebrate FATHER's Day with me. I chuckled and asked why... and without a second hesitation, he said, "Mom, you've been a father to me, and you've got more balls than most men!" Hmmm, that's my man-child! All I could say was, "Well, thank you, buddy — what do you want to do for Father's Day?"

MARCH 6, 2014

I have been thinking about what I can hope to leave my son when I ultimately pass; it will not be much... But then, it occurred to me:

he will have his memories of my pride in honoring his life, and our family photo album. I am now writing stories, as I recall them, and adding captions to the photo album, stories of his childhood, my childhood, etc., hoping someday he can look through that and remember what his brain would not allow him to access dependably.

I am not feeling well these days. When health suffers, it sure makes you take a consensus.

MARCH 12, 2014

I had Monday and Tuesday off, and we had glorious sunny days! I took Matt for a long walk each day and for a workout at the gym. Yesterday, he was so sore no one could hug him and he couldn't walk without "looking disabled" (HIS words)! It feels good to be working out regularly again.

Matt is now down to 267 pounds (from 368); he is very proud of himself and I am oh so proud of him! It's fascinating that no one else has been successful in getting him to weight train but me. He just turns into a donkey and shows nothing but apathy to every other individual that has tried. In his traditional hilarity, he told me, "Mom, I am proud that I can't sit a plate on my belly anymore!" Dropping over 100 pounds renders physical results!

THE CIRCLE OF LIFE

M y health was ailing this weekend, but Matthew wanted to spend every day with me, bless him. He helped around the house a lot and told me he was just happy to watch movies with me and hang out. He said, "Mom, I value every minute I get to have with you" (his words). Wow. He's come so very far.

APRIL 23, 2014

Two days ago, Matt asked me why I was giving $10 to a homeless man when I was about to have no job and no income for a few weeks. I told him it was because he had a lot less than me and needed it a lot more than I did, and because I *could* give, I SHOULD give. I told my son, "Buddy, I have learned to give — not because I have too much, but because I know what it feels like to be hungry and to have almost nothing."

As usual, with such moments of realization, Matt cried and told me he loves me.

MAY 10, 2014

I am one week into my new fitness regimen. I have been weaning off medications from nine per day to only two. A high-fiber nutrition plan has been in place for seven days. Doing all that simultaneously did not allow me any exercise, as I was physically and emotionally ill all week. Today, at least, I can feel "light in the middle of the tunnel." I hope to hit the gym today or tomorrow, or at the very least, undertake a good walk outdoors. Focusing on the positives, I could not have started this regimen if I was still working.

MAY 11, 2014

I had such a lovely mother's day with Matt. But we received sad news this afternoon that one of his friends (George, a resident at the group home), took a fall three days ago. He was not taken to the hospital or to see a doctor after the fall. That information was disconcerting.

George suffered an aneurysm this morning and was in a coma in the hospital. With no brain activity, they are now waiting for him to pass. His family is not even driving down to pay respect, which both Matthew and I found utterly shocking. We visited George in hospital, and he looks to be sleeping peacefully, snoring to beat the band. Matt prayed, and we talked to George for 30 minutes... We witnessed two tears come down his face, one from each eye...

"Mom, he knows we're here. I knew you were there with me after my brain injury, too. I remember you telling me to fight." Wow.

We will visit again tomorrow if he survives the night. Life changes without warning, sometimes. Matt handled things remarkably very well.

MAY 12, 2014
Matt and I visited George in the hospital again... A doctor attended briefly, and I asked, "If he had received medical care more promptly, might his recovery be better right now?" The doctor must have assumed we were family, and replied, "There's a good chance he could have fared better if medical attention had come more quickly."

Now his breathing is so labored that he requires oxygen... but no water and no feeding tube. They say it could take as much as one month for him to die... He will probably die of *starvation*. How uncivilized and inhumane that is; we can put our pets out of misery, but beloved and helpless humans die a slow death. Every time we held his hands, his breathing was less labored, so again, we feel he was aware we were there. To be alone in his last hours of life would be such an unbearable and lonely dishonor. My heart aches for his suffering, and that his family has still not shown. I will return to see him tomorrow too.

This was a client that arrived in the group home shortly after Matthew began his residence there. George was considered another high-risk patient, with underlying former addictions and mental health complications, besides TBI. The home first sought to keep George distanced from Matthew — but George ended up becoming Matthew's most trusted and beloved friend in the home.

ALL THE LITTLE THINGS

One worker at Matt's group home told me he has shown none of his usual procrastination and laziness this week. I asked Matt what was so different now, and he said, "Mom, you told me every move I make burns calories and to think about that every time I was being lazy! You said that was a healthy obsession, right? Well, I really want to lose more weight! I'm going for the calorie burn! Besides, keeping my focus on getting better takes my mind off of being unhappy in the group home."

Matt and I are competing with one another to determine who will have smaller boobs first, and bless him, he's winning, as it should be!

JUNE 6, 2014

Weigh-in time! Mattie just reached 260 pounds! Four more pounds and he's down 100# from his heaviest! He's going to be with me four days a week through to September, so I can help him with his next fitness regime. This week, the group home took the residents out for ice cream. Matt said he didn't want ice cream but wanted to come along for the ride... to get out of the house. They denied him the outing, but he stood his ground and said no to ice cream. Some days, I really think the group home is trying to sabotage his success; I cannot see any logic in that.

I will pick him up at 11 AM this morning!! We will head straight for coffee, then to the outdoor circuit machines at the Recreation Center!

He enjoyed the circuit training! After that, we went back to my place, and each had an egg-white omelet with celery, onion, red peppers, and half an avocado. Matt also had a meatloaf muffin! Yes, I keep meatloaf muffins on hand as a healthy protein snack!

Matt phoned me after his group home dinner this evening, thanking me for the great outing. Refusing the bread provided with dinner tonight, he was admonished and told to eat it because it's good for him. "No disrespect intended, but it is *not* good for me." He did not eat the bread. Another proud mama moment — not simply because he stood his ground and made one of the few choices he can make for himself, but because he remained polite. This was adult behavior.

JUNE 8, 2014

As of today, I am down to 207 pounds. I should break 200 in another two weeks! Matt and I both had to keep pulling up our trousers on the power walk this morning!

"Mom, this is so freakin' awesome! I love the way I feel now! Thank you for always being here for me! And thank you for seeing the man I'm trying to be — and not just the man I've *been*."

JUNE 11, 2014

A friend's husband worked on my car again from 8:30 am to 2:30 pm today. Between yesterday and today, he saved me about $900. My cost for parts, oil, and fluids was only $300. What an incredible favor that was. He says my car is fine to drive on the Coquihalla now... He said he wouldn't hesitate to drive it across Canada! I am so very blessed... Broke, but blessed!

JUNE 15, 2014

Poor Matt. Yesterday I introduced him to deadlifts, with only 12-pound weights in each hand — one set of 20 repetitions. Today, he can't bend over without major discomfort and can hardly walk! But, in his usual tradition, he giggles with every step!

JUNE 17, 2014

Holy crow. I decided it was time for training today *in the gym* today! No more outdoor circuit! What did I start with? Legs & shoulders!

I walk like I'm disabled right now, and I had trouble unlocking my car door! Outstanding return to the weights! And I forgot how great salad, salsa, chicken breast, and brown rice taste after training!

Today, while driving home from the grocery store, listening to Nelly Furtado — CRUNCH!! A huge rig plowed into my driver-side rear door. Wonderful... Police ticketed the chap for making an unsafe lane change. I'm grateful I wasn't hurt, but MY POOR CAR! The insurance deductible for bodywork will cost me another $300, but the full repair is estimated at $1,700.

JUNE 18, 2014

Whew. What a day. We met with Interior Health. Matt is hopeful for an opportunity to be moved out of the group home and into a family care home. Excellent news. He might not remain in Kelowna but will stay in the Okanagan. This is very promising news.

There are immense differences to be observed between health authorities. After discussing the next placement considerations for Matthew, the director of funding asked me, "How can we best support YOU (me) through this next transition?" Wow!

JUNE 21, 2014

When it rains, it pours. My home computer is on the fritz, and my smartphone collapsed too. I have a loaner phone, but it is also malfunctioning. Today, I will have to attend an internet café for communications.

JUNE 24, 2014

We had a good meeting with Interior Health, in that they are actively seeking a new placement for Matt in a family care home. They might not have a placement for him in Kelowna, and Kamloops is our last-resort city (neither of us has fond memories of Kamloops, with the fiasco experienced with Hillside Psychiatric in the past)... But we keep fingers crossed; Interior Health says they want this to happen sooner rather than later, thank goodness.

He was, unfortunately, not a candidate for the family care home, but there are considerations for a well-established group home in Kamloops. Again, we are hopeful.

JUNE 26, 2014

BUT WAIT! There's more!

We were involved in a head-on collision in Kelowna yesterday; Matt was in the car with me. Fortunately, we could self-extricate, though being stunned and particularly shaken... An elderly couple ran a red light and made an illegal left turn from the other side of the highway. I had the green light to proceed through; they hit me head-on in the middle of the intersection. My car is a total loss, sadly — just two weeks after undertaking a lot of mechanical updates and seeing it in pristine condition again.

Kelowna is not where we should be. It feels like I am reminded of this at every turn.

JUNE 27, 2014

I am trying to focus on what I *can* control — and I *can* control my fitness regimen. I am making significant progress with training and a preliminary diet down. Weight is inching down, fat is decreasing. Muscle memory is amazing, especially on my shoulders! Deltoids are returning faster than I could have expected!

Today and tomorrow will be weight training recovery days, because of sustaining some soft-tissue injuries in that head-on collision yesterday, but all good.

I am at 149 pounds this morning, with that one-pound drop definitely exiting from my love handles! I want that particular "meat" gone forever! Time to go strut more off around that track again!

JULY 3, 2014

Matt's visit to the doctor went well. Mattie's soft-tissue injuries are worse than my own. They referred him for massage therapy, which made him happy! "Mom, at least there's good news in with the bad!" He also suffered a TMJ inflammation, which is predicted to settle down soon. His neck, right shoulder, and back range of motion are still not great, but about 40 percent improved from last week.

I am glad I have time off work to ensure Matt gets to the massage therapist because his consistently inept group home told me they do not have staff to accommodate driving him to massage therapy! Still another WTF maneuver, considering their remuneration of $6,500 per month, per client. I truly try to understand the home's management response, and I suppose Matt is a problem for them because he is so high functioning. The other six residents are very low functioning, with three in wheelchairs and two unable to even speak. This type of group home just likes to sit them in front of a TV and feed them and ensure they're reasonably clean. Matt, conversely, requires stimulation, conversation, and structured activities. He deals with the absence of that by hibernating in his room and trying to sleep until he sees me again.

The health authority seems dedicated to finding him a private placement that will accommodate his needs more realistically, with a view toward moving him as far as possible toward assisted living & independence.

JULY 12, 2014

I am often criticized by friends and coworkers for spending three to four days a week with my son. I am criticized by "caregivers" for speaking with my son by telephone every single day. But I am committed to doing this because we never know when our numbers are up. I never want to see a time when I say "I wish I had." I always want to say, "I'm glad I did."

Plus, the fact remains that I enjoy about 98 percent of my time with Matthew — the other two percent being merely the price I pay for the privilege!! I'd assess that as a bargain!

I do it because I can, I can because I want to, I want to because everyone said I couldn't.

JULY 13, 2014

Mattie and I trained chest & biceps today. It was a day of effort to push through his apathy, but I did — and he allowed it. THEN, we were ready for "finishing exercises," with his favorite chest exercise, the *pec deck*! He showed in short order that he could outperform me on that one!

And at the end of it all, he thanked me profusely for pushing him — and he graced me with more of those silly giggles of his, for which we know him when he's so sore he can hardly move!

I am incredibly proud of Matt. When he trains now, his pectorals, shoulders, and biceps show through his shirt! He keeps bragging, "Mom, my boobs are finally smaller than yours — as they should be!"

We both look forward to pushing past limitations again tomorrow! Our shoulders and back are still too sore to train again, so it looks like legs again tomorrow for both of us! "If ya don't have sore legs 24 hours after working them — then ya didn't do enough."

"Mom, is that science?"

"No buddy, not science — just no excuses!" My son's efforts toward multi-tasking continue. He exited the washroom just as I was serving our 3 PM meal and says, "Mom, I already said grace while I was on the toilet — and I washed my hands, so it's okay to eat!" He was hungry from the weight training earlier in the day!

JULY 15, 2014

Well, no more denial. The whiplash is not improving further (although the discomfort is not debilitating; I do have persistent issues with head-checking when I drive, on both sides). I have my first massage therapy appointment scheduled for Friday. My knees are still physically bruised and sore to the touch (as both knees struck the dashboard on impact). I am to continue with the tensor support on my right knee.

I see so many serious injuries in my line of work, however, I almost feel I'm being a bit of a *princess* by admitting I need an RMT.

JULY 20, 2014

I have to share another moment with my son today. After taking a bath, he came to me and said, sheepishly, "Mom, I don't mean to criticize, but I found marijuana in the bathroom; I know it's not my business, but—"

I almost choked on my water, and could not withhold my laughter, asking him to show me what he found. He found oregano from the salsa I made the day before yesterday. I had not yet cleaned the bathroom floor and it must have been on my clothes or in my hair. I actually brought him to the kitchen and gave him a taste of dried oregano! He laughed loudly and apologized at the same time! "Mom, you know you can live your life as you want it, but I am trying SO HARD to stay away from marijuana! Let's have some salsa with our next meal. I like the taste of oregano!"

Dreading a return to work tomorrow, and Mattie equally dreading his return to the group home in the morning, around 7 PM this evening, he asked me, "Mom, is there anything I can do for you? Anything I can do to make your life better right now? You always give me total support, and right now, I think I might be better than you inside my head. If I can do anything for you, I sure hope you will let me know. It would make me *happy* to help you. You're always telling me we all need to feel value. Well, I do too, Mom."

"Honey, that question makes me feel the best I could feel about anything and everything; it makes everything else irrelevant. I feel better just knowing that you see me and *want* to make things better. I love us."

"Mom, I love us, too."

SUCCESS IN THE FACE OF ADVERSITY

The day just keeps getting better. We concluded our meeting with Interior Health and the Kamloops group home — and all is a go! Matt will move next Wednesday! The woman who owns the home is German (I have always, for some reason, had a very good rapport with German people... I know I cannot paint all with the same brush, but that's just how it has happened for me through the years). She has multiple decades of extensive experience with brain injury and is a registered nurse. Her husband also worked in mental health previously. The facility is co-ed, but genders are housed in separate buildings. Total capacity: nine patients.

We also got to meet two of the other residents there (they drove over with the owner to meet with us here in Kelowna), and Matt bonded with them both right away. The male, R, is First Nations, age 46, and higher functioning than Matt in most regards. He takes part in the Special Olympics, and he is trying to talk Matt into getting involved in baseball. They also have a street hockey team for the disabled, and they speculated on the idea of Matt trying out for a goalie position! They also are very involved with the First Nations in Kamloops, and Matt will get to go to his first Pow Wow next week! He is incredibly excited.

They also have a pool and a hot tub there! They also arrange for their residents to have part-time jobs, in those cases where they are capable! This has been the G_D-send we were hoping for all these years, and I can finally step back with confidence that will finally be proper management and supervision for Matt. Oh my goodness, I cannot imagine having only my own life to manage! It will be a first for me! It is fortuitous that I have bodybuilding to fill the gap of the empty nest syndrome that may visit me!

JULY 26, 2014

With Matt heading off to Kamloops, and me being able to take a less active role in his therapies, advocacy, and planning, this is going to open the door to decisions I can make solely based on what I want for myself. It is my present line of thinking that I will *not* remain in Kelowna. I moved up here almost three years ago, solely to get Matt situated and into a better health authority. Goal completed.

If I am honest with myself, I must state that I have never liked Kelowna (it's just not a good fit for me, personally). Staying here holds no logic. I will keep my eyes and ears open for employment opportunities in other areas (Chilliwack, Abbotsford, Langley, Surrey, and Penticton, although I cannot envision myself living in the city limits of Vancouver again). I am also considering pursuing part-time work, as well.

I am in no hurry to return to the workforce but would like to be working by December or January. I will not require a high-end remuneration, as a reduced workweek has a definitive monetary value for me.

JULY 28, 2014

Bittersweet realization: today and tomorrow are the last full days I will have with my son for about six weeks. We will assuredly make the most of these two days ahead, starting with coffee and the gym, and a walk through nature. I want him to remember the sounds of birds in the woods when he falls asleep at night.

He was SO pleased with having sore legs and back yesterday, and some muscle definition is showing in his arms, too! I must remember to take a photo of him today!

"Mom, you sure don't let the dust settle when you decide. You are the opposite of lazy!"

No, I have never been accused of procrastination! Because I am definitely not staying in Kelowna, I have listed my sofa on Castanet, along with two nice shelving units and my dining set. Those can be repurchased when I get where I'm going.

I have already created a scale drawing of what will go into my back seat and my trunk. I will buy an air mattress to sleep on initially and save that for visitors in the future. I will buy a proper bed with my first payroll.

So exciting! I have ZERO regrets about moving to Kelowna so that Matt could have the opportunity of his lifetime. If I had it to do over, I would do it again in a heartbeat. But I am so crazy happy to do something wholly for myself.

In almost three years in Kelowna, I can count on one hand the people I could call friends and have fingers left. But reality dictates that I have been extremely unhappy and unfulfilled here. My life is in the Lower Mainland and I am happy to make plans to return!

JULY 29, 2014

Matt had his semi-final appointment with his Kelowna psychiatrist today. The assessment was that Matt was continuing to exhibit cognitive improvements and the ability to start some complex thinking. Of course, the impulsivity problems will always be there, but the doctor said Matt was showing signs of recognizing his impulse tendencies. He also said that the need for supervision was likely to be permanent. He remarked about the significant progress in Matt's response to extremely stressful and inappropriate scenarios (like he has experienced in the current group home) and said that this was tremendous progress, adding that Matt would have responded with violence three years ago, or would have completely decompensated. The psychiatrist will see Matt one more time, for a summary assessment, before another Kamloops psychiatrist assumes Matt's care. The existing psychiatrist has affirmed, in writing, that Matthew is no longer high-maintenance, and only needs to see a psychiatrist every four to six months for strategic follow-up.

JULY 31, 2014

A Facebook memory post surfaced this morning and I am missing my young man more than ever! I need to see that smiling face again soon! It literally brings tears to my eyes to see the goodness in his face, and to know it is there at his core now. My young man had *such* a dark past for a few years, so lost for a while to what boils down to *succumbing to peer pressure*... making the wrong decisions and opting for the absolute wrong associations. I am so grateful his life was only interrupted, and not taken 15 years ago. He has made good with what he was blessed to have left in brain power and is still pursuing improvements every day.

He told me recently (after seeing his psychiatrist again) that he told the doctor, "I am worried that bad man is still under the surface. I am afraid of that man and I hate him. He is in me, but he is *not* me. I thought he was dead, but I still see him in my nightmares." The doctor told him he was doing really well from all accounts and not to be so hard on himself.

Ironic, isn't it? After my son went "sideways" I strove so diligently to have him understand he needs to be hard on himself, to take ownership of actions and consequences... and now he must learn to redirect that.

My greatest teacher in life has been my son.

One of my neighbors here, with whom I have been friendly, just phoned and said "Please come up — it's important, and bring Matt." So we left right away to see what was awry. She was crying when she opened the door, and I asked what was wrong. "What can we do to help?"

Her husband died 16 months ago yesterday, and she decided she wanted Matt to have his wallet. She told Matt she had been wanting to give it to someone special, and until now, she didn't know who to give it to. She asked Matt to promise to cherish it and keep it forever. Of course, Matt cried and promised to cherish it for as long as he lived. We are both stunned. She told Matt she loved him, was proud of him, and wanted him to have this special gift as he left for his new life.

WOW... I am speechless (and Matt has put all his ID inside the wallet, and is crying again, as he sits on the sofa looking at the beautiful leather wallet with embossed flames on the leather).

The gifted wallet...

AUGUST 1, 2014

Big transition day. Matt always awakens with a smile and a soft-voiced, "I love you, Mom. How did you sleep?" I am going to miss that. The gravity of it all hit me this morning, and I finally cried. This time, my big young man was comforting ME.

I just told him how much I love him and how this is a great opportunity for him, and for me... and he said, "Mom, this IS good for me and it's maybe even better for YOU. I don't like that I've made you cry already this morning. Do you need a hug?" He added he *knows* he is going to do well because he *has* to do well (yay, he was listening to those countless lectures that Mom could not bail him out if anything went wrong this time; he was an adult and if he wants to try for more independence, he was facing adult consequences).

Big day ahead. I pray that my $800 Dodge Neon does alright on the trip from Kelowna to Kamloops (and back again). I bought a fuel conditioner last night and checked the oil. She doesn't run hot and the tires are acceptable. I suppose this is a good test drive, because in a week — she has got to make the journey to Vancouver!

On the road in one hour; coffee in right now.

My transition with the "empty nest" is going to be counteracted with tough-arse cardio and gym training, first thing tomorrow morning. Time to bump it up a notch now (now that the track pants I bought just one month ago are literally falling off me this morning)! Matt told me it looks like I "dropped a load in my pants." A traumatic brain injury will get you the truth of the matter, whether or not you want to hear it!

Matt just poked his head out of the bathroom and said, "Mom, your friend Zoa is probably starving right now, eh?" He remembered she's in Florida now and in final prep for another pro-level competition!

AUGUST 2, 2014

I love the experience of having qualified coaching... After having to take three consecutive days off from the gym, and missing a full week of cardio (because Matt was needing full attention), I've been told, simply, to get back to it "and have that scale under 200 pounds by next Saturday!"

AUGUST 3, 2014

Well, Matt went to his first Pow Wow yesterday. Bless him, given his deafness in one ear and hypersensitivity in the other, he couldn't handle the beating of the drums and all the exciting stimulation. He had to leave in short order.

Had this happened with the prior group home, they would have been infuriated and would have ostracized Matt. Staff accompanying Matt from this group home, however, were understanding and assured him "No worries." They returned him to the group home with no guilt attached. What a relief to see an appropriate caregiving response in the face of the unknowns!

Matt now has his room fully organized and says he really likes EVERYone there, residents and staff alike. Hopefully, he can remember to take pictures of his room and learn to attach them to an email today!

He sounds so much more relaxed now, too. What a relief!

AUGUST 5, 2014

I just had THE most-hilarious thing happen. One senior in my building just asked me if I was *really* going to the gym every day because I was thinking about a bodybuilding competition? I laughed and said I was *planning* to do ANOTHER one. She could not hide her disbelief – her expression showed she was certain I was delusional! My neighbor (a man who also attends the same gym) said, "OH, she's serious!" Then he left. I had a cup of coffee with her and we chatted about nothing of consequence.

The man (Ian) returned with a magazine 12 years old, which featured one of my former stage pictures in it. TOO MUCH FOR TV! Who would have ever thought someone I barely knew would recognize me from an old magazine pic — AND have a personal copy of the magazine in his possession? He told me before that he saw me in a magazine years ago, and I just chuckled it off. Sweet thought or mistake — I was sure it wasn't me. I was only featured in one obscure production years ago. Lo-and-behold, random but less than obscure, after all!

The magazine spotlighted a former "before" shot (at 246 pounds) and a stage shot at eight percent body fat, and this man remembered it. My son has a copy of the same magazine; I thought that only my dear Mattie would be one to remember that!

Life can be hilarious and filled with so many interesting and unexpected moments! "L'chaim!" To life.

AUGUST 7, 2014

Today, I received an email update from the director of my son's new group home. She entitled it "GOOD message!" Matt has told me repeatedly that he is doing well and is thrilled, but there's nothing to compare with hearing it from the director of the facility!

Email from the director:

> Sorry I haven't sent you anything, but so far so good with Matthew! I'm actually amazed at how well he manages his cigarettes, even though we have a lot of smokers. We sat together, and he made his own

smoke schedule with us. He also began a job here, and he will earn extra dollars because he needs to have his own TV cable box. We will ensure parental controls are in place. He has been responsible for watering the lawn every second day, and another client has mentored him. He seems to adapt well, is very friendly, and follows directions. We keep him busy during the day, and he also started working with his Therapy Assistant.

Matthew self-implemented a plan that involved smoking half a cigarette at a time, which helped him honor his commitment to smoking only ten cigarettes in a day. His catch-phrase became "I'm gonna finish it." To this day, if I see someone going out for a smoke, I remember my son's voice, "I'm gonna finish it."

AUGUST 12, 2014
I am bursting with pride. Matthew has had immense apathy toward rehabilitating his limitations; until now, I have been the only person who has been capable of pushing him forward. He has now had additional funding approved for cognitive therapy; when I first heard this, I thought, Ummm, been there, done that... that's wasted funding (though I did not voice my thoughts; many times, things are left better inside my head).

I stand corrected! If we reduce TBI to either "as expected" or "beyond all expectations" — this is the latter! Funding was not wasted this time! He has been taking part in cognitive therapy since he arrived at the new group home. First, for ten minutes, then 15. Yesterday, he achieved his first FULL HOUR! He says he loves the therapy, now. His emails are already becoming better (yesterday he sent me an email telling me Robin Williams had committed suicide and how sad and shocking that was). Most of his emails have been one-liners until now.

He is not being taken to the gym as yet, but last night on the phone he was so proud to tell me he did three sets of push-ups on his knees (20 reps, 15 reps, and 10 reps)! He asked for other exercises he could do just in his room and I reminded him of crunches, arm circles, bicep curls (suggesting he hold one of my bodybuilding trophies), touching his toes, and squeezing his glutes on the way up, and he was stoked!

AUGUST 22, 2014
Progress continues for Matthew. He remains completely stable and happy and is putting forth extensive effort to improve.

He's been averaging a full hour daily with cognitive therapy. This has been his first success with that since the TBI. Until now, he has never lasted over 10 minutes with any task requiring concentration and analysis.

He no longer takes daily naps, either; they keep him active and stimulated. They are professionals. If "it takes a community," they are the community. I cannot sufficiently express in words how grateful I am for the hand of true professionals.

The increased activity with no afternoon napping has, however, resulted in a return to incontinence, much to his humiliation poor guy. He has ruined his $1500 bed (which I purchased new for him three years ago), but the home immediately got him another one. They emailed me for consent to dispose of the other bed and said Matt had begged them to bring it back when it dried out. He suggested using Febreze, poor guy... adding, with tears, "My Mom spent too much money on that and I want it to last the rest of my life. There's a 25-year guarantee. She has never had a bed that good, so I need to keep it." Wow.

I explained to him that the incontinence is probably because of overstimulation and exhaustion *because* he is trying SO hard... and reminded him how far he's come. "Buddy, remember: we don't sweat the small stuff or material possessions — EVER. We have our health, our love, and our FREEDOM. We are both safe and not homeless." Of course, he cried and thanked me for loving him "in spite of all the trouble."

"Mattie, buddy — THIS is not trouble. We have SEEN trouble, and this is not it!" He laughed hard... I believe in always making a serious point clear, but reinforcing and redirecting with humor. On a litany of levels, we are seeing success in the face of adversity.

AUGUST 28, 2014

Today, I chatted for 30 minutes with the director of Matt's group home, who related how incredibly well he's doing and how well he fits in... adding that he has lost another four pounds! She has requested a clothing allocation for fall and winter clothing for him, too, since most of last year's clothing is way too big for him! This home is SO on top of things! It is the first time I have not had to effect "behind the scenes" advocacy.

If I'm dreaming, please don't wake me up!

AUGUST 31, 2014

I am missing Mattie... October 9 marks his arrival in Langley for his first visit home! This marks our longest separation in eight years, but our first "positive" separation. I am proud of our healthy relationship. We've broken the constraints of codependence after his brain injury. Many predicted we could not succeed.

Well, *sometimes*, we failed. But we fell down seven times and got up eight.

SEPTEMBER 1, 2014

Matt asked me to confirm his understanding of nutrition and training basics. "So, Mom, if I work out, I should eat within an hour, right?"

I affirmed yes, healthy food, of course.

"And if I take a walk after that, do I get to eat again?"

Look at that analysis! I told him if he takes a 1.5-hour walk, he can probably have a protein shake!

"That's what I thought you said, but then I thought it must be too good to be true!"

SEPTEMBER 9, 2014

Just when I think "it's safe to go back in the water," drama rears its ugly head. A staffer from Matt's former bad group home telephoned him yesterday. "Mom, I was polite, but that really sketched me out."

Well, this mama laid down some laws to the former home vis-à-vis the health authority today. Now, all incoming calls for Matt will be screened.

SEPTEMBER 13, 2014

Matt just emailed, happy to tell me he's going to church again. He goes every Saturday to a 7-Day Adventist church and loves it.

Matt was asked to select a favorite meal at his wonderful group home and last night they made my recipe for cheese-baked prawns!! How exceptional is this home? I talk a lot, and yet, I have insufficient words to express my delight!

I created a family cookbook with over 500 pages. Matt took the recipe from his binder copy!

SEPTEMBER 20, 2014

Matt and I are both getting so excited about his approaching trip via Greyhound! Last night, he said, "Mom, I am so proud of you. When you see me, I hope you don't expect me to have dropped as much weight as you. You are more disciplined than I am!"

Bless his heart! He is holding his weight, which is extraordinary, considering the brain injury and so much incredible food being cooked at the group home! He also added, "Mom, I am so glad we are both doing so well and that we are so happy!"

I miss him so much, but in an absolutely healthy way. We faced some immense struggles over the past 13 years, but now we can say it was worth every traumatic experience because *we came through* to the light at the end of the tunnel. Not every brain injury survivor, particularly at Matt's level of injury, comes out on the good end of the stick. Not every survivor family comes out "right in the head" either. We make it a daily habit to speak our gratitude "out loud."

Absolute success in the face of adversity. I think we deserve the new karma.

A PROGRESSIVE GRATITUDE

M atthew was a person "known to Police" two decades ago. He was, at the time, the quintessential example of all that Police encounter on a daily basis and strive to withstand with dignity and decorum.

While I have never viewed Matt's C-PIC file, I *have* perused his medical records. Specifically, the clinical records of St. Paul's Hospital, positioned in downtown Vancouver, are enlightening. He was treated for multiple head injuries, gunshot wounds, knife lacerations from stabbings, and more. In all circumstances, he received treatment and left the hospital premises before discharge.

He feared Police — yet he could understand they were doing a job — one that involved extreme risk and a loss of life or quality of life. When he was not in a dissociated gang persona, he respected authority. In the years after his TBI, and on those occasions where he achieved stability, he was *drawn* to Police. When we passed a Police cruiser on the road, he invariably said the same words as he pointed, "There's our friends. I am so glad the Police are not looking for me now. I will *never* go to jail again. I'm so proud to be able to say that and know it's true."

He literally *smiled* each time he saw a Police cruiser. It made me proud.

FROM HEALTHY DISTRACTION TO POSITIVE OBSESSION

How very interesting that our perception of old age alters as we mature... I remember my son asking me, when I turned 30, "Mom, you're 30. Does that mean you're going to die soon?" Mattie was six.

I remember being 55, and extremely unhealthy and equally unhappy & exhausted from fighting a health authority for my son - and thinking I was ready to die, and that I was in the last years of my life. Now I will be 60 in December, and I feel like another aspect of my life is just taking off. I am becoming more accepting of the aging process now, and never ever dreamed that would happen to me... It boggled my mind that it happened to others; I had only read about it.

Regrets? You bet I have regrets. I wish I had smartened up three decades ago regarding my health and my outlook, but it is what it is. Today, however, is the focus. The NOW is shaping my future (and my son's future). I regularly consider how it will affect Matthew when I pass; he will be devastated, although I hope that the regular discussions we have had about the inevitability will help prepare him "when the time comes." Being attentive to our health, mine included, is what I can best contribute; the longer I can keep myself active and stabilized, the more time I will have to help him.

SEPTEMBER 23, 2014
Matthew begged me for an updated headshot photo, so I snapped a selfie and sent it to him. Bless his heart, when he phoned me tonite he said, and I quote, "WOW Mom, you've lost so much weight! Your face is so small now and you don't have any meat under your chin anymore!"

He asked me if he could show the pic to his friends at the group home and I said sure. I thought he meant later! But no — he put the phone down and I could hear him saying, "How old do you think she is? Tell the truth: no BS." I heard people saying 50, 45, 49... which made my day of course! Then I heard one guy say, "Wait, dude, that's your MOM?" She can't be 45 if you're 35! Loud hilarity followed!

Then Matt returned to the phone and said, "See, Mom?"

Nutrition, exercise, weight loss, positive friends, a positive attitude, a stable son, enough vitamins in a day to constitute another meal — and a mix of vitamin E and coconut oil on my skin are all making a difference! And for once in my life, I actually feel that I deserve all the goodness that surrounds me!

OCTOBER 7, 2014

I visited friends in Chilliwack this weekend. Had a great walk down the Vedder Trail with Val yesterday, and a two-hour lunch with Gloria. Then, I spent Saturday and much of Sunday at Harrison Hot Springs Resort, where I met friends Rob and Natasha, and their friend Pedro. My friends had made an attempt at match-making, but "that bird didn't fly!" In fact, that bird has not even ventured far from the nest since Matthew's TBI of 13 years ago.

At Harrison, I was up at 5 AM and in the hot springs; then I swam ten laps in the pool and returned to the hot water. There was an excellent buffet breakfast (egg white omelet, oats, blueberries, watermelon, cantaloupe... black coffee), and I then had a full-body workout in the hotel weight room. I met my friends for Meal Two (the same buffet options again). Harrison Hot Springs Resort is w onderful... and it was a nice little luxury waking up to a copy of the *Globe and Mail* at my door, too!

My Mattie arrives tomorrow! This is the longest separation we've had in many years. Even during institutionalization, we spoke on the phone almost every day and I visited at every opportunity permitted. We were apart for the eleven months he fled to Ontario, running from those who had placed a contract on his head in Vancouver, but we also spoke by telephone during that timeframe.

It will be so nice to hang out, go for walks, train together, grocery shop together and TALK! I am so impressed that my young man has matured since last we were together, too!

OCTOBER 9, 2014

I forgot to step onto the scale this morning, and Matt wanted to see what the scale said. HOLY CROW: 173 lbs. I am thrilled! That is why the muscle in my arms is more visible; I am leaning out!

OCTOBER 10, 2014

My "little" (6-foot 3-inch, 250 lb) buddy is so sore this morning we had to get out the heating pad and the massage unit. Squats have just killed his legs! But he's also sore from just picking up the 45-pound plates to rack up and de-rack my leg press yesterday! Still, he vows he is training chest with me today!

OCTOBER 12, 2014

It still makes my day when my son tells me he thinks I'm beautiful! We were in HomeSense yesterday and Matt had a big grin on his face coming out of the store... I asked, "Whassup, bud?" and he said, with a bigger smile, "Mom, two different men in there were checking out your butt — and that made me SO proud!"

Cardio done, Meal One in, and shoulders & abs trained, all while Matt slept! I returned home to find him up, bathed, shaved, dressed, and the sofa bed returned to its position. His bed linens were folded and placed inside the closet with his pillows. He had made my COFFEE, had oatmeal cooking on the stove and my bath running! HOLY CROW! I asked what prompted all this and his reply was, "Mom, I think I am holding you back being here. You have *so* much energy and I just don't, but I want to make things easier for you and NOT hold you back. So, this is what I can do!"

Matthew is an absolute walking miracle, his progress is simply mind-boggling.

Crap, I'm all teary-eyed once again. Time to get oatmeal down and enjoy that hot bath with Epsom salts!

I made a new batch of salsa today, seven jars of mild, nine jars of spicy, and seven jars of "Burns Ya Twice," especially for my coach, who tells me it can never be too spicy for her family. Her version has eight different peppers in it... Matt had to go outside, and I coughed and shed a few tears until the jars were sealed (for 20 minutes)! I also have blisters on my hands, forgetting to have worn latex gloves again when I handled the peppers!

Matt wants to take one jar of the spicy and two of the mild to his group home, so I will ensure those are carefully labeled!

OCTOBER 13, 2014

Matt was motivated to train. We just returned from the Steve Nash Gym in Whalley, where we trained chest & triceps (light for me, since I trained shoulders this morning). He finally stopped trying to prove his manhood by lifting heavy and followed my advice to test the range of movement and start with super-light weights. Some range of motions he simply could not perform, as he has a serious right shoulder deficit from the paralysis stemming from the brain injury, but we found machines that facilitated a movement that would let him work around his issues. Bless him, he kept apologizing for the lower weight used, and I kept telling him to only feel sorry if he gets stupid, uses too heavy a weight, and injures himself! He finally understood the concept, and after the workout said he was proud of himself and SO proud of me. Bless his heart, he is my greatest inspiration and my greatest fan!

He asked what we will train tomorrow, and I said, "Baby got back!" He gave a thumbs up and said, "I think my back is strong!"

And yes, Matthew is blessed with a strong back.

In a reminiscence with gratitude, I note that weight training has presented the perfect healthy distraction for us both, and now see it transformed into a positive obsession. I have been here before, but this is a first for my son.

A BROADSIDED TURNING POINT

I love my son's emails. "WHAT SIDIE TO U LIFE IN AGAIN?? PEOPLE HERE WANT TO NOW!!"

This one translates as, "What city do you live in, again? People here want to know!"

The next email is brief, "HOW MANY MINUTES????? HAHA!!"

Of course, he was asking how many minutes before he could see me again.

I attended with my coach today, and I am on track. I'm down another four pounds and continuing to "do the work and trust the process."

Right now, my next mini-goal is to be 169 by the time Mattie arrives for his next visit on November 5th! I have not been in the "160s" since 2004, one month after my last competition. So, no matter what the mirror tells me, progress is in the works!

OCTOBER 31, 2014
Five more sleeps and my Mattie is back for another visit! So excited! I don't think he realizes I obsess with excitement over his next visit, in the same context that he does!

NOVEMBER 3, 2014
Two more sleeps! I truly look forward to celebrating his 36th birthday with him! He's more excited than a child at Christmas. Last night when I talked to him on the phone, he actually *remembered* the name of the resort we're going to. *That* is real memory improvement! Stable, consistent, patient & loving caregiving, along with a positive environment and cognitive therapy, has changed his life!

NOVEMBER 4, 2014
So very pumped that my Mattie arrives tomorrow morning! I made a monster meatloaf (no fillers, just meat & healthy veggies), pre-cooked some yams, and have the cooler ready for filling. This will go with us to Harrison Hot Springs tomorrow!

His group home is also sending a surprise birthday gift for him down in his luggage. HOW nice is THAT?

Wednesday: arrival, then weather permitting, out for a walk thru the bush.

Thursday: gym training at Steve Nash Whalley, where the chap who signed us up shares the same birth date with Matt. Matt is taking him a present! Then, off to Harrison Hot Springs Resort for training and hot springs extravaganza!

Friday: buffet breakfast at Harrison, more hot springs, and training again; then leave & return to Langley. We will stop in Surrey to see one of his former psychiatrists from Forensics. "Mom, I want to show Dr. H how far I've come — how much I've changed!"

Saturday: gym and another walk (weather permitting), and evening go to watch a bodybuilding competition

That'll get us started!

In our evening phone call, Matt reports his weight, feeling guilty about not having lost more. "Mom, sorry, but I am still 260 pounds, but at least I haven't *gained* any weight, because I sure have been eating some crap!"

We both laughed. He's adopting the mindset! So, we made a mini-goal for him to drop five pounds over the week he will spend here with me. Awesome!

"And Mom, I've been counting — you know I'm good with numbers! I am still 94 pounds less than my all-time high!" I took his photo!

WOW, the cognitive improvements absolutely boggle my mind.

"Mom, will you ever let me take a picture of you again??"

"Oh buddy, I'm no longer afraid of the camera; if you want to take a picture, you take a picture!"

He cried. "Mom, I have really missed having new pictures of you, because I love you no matter what condition you are in — but I know you don't love yourself when you are self-conscious. I get that because it's the same for me."

It's nice to realize that we both have a good life and a better one on the horizon!

NOVEMBER 5, 2014

So nice to have Matt home! He greeted me with an ear-to-ear grin!

Then, the bear hug and the affirmation that I have dropped more body fat. "Mom, you're freakin' me out — you get smaller and smaller, but your muscle is bigger and bigger!"

"Buddy, well that's the idea, eh? Muscle is not getting bigger now, but the quilt of body fat that was hiding it is disappearing now! Thanks for the positive feedback!"

I've been struggling with a bit of "muscle dysmorphia" recently, so it was lovely to hear that from my young man. I look at myself every day and just don't really see it, as I should strive for more and more! But I am trusting the journey, not cheating, and doing the work!

From the Greyhound station, we immediately went to get him a haircut — then out for sushi! Now, we are home watching animal videos on the computer! I love that little custom we have made our very own.

And I love my son's unabridged honesty. "Mom, your house smells good... Mom, your FRIDGE smells good... Mom, what is that on your face?" (I tried shaving my eyebrows cause I couldn't find the tweezers and cut myself). "Mom, you're freakin' me out again" (after giving me a wee shoulder massage and being stunned at the muscle there as I lean out)!

NOVEMBER 6, 2014
I was up around 5:30 and Matt already had my coffee waiting for me! As he handed me my coffee, he grinned widely. "Happy Birthday to ME! Birthdays are good for me — the more I have, the longer I live!"
"Indeed! Happy birthday, buddy!"
He asked me what time he was born, 36 years ago today. I don't think he had ever asked that until now.
I again recited the story of how I owned five taxi cabs in Ontario. I was driving the day shift and knew I was going into mild labor, two weeks before a scheduled caesarian section. My mantra that day was, "One more trip; one more trip." Around 3 PM, I had my $100 daily goal (back then, $100 went a lot further than it does today; $100 back then was more like $400 today) and I drove into Metropolitan General Hospital's parking lot, parked and walked into the emergency department. I underwent a c-section with my requested spinal anesthetic (so I could be awake for Matt's birth) within 2 hours. "SO, buddy — you breathed your first breath around 5 PM on this day, 36 years ago!"
"I got to *feel* you being pulled out (despite the spinal anesthetic) and hear your first cry. When I spoke to you, I said 'Matthew, don't cry: no one is ever going to take you from me' and you stopped crying!"
He giggled, "I guess after nine months in your belly, I knew to pay attention! I already knew that a smart man says nothing!"

I have honored that promise to him all these years... Who knew I'd have to fight to keep him alive and in expert hands after an adult brain injury? Heck, who knew that my bodybuilding pursuits would help me with the physical endurance required for his rehabilitation in the years ahead? G-D knew, and it's not lost on me how very blessed I am to see Matthew alive, well, stable, happy, and thriving.

While Mattie watched a comedy on television, I made a special birthday breakfast for him. As I whisked eggs, made pancakes from scratch, and sliced bananas, I recalled silently that his father was nowhere to be found for days after Matthew's birth. With the further and similar events that followed, I ultimately concluded the relationship when Matt was six months old.
Last night, in one of our many touching talks, Matt said, "Mom, I don't want to use the 'H-word', but you know I feel it only for one person."
"The 'H-word'?"
"Hate," he said. But he added, "Mom, I forgive him, but I still hate him. I never want him in my life, and I don't even want to know when he dies. Thank you for always being here for me. Thank you for loving me, REALLY loving me." WOW.

NOVEMBER 7, 2014

LOVELY time at Harrison Hot Springs. We had pizza from a local pizzeria, the owner of which is a client of the lawyer for whom I work. I think it was the best pizza I'd ever had!

On our way to Harrison, I knew Matt's group home was going to call, but it was to be a surprise, so I didn't tell him. When the phone rang, I asked, "Buddy, could you answer that, please?" He was slightly concerned when the call display registered the group home, with his history of hearing from group homes as invariably being "bad news." But WHAT a surprise for him! He was stunned and thrilled! EVERY resident was there and spoke to him and wished him a happy birthday, as well as the staff! In Matt's 13-year history of brain injury recovery, THAT has never happened. He loves his home so very much!!!!

And I am so very grateful.

Mattie, breakfast
in Harrison Hot
Springs, BC

NOVEMBER 8, 2014

I just viewed the pics posted by the 2014 Sandra Wickham Fall Classic competitors from the morning show. Very nice to see good quality athletes on that stage! I sure wish we hadn't needed to sacrifice our tickets for tonight, but I returned from Harrison with an ear infection that has my balance impaired. I have trouble driving and walking, so driving at night and being around a crowd would be an absolute no go for me. Matt is SO good about everything, and despite looking forward to watching the festivities of another bodybuilding competition and seeing many people we know there, he never once complained. He's really trying to take good care of me, bless him!

My fever has broken, but I cannot even close my jaw fully, because of the pressure that creates on the eardrum. I have no hearing in my left ear, and when I talk, it sounds as though I am underwater.

Determined to sleep without a sleeping pill, I made it through, but not without vivid, strange dreams (including talking someone out of going drinking and then inviting eight people into my home for chicken soup, one of those persons being James Spader???!!!). I also had night sweats, probably waking up about 15x, but all good. The ear doesn't seem improved, but perhaps it is just going to take more time.

There can be no cardio or training today. I think my body needs to fight this infection. I suspect I have pushed my immune system to its limit. Slowing down for a few days may be in order.

Mattie must have asked me 30x last night if he could do anything for me, bless his heart. He made me chamomile & valerian tea before bed, and sweetly apologized for being so tired and needing to sleep! I am so proud that he has progressed so far!

Getting ill is an excellent opportunity to refocus on what is MOST important, and not on secondary goals.

NOVEMBER 9, 2014

I had the biggest "treat" of my weight-loss journey yesterday; Matt and I each had a cup of raw cashews. Sure felt good, and I refuse to feel guilt for the healthy fats.

When I told Matt the calories in the cashews (just under 1,000 calories for a cup), he promptly put the jar back in the cabinet with a look on his face as though he'd just swallowed a mouse!

And dinner is now served: roasted chicken breast, salad, and asparagus! Matt ate 20 percent of the asparagus raw before I stopped him! It's hard to believe that he would not touch asparagus two years ago — whether raw or steamed! He has come so very far!

NOVEMBER 12, 2014

So very nice having my Mattie train with me today, and I quickly realized the insane value of having a spotter for chest presses and overhead delt work! Matt was a HUGE help. I could press 40# (each dumbbell) on the overheads, simply because he could help me get the initial movement started. With my double-jointed shoulders, pressing a heavier weight is problematic and risky for me, but once it's up there, I am good.

His legs are sore now, as are his shoulders and arms — and he is loving it! He kept wanting to use heavier weight for our shoulder exercises, but I wouldn't let him (he has frozen shoulders from the TBI of 13 years ago, so weights are not good for him just yet with shoulder work)... I taught him how to do the exercises (with me) to the beat of the music in his ears, and he found a new training joy! "Wow, NOW I see why you have music blasting in your ears every time you train!"

I will miss him when he leaves tomorrow, but I am SO thrilled that he loves his group home and everyone there SO much. Sometimes I just cannot believe how fortunate we are.

We realized yesterday that his being 36 now also marks him living a year longer than the initial doctors predicted his life expectancy to be, and he is thriving. Matt is walking proof that NO ONE should ever give up, despite limitations, despite challenges, despite a lack of funding, despite a system trying to fight against you at every turn (until he changed health authorities, that is).

I am counting blessings like a child with an ice cream cone today.

NOVEMBER 13, 2014

As we were driving to the Greyhound station this morning, Matt said, "Mom, what happened to your face?" A good chuckle ensued, knowing with TBI in the mix, he doesn't always communicate exactly what he means (OR he communicates what he is thinking, but with little discretion). I said, "Hon, I don't know! I didn't leave it at home! What do you mean?"

LOL, "Mom, your face looks better than it did yesterday — your skin is better."

My sweet young man. He loves me so much, and ditto. And he misses nothing.

NOVEMBER 15, 2014

Gotta love renewed beginnings. I just reconnected with my dear friend Desi. She heard a rumor a few years back I had died of a massive heart attack. WOW. I had not heard that one. It could have just as easily been true, however, given the state of my former health decline.

SO happy to be in contact with her again. Life is damn good... So grateful for every single twist and turn in life that has brought me (and my beloved Mattie) this far.

NOVEMBER 20, 2014

Today, I received an email notification that the director of Matthew's group home was involved in a head-on motor vehicle collision yesterday. That is all I know at this moment. Matthew and the other clients of the group home will not be told until more is known about her condition. Apparently, the accident was significant. I have written to the managing partner of my former Okanagan law firm, asking him to represent her. He will drive to Kamloops to speak with her personally in the hospital.

For now, the assistant manager of the home will assume duties for the director.

Left with no words, numbly, I prayed.

NOVEMBER 22, 2014

My friend Liz visited this evening. We went through my closet, and she made me toss about 70 percent of the clothing... "Nope - that's too big already, it will be ridiculous on you in the new year... Nope, that one makes you look 50."

"WAIT! Isn't that GOOD? I'm 60 in two weeks!"

"Nope — you need to look 40!" And as she tossed another pair of trousers my way, she said, "Here, this one is too big, too — it's gotta go!"

I said I thought it was probably okay. She told me to "Put it on!"

YIKES! She was right. I now have LOTS of good-quality clothing going out to my son's group home in December!

"No blazers for you, now. With the size of your shoulders already, you're going to look like a man in drag... and no skirts, with those calves, you're going to be called a tranny — so if that will bother you, no skirts! And just so ya know, they're gonna say your calves look like a giant ball sack!"

I am going to take it as a compliment and NOT hear it as an insecurity trigger, as I might have a year ago!

The two bomber jackets I bought (purposefully) one size too small (one month ago) now fit perfectly. I will need a pair of black trousers now for a job interview in the new year!

NOVEMBER 25, 2014

Mattie phoned early tonight. He is now aware of Angela's accident and that she is in hospital presently. But it is apparent he has not had the severity of the MVA explained. I will not share further details with him.

He apologized for calling earlier than our scheduled time but explained he was going out to celebrate a birthday "for PIE NIGHT" at a local senior's residence. He didn't even mention the pie, adding, "And Mom, you know I love seniors!"

The distraction of this outing is an excellent strategy. Certainly, he has not been told the home director has suffered spinal and head injuries. I am not sure how he would manage that kind of information.

Sometimes I have to ask myself if I am dreaming. I feel great pride in what I see in my son now. I say it a lot, but he has proven to be the son I always hoped I was raising. Oh, the profound difference QUALITY CARE has made. I pray that there will be no interruption to the proven protocols in place.

NOVEMBER 28, 2014

Matt sent a handwritten note to Angela. "It's not the same without you. I hope you recover well!" Angela was struck head-on in a tragic motor vehicle collision and has suffered a head injury, spinal injuries, back injury, and more. She has significant therapy ahead of her, and multiple surgeries. We have not told Matthew the depth of her injuries; he would not manage the severe anxiety and worry associated with that.

I wrote back to her, "Bless him, he truly loves you, Angela. He has told me more than once that you are the 'Number Two' woman in his life. Last night he was so cute, he said, 'Mom, I'm so glad you're not jealous that I love Angela!' You make such a difference in both our lives. I just wish I could do something miraculous for you right now."

ALL THINGS WITH LOVING PURPOSE

December 1st... Wow. It's hard to believe we are almost finished with what turned out to be a wonderful year for Mattie and me! 2014 has marked a dramatic and very strategic landmark in both our lives.

And in two weeks and two days, I have him back for another two-week visit! He told me two days ago his goal was to drop 10 pounds while he is here with me. I asked, "So, you're willing to do the work? To push past your comfort zone?"

He hesitated, "I *think* so!" We laughed in unison!

DECEMBER 2, 2014

Part of my conversation with Matthew tonite...

"Mom - you sound happy, but are you okay?"

"I am happy buddy; things are great! I'm just tired!"

"Mom, you sound like you're in pain."

"Buddy, I AM; I am perpetually sore ALL the time."

"That's eff'ing awesome! Did ya notice? I'm trying not to swear!"

"Fucking A!"

"I'm proud of you, Mom."

"For swearing?"

"Mom, you're silly. Did you lose track of our conversation? I'm proud of you for hurting yourself in a good way, every day!"

DECEMBER 5, 2014

My Mattie... I've raised my son twice... I've changed adult diapers and reinforced that it is his TBI that causes him to suffer through a wet bed again. I've literally picked him up when he's fallen — while learning to walk as a toddler, and as a more-than-300-pound man as an adult. I've sold everything I owned four times, just to get medical reports to protect him from an apathetic or begrudging medical system, and I've taught him to read, write and walk twice... But I would do it ALL over again, despite the tragedies along the way.

He is my greatest accomplishment, my greatest joy, and my most revered reward. Being an exemplary mother has been my lifelong goal.

I note how he is so conditioned, all these years, to understand that my birthday warrants a precarious approach every year. His email to me this morning never referenced "birthday."

> I LOVE YOU, SO MUCH, AND ESPECIALY 'CAUSE OF TODAY!! I LOVE U, AND WISH U A GREAT-DAY!! DON'T FORGET: this is the day G-D decided you were important.

And he just phoned from the group home. He and some of the other residents sang happy birthday to me! He was so proud of that!

Within seconds of the birthday adulations by phone, he emailed again. "THX, EH, MOM!! I WAS HOPING THIS WOULD BE A GOOD DAY 4 U!! THIS IS GREAT TO ME, TOO, 'CAUSE WITHOUT YOU, THERE WOULD BE NO ME! HAPPY B-DAY MY SWEET MOM!!"

Today I turned 60. I shared a story with friends on Facebook this evening, in case it could help any other individual reading to understand that we all have baggage to carry.

I have dreaded birthdays and Christmases in my life for as long as I can remember, but every year, I endeavor to get past the pain there for so long. At about age five (and these many decades later, it is still active in my memory), my mother told me to "Get past the birthday crap." She told me it was JUST another day and a reminder to her of her greatest mistake. "It's just the day my pregnancy was finally over. Don't go fooling yourself into thinking you deserve something special just because you were born."

So for 55 years, I have never gotten past those words... Odd, isn't it, how such hurtful commentary can stay with us for so long? I've heard the phrase "You won't remember how someone looked, but you will remember how they made you feel." I find a lot of profound truth in that.

But my SON adores this day; he tells me EVERY SINGLE YEAR he is SO glad I was born, because he loves HIS life, and without me, he wouldn't be here and happy. He tells me every single year that this was the day G-D decided I had a purpose, that G-D decided I was important. Well, happy birthday to me!

DECEMBER 9, 2014

I just spoke with Matt on the phone. He's so excited about being here in one week! Said he's definitely like a little kid at Christmas — and then added, "OH YEAH, but it *is* Christmas! HAHAHA!"

"MOM, I haven't lost ANY weight, but I'm still holding steady at 260. At least I haven't gained any back — and sometimes I eat like a madman!"

It is not lost on me how much he wants to please me, impress me, and excel with his weight loss as I pursue my own. This is precisely what I had hoped would happen — but one can never predict the efficacy of a well-intended plan.

And then... "Mom, I hope you aren't wasting money on me or spending too much on my trip down there. I don't want to be a burden."

"Don't worry. That's how you're going to lose weight while you're down here — you're not getting fed."

Without a moment's hesitation, "Mom, that's not the way to lose weight! I know you'll feed me six times a day! Thanks for that!"

"So, Mom — are we still doing our usual and seeing a new movie on Christmas Day?"

"Do you still *want* to do that, buddy?"

"Oh, heck yeah — if you can afford it. That's our thing. I love us!"

For the past five years, Mattie and I have made a personal family tradition out of seeing a new movie opening on Christmas Day. This year, we will see *Unbroken*. I like to introduce him to movies with a message, particularly if we can take something from the cinema message into our current lives. The main character is a boy named "Louie" Zamperini. He was always in trouble, but with the help of his older brother, he turned his life around and channeled his efforts into running, later qualifying for the 1936 Olympics. When World War II erupted, Louie enlisted in the military. After his plane crashed in the Pacific, he survived an incredible 47 days adrift in a raft, until his capture by the Japanese navy. They sent him to a prisoner of war camp, where he became the frequent target of a cruel Japanese commander.

Matthew loved the movie. As he wiped away tears, he told me, "Mom, thank you for always loving me — and for *teaching* me lessons I need to know, even with a Christmas Day movie."

PURSUING HEALTH

M attie is SO excited about coming back to visit me in less than a week. Just got an email from him now: "45 MINUTES AND WE SPEAK!! AND IN ONE MORE WEEK I WON'T BE CALLING!"

It is THE most incredible elation to know how much I am loved and missed!

> "Give the ones you love wings to fly, roots to come back, and reasons to stay." ~Dalai Lama

This is what I always hoped I was doing for my Mattie, and now, 3.5 decades later it would seem that (maybe) I got it right. That's a relief because they certainly don't come with a book of instructions!

DECEMBER 16, 2014
"One more sleep — I want to go to bed right after I talk 2 u at 6:30 so the time will pass faster!" That was Mattie's final email to me this evening.

I'm very excited to see him tomorrow morning, too! Hoping for decent weather so we can walk through nature — exercise, breathe good air, laugh, and talk! Then Thursday morning, we are in the gym training together, bright and early! I know he'll poop out before I finish with mine, but he can sit in the hot tub and socialize while Mom finishes tearing up pecs and triceps!

DECEMBER 17, 2014
There is never a night that I don't hug Matt and kiss him on the cheek before bedtime, still, after 34 years of life together. I also never leave the house without saying "I love you," as I always wonder how I would feel if I never had time to say it again. I think about that a lot. Traumatic brain injury makes the survivors and all who love them consider the future with morbid analysis. I have witnessed, firsthand, that we don't always get second chances.

DECEMBER 18, 2014

Great workout with Matt this morning (biceps & triceps). Bless him, he pooped out long before I was done, but he was giggling at the pump in his arms and was shaking, so I knew he'd really had enough. While I continued persevering, he spent an hour in the hot tub and returned SO very relaxed and grateful to be there, saying, "Mom, I *love* this gym! Heck, I love my life so much now — especially when I am with you!"

We just finished meal three, a nice extra-rare sirloin filet, browned in macadamia nut oil and onions, and topped with a small amount of tamari soy sauce. Then with that, braised eggplant with a little walnut oil, and garlic tossed with cooked brown rice, and served with a decorative drizzle of Hoisin sauce! All the while, we listened to the "gangsta rap" music selections on Mom's MP3, which utterly amazed Matt. He said, "Mom, where did you find some of this underground stuff? I haven't even heard some of these!"

"Mom, you know I would be happy with a bowl of cereal, eh? You sure go to a lot of trouble with food! Why do you do that?"

"Buddy — do you not *like it?*"

"NO! I love it! I'm shocked — I'm impressed, but it is so much work, and then we eat it and it's gone!"

"Buddy, that bowl of cereal would be gone, too — right? I want you to appreciate the work that goes into the flavor combinations, and the caring that goes into making a plate of food look *pretty*! Then I want you to savor every bite."

"Savor the flavor! Okay, no problem with that!"

WHAT A GREAT visit!

Now, I'll sit back down with my young man and enjoy a sugar-free Tiramisu-flavoured coffee (just the flavor with none of the calories)!

One more hilarity to share from my son. After his haircut yesterday, I needed a couple more items from Superstore. As we were walking back to the car, Matt said again, "MOM, I'm so proud of you."

"Oh thanks, sweetie. I sure appreciate that!"

"NO, MOM, it's not just me — it's about so many people checking out your butt in there. I'm proud other people are noticing your butt, because it's *much* better!"

Leave it to my son to blurt without a filter!

SO nice to have my Matt back home for the holidays! His bus was 1.5 hours late yesterday, but all good. I'm so proud of how calmly he takes everything in stride now... so consistently! Right away, he was stunned at the changes he saw in my conditioning. "Mom, it's only been a month... well, 35 days, actually. Wow! I'm shocked!"

We laughed until we hurt about how much his hair had grown, how much more grey he is now than me! He had applied gel to the front part of his hair, making it stand straight up — so the balance of the day included my joke to him as "HELLO," while holding my hand straight up at my forehead and making my eyes wide! We giggled like little children, and got him a haircut immediately after having sushi!

We were both exhausted and retired to bed at 7 PM last night. I woke up around 5:30 and considered cardio, but went back to bed. "Mom, I hope I'm not holding you back." I said, no, not to worry — I won't let that happen, but my exhaustion is holding me back. I slept until 7 AM and so did Matt.

Now, oatmeal & protein powder for him (with some blueberries) and oatmeal & chicken breast for me — and we're out the door to the gym to train our arms. When Matt has had enough (his endurance will definitely be less than mine), he will go to the hot tub! And he remembered, with no prompting, to ask for a towel to take to the gym! How remarkable his memory function is now.

All that cognitive therapy and absolute perfection in a consistently managed group home with structured outings for residents every single week have changed my young man completely. He even wanted to phone his best friend, R, last night, saying R might miss him. WOW. I find myself again pleased and proud of Matt's respect, care, and empathy.

I realize I say it a lot, but I think it even more: he is the son I always hoped I was raising. So incredibly proud that he has managed (with lots of help and assertive advocacy) to overcome so many purposeful obstacles that were placed in his path all those earlier years by inept (and sometimes, negligent) care providers. We're lucky to be living a true success story in what funding and proper care (not just a bed-park & collect-a-cheque syndrome) can bring.

DECEMBER 19, 2014

I really have my schedule turned around and upside down. When I am up at 2:30 AM and doing cardio by 3, meal one in by or before 5 AM — by 6 PM, I am exhausted. Today, I exclaimed, "Wow — it's only 3:30 in the afternoon and way too early to go to bed, but I feel like I could!"

I need to stay awake until at least 9 PM tonight, to get myself back into a semblance of a logical timeline. It doesn't phase Mattie when I am out the door for cardio by 3 AM. He wakes up briefly, says "I love you, Mom; I'm proud of you," rolls over, and falls fast asleep again!

This morning, when I returned, he awoke to say, "Wow — are you okay? Did you decide NOT to go do cardio?" He did not know I had been gone for an hour! At least I know he is not wandering the neighborhood in the wee hours of the morning.

It is incredibly wonderful having him here. We plan to train back together in the morning. I have had Mattie on the same eating plan and schedule as my own. Every 2.5 hours, we eat. Now, at meal four, he asks, "Do I have to eat?" Yes, sir, you do!

Just to get his reaction, one hour after our last meal, I said, "Okay — time to eat."

"Mom, you've got to be kidding?"

"Yes, buddy — gotcha! It's a joke!"

"Mom, you KNOW I love to eat — but this gets intense sometimes!"

Already, he is conditioning to the process. He just asked, "When do we eat again? Oh wait! We get a protein shake with frozen broccoli at 6:30! I can do that! Can I put some cocoa powder in it, too?"

"Cocoa powder?"

"Did I stutter? SORRY MOM, bad joke! My mouth doesn't always say what my brain wants it to say!"

DECEMBER 20, 2014
Another funny Matt story to share. Matt goes out for his first cigarette this morning; because it's still dark out and my little area is quite private, he opts to wear my leopard velour bathrobe out. I then hear him outside, in his deep and manly voice, say, "Whassup?" LOL, of all times for my neighbor to be entering his car and see big 6-foot three-inch, 260-pound Matt in a woman's leopard bathrobe! I laughed so hard my abs hurt!

I completed fasted cardio this morning while Matt continued to sleep. He didn't even hear me return, but I got him up and moving as I need Meal One in, and then out the door for training!

He kept up! His biceps were so sore from two days ago still that it limited him from completing movements on back training, but he pushed through a few and then enjoyed the hot tub. I had a great back workout and then threw in four sets of leg extensions at the end, just for posterity! Just about to put in meal three shortly, then we are off to see *Horrible Bosses 2* at the movie theatre!

The movie turned out to be one of THE funniest movies we have seen in a long time!

I saw my coach and her husband at the gym this morning. It was nice to hear complimentary feedback from both of them on my conditioning! Today was the first time I felt comfortable wearing a clingy tank top! After the compliments, Matt quietly said to me, once we were out of ear range, "See Mom, it's not just me; you really *are* changing!"

DECEMBER 21, 2014
Meal Four. Of course, I love exotic foods. So, I'm trying something new (still again, compliments of the impressive selection at Heritage Meats in Langley)! We're having sauteed mushrooms & onions, brown rice with lemongrass & dill, and — (roll drum, please) KANGAROO STEAK!

Matt looked at me with mixed emotions... thinking how cute a kangaroo is. I reminded him of how cute cows and chickens are, too. This prompted another conversation that he would like to become a vegetarian. Matthew's assessment of the kangaroo steak dinner? He loved it but said f I make it again, just don't tell him what it is!

It's very solid but tender meat with a completely unique taste and texture from beef or chicken — or anything else we've had. It was filling and tasty! Given that one $5 steak was enough for both of us, it is a dense protein with almost zero fat, it represented good value.

I braised it in 1/2 tsp of walnut oil, on both sides, then turned off the burner and let it sit. Made a sauce from 1 tbsp catsup, 1 tsp Hoisin sauce, and 1 tsp sriracha, and let that sit atop the resting kangaroo steak. I combined the sauteed fresh mushrooms (sauteed in 1 tsp avocado oil with 1 tbsp minced garlic), adding 1 tsp tamari soy sauce when turning off the burner. Then I tossed in the sauteed brown rice (to which I'd added 2 tbsp lemongrass paste and 1 tsp dried dill).

Matt reminded me he didn't eat mushrooms, and I apologized profusely, that being a food boycott dating back to his time in Japan when other children laughed at his name and called him "Mush-u-roomu."

He told me, "Don't worry, Mom, it's been a long time; I know you forgot. I will try the mushrooms. You're always telling me to push past my comfort zone!"

I put the rice mix on our plates, then added the steak on top, with drippings over all that (only oil in the drippings was from the walnut oil — this was a VERY lean red meat). It was a unique and filling dinner, and Mattie absolutely loved it. Once again, his designs of becoming vegetarian have been thwarted!

Certainly, I would wholly support his goals of vegetarianism, but only IF the new management in the group home can maintain good protein substitutes for him. I don't have the confidence that they would consider accommodating the inconvenience.

DECEMBER 22, 2014

We trained chest and shoulders and threw in a few leg presses, some glute kickbacks and a few hamstring stretches with a 60–pound barbell. I would have performed two more chest exercises, but Matt was having a hard time, so I cut it short.

Poor guy, he has now gone so long without weight training, it really messed his shoulders up. I suspect the issues are permanent now... He can't do shoulder or chest exercises without instant pain (using extremely low weight). He was okay on the calf raises, and he did a few leg presses, with one 25-pound plate per side, but he gave up on that quickly; his right-leg deficits are worse (having not had weight training all this time). Left-brain injury renders right-body deficits. His right leg is very weak and shakes with the slightest exertion. It is also apparent in his gait because he still has numbness in that leg and foot.

We will try to get some walking in if the rain stays away long enough. Fingers crossed on that, as he really needs walking. His balance is also especially bad, again.

"Mom, are you going to send me back early?"

"OH BUDDY — why would I do that?"

With tears quietly streaming down both cheeks, he told me, "I just don't want to hold you back. I am slower than you, and I am sorry I need so much attention. I want to make you better, not be a truck in your way."

"Oh, Mattie — I love having you here. Don't you EVER doubt that, okay? Did you forget that this competition is for *you?* Remember, I will be on that stage for your birthday next year, buddy!"

"And, this Bud's for you." I laughed at his recitation of the Budweiser slogan! Now sobbing, and so emotional, he added, "Oh wow — I forgot about that. You're really doing this for my birthday. You love me so much. Thank you, Mom. Thank you for loving me."

It actually broke a little piece of my heart to think he would worry about me sending him back early because I would consider my training a higher priority than him. That actually made me a little nauseous.

Love what matters. Competition training can be "turned up" in January after he has returned to Kamloops.

DECEMBER 25, 2014

I am so proud of my son... He never complains about ANYTHING (other than what he believes to be disappointing to me from time to time). We just had chicken breast and salad, and he couldn't care less about turkey dinner and fixings. I am so grateful for that!

I just let him choose our Christmas Day movie, and he chose "The Gambler" (instead of Big Hero 6). So the Gambler, it is! Popcorn is about to be popped here at home, with some pink Himalayan salt (coconut oil spritzed over half; avocado oil spritzed on the rest)!

We are 100 percent eating clean for our Christmas!

DECEMBER 26, 2014

Just finished watching *Guardians of the Galaxy* with Matt! Very entertaining! Matt said, "I wonder how much Vin Diesel got paid to say 'I am Groot' 50x as his only line?"

DECEMBER 27, 2014

Another Mattie anecdote. Today in the gym, he whispers to me, "Mom, can I swear?" I said, "Faak yeah, buddy — whassup?"

"Mom, your shoulders are freakin' huge."

"I thought you were going to swear."

"You always do it for me; it reminds me it's conduct unbecoming. Oh, sorry... But hey, did I say that right?"

LAUGHING LOUDLY, I reply, "Yes, buddy — you got that *absolutely* right. So glad I can set a good example for you."

"Oh, Mom."

DECEMBER 28, 2014

I had to have a chat with my beloved son last night about his choice to behave childishly. At that moment, we had an "adult to adult" conversation, and I gently directed his attention to that point. I had to tell him that the child-like and the near-continual need for positive reinforcement, approval, and such were actually draining me. He admitted he saw that, and he wants to change it. He took full ownership of his behaviors and since 7 PM last night, he has wonderfully put a lot of attention to detail in "growing up a notch."

Good man. Dutiful son, most days... I felt a *little* guilty for calling him out on childishness, but he insists he wants to be treated like a man in the community. I admit I am torn. If showing adult behavior results in a lesser kindness and appreciation of life, let's stay in the man-child mode. Every day presents such a delicate balance with TBI. When to push? When to let things sit?

Life is good — often *draining*, but thank goodness most of us can choose to effect change and push forward repeatedly!

Well, Matt has absolutely collapsed. Instead of hitting the hot tub today, he spent 30 minutes in the sauna instead. Good grief... another reason my buddy needs supervision. He was so proud of himself, but I recognized dehydration and had him drink a Gatorade... When I asked him why so long in the sauna and no hot tub, he said, "There were a lot of nice people there, and you know how I love talking to people." My social butterfly! He has been social since he was a toddler.

Before retiring for bed, Mattie told me, "Mom, sorry I disappointed you again." Yikes! His awareness is a double-edged sword for me. On the one hand, I am proud that he is "getting it" but, conversely, my heart aches from the lesson.

I assured him we were good — *great*, in fact; but reminded him, "I just worry." It continues to be clear he cannot forward-think to what is always in his best interest. That insight I did not share with him, however.

I don't even want to think where either of us would be without the blessing of the Kamloops group home. I hope Angela can return but am trying not to obsess over that speculation. Much more than that, I want her to be *well* again.

JANUARY 1, 2015

Mattie is now back in Kamloops. It was probably about a week too long for him to be here. We talked about this openly, as adults. He concurred, which made me very proud of how far his ability to reason has come.

I miss him horribly. The house seems so empty and quiet, but I truly need this time for myself at this age. Again, I turn to thoughts of gratitude that he is privy to such quality caregiving from attentive professionals. I am no longer capable of giving him the care, attention, and redirection that he needs so extensively, so frequently...

When Mattie was here, I think my weight training was about 70 percent less effective, because I was rushed and distracted, needing to monitor him and needing to be ready to leave when he had finished his visit to the hot tub. His TBI just doesn't permit him the endurance levels, and I don't dare leave him to any potential social "misintention" because of an absence of supervision. He needs the supervision and deserves it. Conversely, I deserve to be a mom from a distance from time to time.

Mattie phoned right on time tonight, so excited to tell me how welcome everyone made him feel when he returned to the group home, and to tell me all about the presents he came back to find there for him. He could not remember what they were, but walked up to his room with the phone and named them off to me! He said, "Mom, I know YOU love me and want me, but these people here do too! I am so happy to be wanted by more than just you. And I'm glad that doesn't make you jealous!"

Of course, that made me cry. It brings me to tears again just typing it. Nothing could have pleased me more... and to know he is so ecstatically happy to be back HOME — in HIS HOME? I can imagine no greater progress.

I feel like a thousand lead weights have lifted from me, and from Matt. The past 13 years of TBI have been so challenging — for him and for me as his Mom and his advocate. More often than not, I thought both of us would perish from the battle — never mind his brain injury and the horrible physical maladies to be overcome and accepted to never change... Every single battle has been worth the journey, however, thanks to his Kamloops group home.

I actually feel I can "let go" a lot more now. I was *almost* there before, but I am SO confident things are and will continue to be just fine.

My young man has permanent deficits, yes — but he is kind, calm, patient, and tolerant. He is unselfish and loving. He is happy.

Whew. From an out-of-control gang member on the fast track to self-destruction, to where we are today? It's nothing short of miraculous.

Now, here's to mom getting a solid night's sleep and tearing down some more muscle in the gym tomorrow!

HEALTHY BODY, HEALTHY MIND

One of my goals for 2015 is to ask myself, "Have I given this my all?" — every single day. That goes for my training, my journey to become more and more emotionally stable (and less emotion-centered), to achieve more independence and less co-dependence where my son is concerned (for him and for me, equally), with wherever my career path may take me, and more. For me, it's all about maximizing improvements in being the best person I can be in all avenues while I am still capable. My life is closer to an expiration date now, although extended beyond what it would have been in my physical condition seven months ago.

AND, another random story... I sent out a few New Year cards this year, including a few to some folks I liked in the seniors' residence where I previously lived in Kelowna. That was where I was when I first began my new fitness journey. When I left in July 2014, I had lost some weight, but I was still obese. In my New Year cards, I included a recent photo of Matt and me at the gym, next to the Christmas Tree, and a tricep pose taken a couple of weeks back when I checked in with my coach.

*Mattie with Mom at
Harrison December 2014*

Well, apparently, the pics made quite a stir. One of my friends there had told some of the "old gals" that I'd gone crazy with fitness, lost 100 lbs, and was going to compete in bodybuilding one last time, but no one believed her. I laughed so hard when she emailed me to say it was great that I sent the pics, and I should have seen their faces when they opened the cards! Still, one woman mentioned "Photoshop" and how you could make any photo believable with that software!

One thing I love more than many other things is proving folks wrong... Absolutely, if I SAY I am going to do something, you can bet money you don't have I am going to take myself to the limits to get it done, especially if someone has said I can't or won't! Guess that's taking stubbornness to the next level!

JANUARY 2, 2015

Well, that was a short sleep. When Mattie was here, I had poor sleep and had to resort to taking sleeping pills again. Now, I am trying to discontinue, but the nightmares resume. I Googled the whys and wherefores of that and apparently it is because of an interruption in neurotransmitters, which interrupts REM sleep. Interesting, and logical...

I think my sleep suffered when Mattie was here, too, because I have so many concerns for him, just under the surface. Changes in a group home environment are something to which I am particularly attentive. While I do not want to overthink this to the point of paranoia, it would be nothing short of foolish for me to forget what has happened in the past — twice.

I am careful to *not* lose sight of the many daily blessings in our presence, however. Matthew's stability continues, and he is happy. Without that, I could not pursue the lofty goal of returning to the bodybuilding stage in my 60s.

G-D bless this health authority and the incredible director of that home for being willing to take a chance on my once high-risk son.

JANUARY 14, 2015

I had a simply outstanding teleconference this morning with the health authority's Acquired Brain Injury Program and the group home. The home allowed Matthew to attend and take part. In other homes, that was always prohibited.

The manager of the home stated, "Matt has been the easiest transition we've ever had here. We have no problems with Matt. He really fits in well and has made friendships here."

HOLY CROW, that is what I always FELT was possible but never happened before (a) because of lower-quality care and (equally important) (b) because Matt was insecure, shamed, and apathetic about doing the work to effect change. He even stated in the teleconference today that he really *wants* to be a good man and he believes he has a future now.

We discussed openly my decisions to bring Matt down for visits less frequently and for a lesser duration. Everyone, including Matthew, agreed it was a good maneuver for both of us! He said he wants to grow up now. WOW.

In concluding the teleconference, the ABI program (the funding people with the Health Authority) asked if there were any concerns, other comments, or changes to be discussed, and everyone concurred all was great!

Matt sees his new psychiatrist for the first time today, who is in place only to maintain monitoring of the medication regimen that works very well for Matt — and to have onboard if (G-D forbid) any change in Matt's TBI conditions or behaviors transpired, for any reason, including the aging process. Besides, funding is contingent on a psychiatrist being in place. Without a psychiatrist on board, Matt would be at the whim of an overworked health care system, and it is almost impossible for a psychiatrist to take on an individual with Matt's level of brain injury. I fought aggressively years ago to call in a favor (from years of working in law) to get Matthew situated with a competent psychiatrist. I did it in Abbotsford, again in Kelowna, and now this amazing group home did it for Matt (for me) in his new location.

We have simply unimaginable progress, goodness, and blessings. I have no regrets about the efforts, the re-education, and the sacrifices made along the way.

THE GEARS BEGIN TO SLIP

I only recently learned how to effectively engage boundaries, believe it or not. Before that, I let folks walk all over me until I, eventually, blew. For decades, I asked myself what that was — why I was walked over AND why I allowed it. The only connection I could garner from my past was my mother. I suppose being bullied and horrified to speak a word in response got that started for me. I still have a way to go, but I am very different now. It took a lot of work.

My son expressed it simplistically and effectively (re my former style): "Mom, you have two speeds — really sweet & loving, or WIN by any means necessary. Bad people first think you're a pussy, but you show them fast it's smarter to back off!" After blurting that out, he immediately added, "Sorry, Mom — that one shoulda stayed in my brain!"

I told him that we teach people how to treat us back, either by having boundaries or by having none!

Weight training is certainly a PERFECT way to work off stress. I was so stressed when I entered the gym tonight, that I actually vomited.

JANUARY 31, 2015

A tiny piece of Matt's drama surfaced today. I received a call from the group home while driving home from posing practice. Turns out one of the other residents was seen with $50, which clearly was not his money. When a care aide asked the young man where he got it, he replied, "From Matt — Matt wanted a stronger pack of smokes."

SO, as the staff was all too aware that Matt was not permitted to have cash, I got a call.

I had to enter my "advanced interrogator" psyche, like other mothers before me. After a chat with Matt, his first response was to tell me "I don't want to 'rat out my friend'." As it turned out, Matt had complained about his cigarettes not being strong enough and had asked the man, another patient, for money. His friend gave it to him, without hesitation.

"Matt, you are 36 — which makes you closer to 40 than you are to 30. The 'rat out' phrase is either a childish or a jailhouse mentality, and I don't want either in my life now. Where you live is YOUR HOME. If you cannot come clean with this, you should take a break from visiting me and consider your options. You are not a child and I am not your codependent mom anymore, buddy. Man up, or suffer the consequences of acting irresponsibly — as the rest of us do as adults."

"OH, MOM! *Please* don't do that. Please don't take away my visit."

I suggested he tell the man who gave him the money that he was sorry but to explain that he has shortcomings and disabilities like everyone else there, and he's trying to grow up. I thought he also should apologize to the man for complaining that he wanted stronger cigarettes. I explained this was manipulation, taking money from another patient in the home because he felt entitled to more-costly tobacco. I reminded him of his earlier days in group homes that involved manipulation and bullying — for cigarettes.

I am grateful for things going well for so long. These are small "blips" in the overall spectrum of what we have survived and endured. So, as Matt cried and expressed shame and remorse, I reminded him we never go to sleep angry.

This is something I have always taught my son, especially after his TBI. I have taken it a step further and taught him to allow himself to feel sadness instead of anger because I believe that anger is rooted in sadness and frustration. I believe that sadness is easier to redirect than anger, and I believe sadness is a healthier emotion than anger. Sadness is more closely in touch with love. Love is the basis for our happiness and fulfillment, and our sense of value in life. And let us never forget that channeled anger found him institutionalized and without freedom.

Interesting that he enjoys an absence of anger now. That, however, has evolved only over the course of his residence in the new group home, where he enjoys *quality* care, and patient, tolerant and attentive staff. The fact he has made several friendships there speaks volumes, too.

I aspire to have more of my son's attributes. He is kind, social, a good listener, easy to talk to, patient & calm, and *now*, he has an absence of anger. Is he perfect? Of course not, but he is as close as he could be, particularly when considering his permanent deficits and from where he started.

Never go to sleep angry. He will not lose a visit home but had there been no remorse and no apology and corrective behavior forthcoming, he would have. Tough love would have been harder on me than on him, too.

FEBRUARY 6, 2015

Special Mattie story to share. I always ask Matt how his trip down by Greyhound was. Today, he said there was a nice girl who, he's pretty sure, was flirting with him. He said, "Mom, you have *no idea* how good that made me feel — it made me feel human. I told her I had a brain injury and everything, but I kept my sunglasses on" (he's very self-conscious about his lazy eye and his double vision from the brain injury).

He tries to wear sunglasses when he visits anyone or any place, whether inside or out. He often shares that he just wants to be seen as a normal man, for a change.

He elaborated that he really needs to feel like someone values him. I told him that was probably the biggest thing we ALL need as humans.

He also told me he is proud of the decent person he's become, that he *knows* he is a good man now, even if he does still make stupid mistakes (I interjected that we *all* make stupid mistakes, but to make them three times is a choice; mistakes are a part of life; good choices are, too).

"Mom, I really care about people — and I really LISTEN to them. I think most people don't listen. People need to be heard."

Wow. I am both proud and impressed with his insights and the way he is thinking things through. That is a LOT of progress.

Yes, he has had some impulsivity issues again recently, but he has also worked through them and faced the consequences, and *moved on*. That's more than a lot of folks with no disability accomplish, frankly.

He'll always be the love of my life. There were no mistakes in having him. I don't regret the fight, either. He's made my life come full circle several times and I'm just grateful he is alive and well-cared for in his incredible group home. If we examine all the turning points we can assign to life, this is the most fortuitous for him, and by proxy, for me.

FEBRUARY 7, 2015

Sure is nice to have Matt here! I woke up at my usual 5 AM and he was already awake and watching HAROLD & KUMAR: WHITE CASTLE on TV! So we rewound it to the halfway point and watched the balance together over coffee! Nice!

We have a big day ahead; lots to do! Matt is really excited about meeting my bodybuilding team because I talk about them so often!

He's funny, too. When he hugged me this morning, he said, "Oh Mom, I think you had another overnight weight drop. You're so tiny but muscular!"

ONLY my son, who hugged me when I was 103 lbs heavier, would call me tiny!

FEBRUARY 10, 2015

I've been up since 4 AM. I didn't want to awaken Mattie, so I just laid there, until I decided I could get down on the floor and do abdominal exercises. Done!

Now energy is waning with the waiting, I need to get up and GO, or I fizzle!

Matt had coffee with me at 5:30 and I could tell he was exhausted, so now he is back to sleep on the sofa!

All good; we just go with the flow. With brain injury, a rigid schedule can not always mandate life. So, we will take some quality bonding time, then exit to train arms at the gym.

Matt can have another nap after that, then we're off to see the movie "Project Almanac" at the movie theatre.

FEBRUARY 11, 2015
Tomorrow Matt returns to his group home, and bless him — it is time. I think he misses being with all the guys there, and I am SO VERY grateful he does. He is blessed to live in such a positive environment.

FEBRUARY 12, 2015
Mattie returns to his group home today. It has been a good visit, but again very draining for me. Six days was two to three too long for me. I find his childish behavior surfacing more regularly again. I don't know if it is for a lack of conscious effort, whether he is so conditioned to manipulate me (and others) with the childish response, or whether it is simply brain deficit wrought by brain injury. I hope the change in behavior is not reflective of changes in the group home. The director has not been able to return to work. Matthew continues to be unaware that she was so seriously injured in the MVA last November.

It is abundantly clear to me now that he will, for the balance of his life, require 24-7 supervision. If left to his own independence, he could not survive.

He has gained 10 lbs again, now again at 270. He is self-conscious about it and has lied to me for several weeks, stating his weight was still at 260, but the moment I saw him get off the bus for this recent visitation, and saw his belly engorged again, I knew the weight was up. Poor guy. I suppose he lied to me because he wants to please and impress me so much.

Four steps forward, stay there a while, then two steps back.

It also seems that he takes no pride in his appearance, now. That is a bad sign, as he has always taken pride in the way he presents.

Each time he comes to visit, he appears disheveled — the first stop being a very necessary haircut and trimming of the eyebrows. He has the worst dermatological condition on his back that he has ever had. The severe acne leaves him permanently scarred. I do not know how to treat this. I have hoped that some physician would refer him to a dermatologist for ten years, but it has never been done. When he visits me, I clean his back with rubbing alcohol regularly, and that seems to assist. Before, one of the care aides at the home did that for him, but it has stopped. It seems apparent that the staff is no longer attentive to patients' pride in personal grooming, and that makes my heart sink.

I am having trouble mustering the energy or the time to keep Matt in proper form; it is so very draining to me. I have talked honestly with him on these subjects, and he seems to understand — but the discussions make him exceedingly sad. It is a precarious balance, being forthright and taking extreme care not to hurt him unnecessarily. But I feel I am losing my balance, and he is losing his.

I speculate he is *afraid* to complain about changes in the home, afraid that he might suffer adverse consequences in the home for speaking up. Maybe, he knows things are declining in the home, and he is afraid to voice it... to "call trouble forward." I think he is hoping things will change as quickly for the positive as they did for the negative. He misses Eva immensely and speaks of her often.

I am again very grateful that he is in good-quality care with his group home, despite things declining at present. If not for quality care, Matt would either be deceased by now or living amongst the homeless, where he could not possibly survive.

I am overwhelmed daily to realize the permanent limitations and precarious future ahead of him. But alas, I have to look at all apples in the apple cart; he is in this position because of terrible choices made in his youth. It is so very sad to witness the consequences that will be with him, unchanging for the balance of his life. My hope is waning.

All this presents the hardest-fought battle I have ever faced. Few around me understand the depth of the battle, how it is ongoing, and how debilitating it is for me emotionally. We all want our children to have better lives than we ever had. We all want our children to make wise choices and to live in peace and harmony.

Sometimes, giving our all is all we can do... but with brain injury, there comes a time when we lose ourselves to the battle. Therefore, I pursue bodybuilding. It gives me an outlet for refocusing, for venting my frustrations without begrudging my friends with that need. Bodybuilding and extreme exercise also make my body and mind exhausted, whereas otherwise, I would be sleep-deprived from overthinking. Bodybuilding keeps the nightmares at bay, too. I know: I have been there many times in the 13 years of my son's brain injury.

Also, where would Matt have been if his mom had not been a bodybuilder? In the early years, Big Mattie fell down a lot. That was something else no one warned me about, but with hindsight being 20-20, it makes sense. He had double vision, impaired depth perception, his right foot was half dead with no sensation, he had tinnitus ringing daily, and suffered acute PTSD. He fell a lot, but thankfully G-D gave me a strong set of legs and a good back. Bodybuilding taught me how to lift.

All things in their time. Whether or not we realize it, every experience has culminated at this moment to position us right where we are meant to be.

Wake up, get up, do
the work...

I had this same conversation content with my son this morning. To be better in ANYTHING is to push past one's comfort zone. I reminded him that athletes do this, good business people do this, good lawyers and doctors do this, and people with BRAIN INJURY do this!

He asked if he could take a second cup of coffee "for the road" and whether I wanted one, too!

FEBRUARY 15, 2015

Brain Injury... five steps forward, three steps back. The dance is always changing, with longer and longer intervals in between, but it is still ongoing. It makes me sad. It utterly exhausts me.

If I weren't so sore from this morning's workout, I would go to the gym and train again to stop myself from wanting to scream.

FEBRUARY 17, 2015

After the scathing reprimand I had to give Matt last night, concerning behaviors, apathy, and trust issues, all of which brought him to a state of sobbing tears, he took my advice and spoke with his primary care aide, B, at the home. He trusts B and I am grateful for that.

Matt tells me this morning their chat went very well. He reassured me he wants to get back on track. He shared, "I know the 'old Matt' is just under the surface and sometimes things happen that can cause that side of him to come through again. NO ONE wants to see the old Matt, including the new Matt."

In trying my best to maintain a healthy distance, to see how Matt progresses with small increments of independence tested, the group home has not shared circumstances with me. Certainly, Matthew has not offered disclosure, either; I have not been privy to what has been triggering changes. But I hear the change in his response — in his voice and in his body language. I am on alert.

As I understand it now, negativity from two others at the home has triggered Matt's personality changes over the past few weeks. I have seen it coming for at least four to five weeks now... just traces, but experience has taught me we cannot ignore these fluctuations.

I am glad things will be addressed before escalation occurs, as it has so many times in the past. It only takes *one* fly in the ointment to offset the fragile complexities of brain function when TBI is involved. Right now, we have a "he said-she said" set of circumstances again. I have not forgotten that Matt is predisposed to conjecture and misinterpretation.

But I have heard, firsthand, the exceedingly negative tone of two staff (in the background while talking with Matt by telephone) and I know those types of responses trigger him. It is far too reminiscent of former poorly managed care homes. This is not a matter of him conjuring up excuses; he is legitimately triggered and horrified that he is going to change again.

There is also the possibility that *his* behaviors have resulted in negativity from the two staff. However, when we deal with people professionally, we task ourselves with the responsibility of managing our stressors and our response. We are even more expected to do so in a home filled with brain injury survivors of varying complexities. We have this same onus upon us in our personal lives, but it is of a significantly higher standard professionally.

However, if I redirect myself to the positives, case in point, 95 percent of everything with Matt and his environment is excellent. His progress over 13 years of profoundly serious brain injury and permanent loss of quality of life, as a result, warrants serious accolades. Most of all staff in his group home are caring, patient, and tolerant individuals, all of whom live with their own stressors and obstacles. So, yes, back to being grateful. Now BREATHE.

FEBRUARY 18, 2015

With all this talk about taking care of ourselves, I finally inspected myself in the mirror and said, "Yikes! I need a haircut!" 1:45 today, that is happening!

I'm really late getting off to the gym for back training, so I should head out now... I had to take care of business first this morning, with two teleconferences concerning Matt. At least, all is well. But change is "in the air." I don't like it.

Wee "funny" story from training legs yesterday at Golds... I'm starting my workout on the leg press... one plate on each side for warm-ups... Let's just call the dude on the adjacent chest press. Mr. "I Think I'm Mr. Hot" unloads my leg press machine of 45 lb plates to put onto his barbells, six feet away. I took my headphones down for a sec, and in my *sweet* voice said (yes, in with my own "two psyches," I have a sweet voice and one that is less confectionary), "I'd appreciate it if you'd not take my weights; I'll be going up to five plates per side on this one and I purposefully loaded my machine earlier to be ready for that." He snarled, "So you want me to put these back?" I said (again sweetly, but more firmly this time), "I'd appreciate that."

SO, "I Think I'm Mr. Hot" *threw* his 25-pound plates down on the floor and begrudgingly removed the four 45-pound plates he'd taken from "my" pre-loaded machine.

He kept snarling over at me in between his sets, so here goes my ego. I've had a bit of steam building inside me for a while. Instead of going from one plate per side to two or three, I totaled five plates per side and executed 15 reps. I enjoyed seeing him walk away from his bench press to exit the gym!

Now, mind you, the five plates per side was too much for me given the "new rules" instituted by my trainer for the style of training I am to be doing, so Sarah's Ego pulled them off and dropped back down to three plates per side.

I sure enjoyed that, though! Yeah — doubt me: that'll be fun!

And, I have a little more philosophical thought on bodybuilding...

Given that my PTSD cripples me emotionally and socially from time to time, and the way even a slight stressor or confrontation can set me back for DAYS (because of that condition), I cannot imagine where I would be right now if not for pushing myself to train — especially on "bad" days.

This has been the best mind, body, and spirit transformation I could have ever undertaken for myself. I've always been a risk-taker. I've always been extreme. One person wants to go water skiing; I want to jump out of a perfectly functional airplane. One person wants to go to Club Med; I want to trek the jungles of Cambodia or stay in a grass hut on a remote island in Thailand. So bodybuilding, instead of yoga, for example, has been the perfect recipe for self-medicating I could have ever started.

I keep getting asked why (at this age) I would want to put myself up on a stage and be compared with other younger women. Why? BECAUSE I CAN! Why? Because many think I cannot! Why? Because I want to do my trainer proud... my team proud. And, perhaps most of all, I want to prove to my son the importance of following through on a promise, pursuing a worthy goal, and doing the work to be healthier. I want to set an example, make him proud and have him follow suit by even five percent of what I try to do.

Why? Because it makes me happy. It gives me fulfillment and satisfaction, and it gives me *healthy* exhaustion. Perhaps, most importantly, it makes me a better mother; it makes me a better employee, and it makes me a better advocate. It makes me better, period.

Why? He *is* my why.

FEBRUARY 25, 2015

In an email from Matthew tonight, I had to crack up at his conclusion: "P.S. This email is confidential and privileged communication!" He must have taken that from one of my older emails, but he spelled everything correctly, which is impressive — because I know he is not familiar with a "cut and paste" function!

And in his usual, *all caps* response (I don't even bother to teach him that in "internet land," that means he is yelling; no need to make him self-conscious on still another level), he sends me this:

> MOM, I HAD A GREAT DAY!! AND, I THINK IM GONNA GET THE STAFF MEMBER THAT IVE ALWAYS LOVED SO MUCH as MY WORKER!! THAT MAKES ME HAPPY! Have a great day!
>
> P.S. This email is confidential and privileged communication.

Thanks for the chuckle, buddy — and thanks to the group home for putting forth effort.

MARCH 1, 2015

There's an adage of negative attention being better than *no* attention in some circles. Dogs do it, horses do it, children do it, women in law firms do it, and adult brain injury survivors do it.

If I have learned ANYTHING in raising my son twice, it is that when negative attention-seeking starts, we *redirect* it to lose it, and REFOCUS on what is important (being all the wonderful accomplishments and positive traits)... and MAKE the time for a bonding moment, or hour, or day. This is what Angela's management brought to the home; in her absence, those premises have fallen by the wayside, sadly.

If we do not create the time for our children NOW, someone will assuredly deprive us of it in the future. More often than not, the child starving for love will ask for it in the most unloving of ways.

The BOTTOM LINE is that there is nothing so rewarding as to make people realize they are worthwhile in this world. I sure learned this recently when my son experienced his own epiphany of finding value in his life... He'd been told he was a drain to the system and a nuisance in his youth as a young offender, and in more recent years, by several bad caregivers... BUT HOW THE LIGHTS went on when he discovered his goodness... his ability to make people smile... his consciousness in realizing people need to be heard — to be LISTENED TO!

MARCH 5, 2015

Well, once again, a female in the workplace affirms something I've been experiencing for years!

Yesterday, a pretty, young female staff (secretary) snapped at me... The first two times, I let it go and simply ignored it, as though I didn't hear or she didn't exist. The third time, I merely acknowledged her comment with a lower tone of voice than the "sweet voice" I try to maintain.

Two other staff heard the exchange, and today the office administrator came in to apologize to me. She asked me to overlook it, adding that "I have talked to the girl frequently." She inferred the gal's days were numbered and assured me the firm has a zero-tolerance for this kind of interaction. I just shrugged it off and said the girl was young; I've seen this many times before. The administrator said, "Young and stupid — and one who THINKS herself smart."

"Because you're confident in the workplace and because your resume was discussed openly before you arrived, some of our girls find it intimidating." I was also told that because I am nice, some would try to step on me to see if I wince. I really chuckled at this one, and just reiterated that the girl was young and inexperienced, guessing she was only about 23 years of age.

Nope — she is 29.

MARCH 6, 2015

Well, my heart aches for my son getting his heart crushed, still again, by a member of the clergy.

Matt took it all very well, but when his professed friend and young pastor recently just walked away, and never returned calls when Matt reached out, Matt finally left him a message saying he wouldn't bother him again but someone from the church ought to be more mature. Matt told me he's now thrown away the contact information with the pastor's number on it. For Matt, who saves every scrap of paper with someone's name and number, every single note or card ever gifted to him, I do not lose the significance of that action.

Time and time and time again, I see those who use the name of G-D flippantly but fail miserably in treating people as genuine leaders of their "convictions" should or would do... It is one of many reasons I have left organized religion. If you profess yourself to be a member of the clergy, you are held to a *much* higher standard. I prefer to never accommodate those individuals with such a position.

Of course, I am not privy to more information. If Matthew was disengaged by the pastor, there could be justifiable reasons. He was asked to leave the Agassiz Anglican church years ago because he was seeking marijuana and cigarettes. For all I know, this could be the circumstance rearing its ugly head again. I surely hope not. Cannabis is Matthew's "first call" for stress relief — and his "last call" before decompensation.

REDIRECTION

B etter day on the job today. From the time I woke up, I made a conscious choice to change my thoughts about it, reminding myself that it is just a job — not a lifestyle, and not a brain injury.

MARCH 11, 2015

More great news from my Mattie. He's finally losing weight again and was ecstatic to tell me so! When he was here to see me last, he was back up to 270 pounds. I gave him a soft but sad lecture about his health and shortening his life with too much weight. I reminded him that excess weight was hard on his heart, his lungs, and his joints.

Today he is 255 pounds! That is an all-time low of twelve years for him! Now, he is finally begging his group home to let him go to the gym. They've told him if he goes for his scheduled walks three times a week without backing out, he can then go to the gym! YES!

He's also motivated to drink more water, finally — and told me how proud of me he is and how I've inspired him!

Bless his heart, he is a BIG reason (pun intended) I have pursued this journey of my own and adhered to it so strictly. I want him to see what can be achieved in the extreme... to see what HARD WORK and dedication can bring... and I remind him almost daily that if he can do even 15% of what I do, he will change his life forever!

And besides, this competition — this health & fitness endeavor — is his birthday present for 2015!

GOOD WEEK/BAD WEEK: THIS IS ONE OF THEM

G ood grief! How wonderful that my clothing is falling off me! I only have two jackets that fit properly. My new skirt of two weeks ago is now too loose in the waist and fits like a hipster! My track pants are falling down, and I have to keep pulling those up during training to keep from (1) walking on the hem or (2) showing my plumber's crack!

I just tried on a dress I recently bought a size too small, wondering how long before it will fit. Turns out, it is perfect for today! Black & white dress, black jacket, and stilettos!

Coming back on the sky train from Vancouver, I ended up seated beside the heater. Given my metabolism right now, that was too warm for me, so I took off my jacket, and sat there in my sleeveless dress. I never considered myself "big" until that moment, when pretty much every person on the not-so-crowded sky train was looking at my arms & shoulders... I could feel the looks via my peripheral vision, and when I turned to make eye contact EVERY person (male or female) looked away. My gym peers and my teammates are particularly muscular, as is my coach... I have (until now) never considered myself overly muscular, though I am working on it.

I guess this is going to take some getting used to... Otherwise, I need to keep my arms covered!

Ahhh, the interesting twists and turns in the journey!

MARCH 15, 2015
Less than two weeks before Mattie's next visit. I miss him so much, and he needs the visit, too! He told me tonight he wishes he could bring Ricky and Lindsay down (his BEST friends at the group home)! I told him, "I know hon, and maybe one day you can!" That would certainly be a super-fun time... but I don't know if the home would permit it, with liability concerns and all.

MARCH 19, 2015

I am pleased that the group home has stepped up Matt's walking! More frequency and longer walks every time! Each day he tells me, "Wow, Mom, we walked further than ever today!"

I reminded him he said the same thing *last* time, and he responds, "But it's TRUE! I don't really like it, but I'm doing it. I remember you always say you have the best workouts when you still go, even when you didn't want to!"

MARCH 24, 2015

I just received an upbeat email from Mattie, saying how *stunned* he was to see the director of the group home return for a visit today! Every single day, he mentions her name. "Mom, the home has not been the same since she had to be off work, and even though we need her there, I want her to be totally healthy and healed again before she comes back." He is unaware of the severity of her injuries, and that it is unlikely she will ever be capable of returning to her position there. I cannot predict how he will take that news when it comes.

I am always amazed at the depths of insight and unselfishness Matt can exhibit. He says he already misses his "brothers" (R and L) and he hasn't even left yet! He says that R, in particular, is sad that Matt is going to be away while he's visiting me. I promised Matt we could call R and L when he is here. He has made a close bond with both young men, and I am very grateful for that. Perhaps R and L are concerned with the group home changes, in the absence of their beloved director, too. R has lived for over two decades at that home.

AND, although this dance is not a brain injury, it *is* a convoluted disruption. We take the good with the bad, but right now, I cannot cry and I cannot scream — but I assuredly can be paralyzed with anxiety.

I am a control freak. I am proactive and I plan well. I am organized... I NEVER procrastinate. When my plans disintegrate because others fail or refuse to advance a plan or cooperate, I become paralyzed with anxiety. Fight or flight. When I have options for neither, PTSD gives me tunnel vision and freezes me in my tracks.

This is NOT a good week, despite how I might want to CHOOSE for it to be!

I had movers scheduled for Saturday morning. The tenant at my new place is already out and merely needs to clean... I have offered to accept the premises *as is* (e.g., do the cleaning myself)... The existing tenant is working on Saturday and Sunday and won't meet with the owner until next Monday. There are zero movers available for a move on Monday or on Tuesday. I have phoned seven. Even the mover who charges $120/hour with a three-hour minimum is not available.

I have a move that takes all of one hour — two pickup truckloads, that's it. One would *think* this could all be so easy.

I asked two friends with trucks if they could help and was told (1) "I don't move anyone and I don't ask for help with moves"... and (2) "Sorry - can't do it."

I am feeling drained, frustrated, sad, and alone. Making matters worse is the fact that I am moving because my landlords want to deny me having Matt over for a visit once every six to eight weeks... saying it would use more hydro, and more water... People interview well sometimes. It's no different with landlords and tenants than it is with lawyers and paralegals.

The issues with dinner guests and my son over with extra hydro charged were never mentioned pre-move-in... I was honest with them to let them know Mattie visits for a few days every six to eight weeks. They jumped on that new bandwagon two weeks after I moved in.

A friend suggested to me that perhaps the property owners had concerns with Matt's size, knowing he has a brain injury. Nope — Matt has not yet visited, to date, but ironically will arrive here on Thursday to help with my move.

Good week/bad week — this is definitely one of them.

THE PHILOSOPHY OF TRUST

M attie is home for a visit. He told me this morning, "Mom, I want you to know nothing you do goes unnoticed by me... I really understand how much you love me and have sacrificed for me. I appreciate you so much."

When you have raised a troubled child twice, there could be no greater words to hear.

MARCH 31, 2015

We went to Ikea today. Matt was so strong lifting the 150 lb boxes! Totally impressive! After that, I decided we both deserved a sushi treat! Sushi California in Coquitlam, BC, here we come!

Actions prove who someone is...

Matthew has worked very hard for me since he arrived here... and we have eaten quite clean. He wanted to weigh himself tonight! He is now down to 250 pounds! That is remarkable. He arrived at 255 pounds on Thursday!

After 13.5 years of mostly profound apathy and hardship after a traumatic brain injury, Matt is taking more and more action toward improvement. I am so pleased to see this. He faces a shortened life expectancy and I want him to achieve that pride that all of us can only know when we push past our comfort zone to a new physical (and emotional) level.

He's quite excited to go to the gym with me tomorrow and I also am ready to get back to training. I have not trained for eight consecutive days now... It would have been WAY too much to handle with the move.

This relocation has made me absolutely hit the wall. Matt has expressed concern about how I am changing now... says I push like I'm younger and never stop. He told me he saw me get a 2nd wind, a 3rd, and more, "But tonight, Mom — you are not right."

Poor buddy, he told me he wished he could be around to help me more. "Mom, you need the help — but you are in denial; you don't admit when you need help." I told him I realize I need the help but there was no one to assist, so it was my job to see that it gets done. He cried on that one... Such a sweet and sensitive guy. I reminded him that this is competition training and not a lifestyle; this is temporary and would conclude soon.

Back to super-strict meal planning again, with fasted cardio too... I will weigh my portions again, at last.

I have selected my music for a posing routine, and have the routine almost put together in my mind and on paper... I hope to render a confident presentation, and no matter what, am proud to have had the health and persistence to undertake this journey, and so proud that Matthew has joined the endeavor with me and excelled beyond my wildest imagination.

This competition is for ME and MATTIE, and for every single individual over the age of NEVER who thinks it's too late to start a fitness regimen!

APRIL 1, 2015
My son and I always have deep conversations when we're together. This morning, we talked long and hard about failed former caregiving scenarios and he has remarkable insights into why he, himself, failed...

In short, he says trying to change is hard work... especially with brain injury because thinking gets confusing and he loses his concentration before he really gets to make much change. THEN, with bad caregivers (and he has experienced many), he stops caring about even trying, because "Why bother? They're just not going to notice anyway, and sometimes they just have selfish reasons. Sometimes, they also just *like* being a bully — they like the power. You can see it when they enjoy it. I know it because I *used* to be like that. I used to love making people 'squirm'."

Many so-called caregivers do not care. Because of the exorbitant cost of quality caregiving, few individuals appointed to the care of the brain-injured (or the elderly, or for others with disabilities... or those in hospital care) are comprehensively trained. Homes and funding authorities look to profit, cut corners, and maximize funds. This is the scenario in MOST group homes. I stand by that as a fact, and not as an uneducated opinion. One cannot hire an experienced Care Aide, with comprehensive knowledge and understanding of the complexities of brain injury, for $12-14 an hour any more than one can hire a decent legal assistant for that.

It's funny, yet not funny, how that same trend carries into law firms. A proper paralegal performs the work of a junior lawyer and is compensated accordingly — but I have literally *heard lawyers say, "This is not rocket science,"* the propensity to need five staff is trending toward hiring one paralegal, and four $12-$14/hour uneducated assistants. They even sell it to their overwhelmed paralegal as "You can train them YOUR way."

Recently someone stated to me that Matt tries very hard for me, and is apathetic to others. I get that... but it is only partially accurate. I feel a little gaslighting has been tossed into the mix here. In my son's present group home, he will do ANYTHING to improve or change for those caregivers and staff that he trusts. The director of that home is a prime example... Angela treats him (and all other residents and staff) with great respect, calmness & understanding, yet with a firm hand. That is leadership. She is also well-trained and educated, wise and logical, and all too dedicated to her own continually developing improvements, on a personal and a professional level. Angela is trusted *and* trustworthy, adored and respected.

Matt has recently encountered reasons to mistrust a couple of staff. Matt will never again "perform" for these individuals because the trust, once assumed safe to give, has been broken. It can neither be recovered nor repaired because circumstances have been mismanaged, misinterpreted, and misdirected.

Matt said to me, last night, "Mom - once someone has broken trust, I just don't care about them anymore, so why should I try just because they *tell* me to? How do I know what they're asking me to do is for ME and not just for THEM? They don't matter to me or my life anymore. They're just liars. I totally get why people stopped trusting me, but I am really glad that *smart* people get I am trying, and remember that I have a brain injury. I don't want to blame my mistakes on my brain injury, but it makes improving harder... but I keep trying. Thank you for seeing that."

He also added (and this exhibits great insight developing) that if someone he doesn't trust tells him to do something, he thinks about it — and asks himself if this is something his MOM or E, the director, would ask him to do. Only then does he "perform" because he knows it is right, and not because the untrustworthy person dictated it! He spoke of "under motives" — "Is that what it's called, Mom? I don't think that's right."

I told him he was probably wanting the word *underlying*, as in underlying motives. "YEAH, that's what some of these people have. They throw new stuff into the mix to make a person mess up and then they get to make them feel like a puppet — as though they aren't worth anything at all. Does that make sense?"

Sadly, it made too much sense — but I let him keep talking.

"Mom — I guess it's the same for me, eh? I break trust and no one trusts me again. Only you and E ever did that — gave me more chances. Wow. I am so fucked up."

He continued, "Mom, you give too many chances and you should not let people who don't matter interrupt your day." He told me I think all people have good in them, and only good can bring that to the surface. "But Mom, I hope you know that is just not true? You're not stupid. All people are not good."

Good point, buddy. Mom's working on that, too... I still have lessons in *my* evolution.

And then, the grand epiphany from Matt. "Mom, if I am really honest with myself, I guess people treat me the same way when I mess up and they stop trusting me to do anything right again. But a good teacher sees the truth and knows when to try again. I have trouble with that and I think THAT is because of my brain injury and I don't know how to fix something that big. Angela knows the truth; she takes no crap, but she knows when to try again, and how to make people *feel* like trying."

APRIL 2, 2015

My Mattie is always apologizing for being sensitive. He cries easily. He feels deeply and strongly. Sometimes, I feel his level of empathy is so great that he suffers from it, particularly with the complications, confusion, and deficits of brain injury. Sometimes, I think he just tires of people who are tired of dealing with him and cannot recognize how hard he is trying. He believes that most people do not know how difficult this is for him. On those occasions, I think his mind takes him to a darker place, and on the worst occasions, I believe these times cause him to dissociate. After that, he is no longer Mattie. The Matt personality speaks faster, speaks in a lower tone of voice, is cold and calculating, and seems to deliver some sociopathic traits during the dissociation.

Since his brain injury, we have worked very hard on allowing feelings to be experienced and trying to understand why he feels them. He used to channel his confusion and his hurt into anger, which was invariably an inappropriate response for Jon and Jane Q. Public to witness from a (once) 368-pound, 6▓3▓ man.

I still believe we should allow ourselves to *feel*, then strive to understand from where those feelings originate... Only then can we endeavor to understand from where the hurtful actions or words have arisen. Only then can we hope to see something beautiful come from this mess.

Only then can we learn from the philosophy of trust.

CAUSE AND EFFECT

I needed to reprimand my son for a wee indiscretion this morning. But I never hold a grudge. Life is simply too short. Making the point and moving on is my motto. Besides, with TBI, there is only a small window of opportunity to make the point, reinforce the good behavior that should replace it with a reminder of how he's done the good thing before — and move on. He just can't hold extended "stress-talk" in his mind. It only computes to a point; after that, we're in muddy waters again.

Plus, the group home is in a transition phase — things are changing, and Matthew is especially sensitive to "change," especially with structural changes in his environment. Mattie cannot fathom that different staff and different management approach things differently. He sees it more as a "right way/wrong way" approach. If Plan A works, it's the *right way;* there's no need for a Plan B. "If it ain't broke, don't fix it." He thrives with a consistent structure, positive reinforcement, and simply being confident about what they expected of him and others.

"Mom, thank you SO much for not staying mad at me. That makes me want to try harder."

"Buddy, would it serve any purpose to stay mad at you? What do you think that would do?"

"Well, it would make me feel ashamed of myself, and sad — and it might even make me feel mad if you didn't let it go. I don't want to blame everything on my brain injury — you taught me that. But I am slower to remember and slower to learn than someone who doesn't have a brain injury. So, if you stayed mad, that would just make things a lot worse."

"How about this? What if I never reprimanded you for things you needed to correct? Would that be better?"

"Well, you're my Mom — I think it's *your job* to help me make things right? No disrespect intended!"

APRIL 3, 2015

Sitting here with my coffee, I reminisce about Matthew's leg training with me yesterday, and how proud of him I am. He noticed when I said I was going to do ten repetitions of an exercise, I did 15. So, when it was his turn and promised eight, he did ten! Then, after seeing me perform hack squats with a 45-pound plate on each side, he wanted to try. I warned him it was likely too much for him, but HE WANTED TO TRY. Atta boy!

He performed one rep and said, "HOW CAN YOU DO THAT?" Then I put another plate on each side, and he just said, "Wow, Mom, you don't give up. You inspire me — but on this one? I'm giving up and I'm not sorry!"

I told him I'm beyond doing what's just "good enough" now... To be good enough, I have to push for more.

This morning, he says his whole body aches, and he is giggling as he tries to get out of bed! He asked what he did to make his *quadricraps* hurt so much, and I reminded him of the hack squats with 90 pounds — and that those muscles are quadriceps. "No Mom, you don't understand — these are *quadricraps* right now!"

I feel so proud to see my young man experience the positive power of pushing past a comfort zone to progress! With training, we learn that a little of the "right" pain is taking you to a new level of good things in your near future! We sleep better for it, we look better for it, and we are stronger for it. And we can take these lessons into any other area of our lives — including brain injury rehabilitation and work in personal injury law!

APRIL 8, 2015

I miss my dear Mattie, and as usual, I feel a little guilty about having my personal time and space back again. It slightly restricted training because he needs so much attention. All good, though. He's my reason for doing everything I do, especially the training. Bottom line, time with him is more important than the training, but I am trapped in a web of my own construction with having made the commitment now to see this competition (and my word) to fruition.

I got Mattie on the bus back to Kamloops... He was so tired that he could neither think straight nor walk without being off balance. Poor guy. He had two weeks of heavy activity here with me, but he did so very well! He will probably crash for two days at the group home now. I emailed the standing manager, warning her this was inevitable for him — that he would need rest on returning, adding he had done so very well, remained stable, and was happy. I wanted to prevent the risk of having staff accuse him of apathy. Certainly, on many days, he is the prince of apathy — but not this time.

I sent him back with a meal of chicken breast and yams, and a Gatorade. I also made sure he had a couple of bucks on a Tim Horton's card so he could get a coffee at the stop in Chilliwack. We never let Matthew travel with cash. I am already looking forward to his telephone call this evening — and hearing about his social adventures with nice people on the bus!

APRIL 10, 2015

I was up at 1:30 am with another nightmare. In the dream, I was on an inflatable raft, intended for pool sunning, in a calm area of water that was infamous for its rapids and a waterfall downstream. I had fallen asleep (in my dream) and woke up to air leaving the raft. As my raft advanced down-current toward the waterfall, I panicked, realizing I had no way out from this very serious and imminent danger... Oh my. I always query what caused my subconscious to dream what it does. This one doesn't require a rocket-science analysis, however.

I suppose it is no surprise that I find myself deeply disturbed by my son's return to the Kamloops group home and having his bags confiscated and searched for the first time. He cried last night — literally *sobbed* in anxiety. "Mom, I felt like I was in jail. I felt trapped. I hope Angela comes back because things are really not the same here. Mom, I don't know this place anymore."

He says his friends all say the same thing, but no one dares express their opinions. One of his friends calls the new manager "the Gestapo."

I suspect the home is attempting to determine from where he is getting marijuana since they do not believe that he is getting it from the new female patient at the home, as he asserted. I suspect they think him to be securing it while visiting me, but they do not realize that I am with him every step of the way, other than times when he enters a public washroom. Of course, he could elicit this while traveling to and from, by Greyhound bus. But he never has cash, and never more than $4 on a Tim Horton's coffee card. Of course, he's proven more than capable of convincing someone to share a joint with him over the years; his charm has seen success with far more than that, sadly.

I reminded him to reflect on the history of inept managers we've witnessed in 13.5 years of brain injury. He replied, still in tears, "I know, Mom. I have to be quiet because I don't want to be on the street. But thank you for seeing the man I'm trying to be — and not just the man I've *been*."

At least, he "gets it." What began as an absolutely perfect placement and the best caregiving and structure, to date, reveals evidence of decline now as a lesser attentiveness to patient needs, a more militarily administered discipline, and there seems to be a practice of non-judgment being replaced with suspicion, assertive onslaught and a presumption of guilt.

PERSEVERANCE THROUGH A THICKENING PLOT

M y training continues, and with discipline maintained, I remain pleased with the progress — but in the face of changing adversity surfacing in the group home, and with Matthew's personality changes, I feel my cortisol rising.

APRIL 23, 2015
And the plot thickens. Cause and effect — but what is the cause? Is Matthew going sideways because of group home triggers, or is the group home responding to his going sideways?

Matthew was caught with marijuana at the group home again.

My son, I love him to the moon and back, but sometimes I have to reprimand him as a wake-up call. I know this is the TBI tango, his morbid version of it... but wow. Last night, I was so angry with him for an infraction involving marijuana that the scolding needed to take a memorable tone. He cried... was so remorseful... but I have heard that song and dance so many times; it is a redundant melody now. "I DON'T CARE, Matt. I've heard it all before and I can't sing to that tune." He cried more...

I reminded him of what happened EVERY TIME, without fail, when he sought cannabis. The radical change in his behavior resulted in violence and institutionalization.

Every single time.

I reminded him of the seizure that occurred in Kelowna when my landlord smoked a joint with him, and how seriously he declined after that, in speech, in response, in his ability to reason and remember. It took *weeks* for him to return to baseline.

I told him I might need a break when he phoned the next night... If I did not answer the phone, he could just leave a message. We would talk the next night if that was how I was feeling...

"Okay, Mom. Mom, I love you. I understand. I'm so sorry, Mom."

My heart broke... but these things have to be done sometime. Tough love is always tougher on the parent implementing it. I do not know if my response is the *right* response. I only know that the point needs to be made and that this wouldn't have happened with the former management in the home. Not a chance.

I received an email from Mattie, "HOPEFULLY UR HAVING A GREAT DAY!! DO YOU THINK WE COULD SPEAK 2NITE??"

Bless my buddy... Of course, we will speak, share stories, and find reasons to laugh! We never hold a grudge. Never. If I extended the penalty, the point made (and the lesson with it) would be extinguished. This is TBI.

MAY 1, 2015

Wee bodybuilding chuckle... Yesterday, I went through a lineup with the Vancouver Police Department checking sky train tickets. No worries; pulled mine out and first couldn't find it... Police asked for my ID, so I presented that while I kept digging and did, ultimately, find the sky train ticket. He asked me about my date of birth; I said December 1954. He said, "REALLY? Good on you!"

WOW! Talk about making my day! And I asked the very handsome officer what that ticket would have cost me, had I lost my sky train receipt, and it would have been $183. HOLY CROW! That's a lot of protein powder and chicken breast!

Interesting transitions on this journey. I glimpsed briefly at my reflection as I walked past an enormous window today and hardly recognized myself. I am not remotely the same person I was one year ago.

I wore size eight trousers to the office today and a size ten jacket. That's a FAR CRY from the size 24-26 that I wore one year ago.

Another six months is going to reveal still another new me!!!

MAY 2, 2015

One year ago today, I started my journey... I resigned from a terrible job in legal and opted to change my life, and get healthy (physically and emotionally). Next, I implemented a proper nutrition program and slow exercise, initially walking and using an outdoor circuit. I began substituting organic vegetables & herbs for medications — all under doctor supervision (but not under his recommendation; had it been up to him, I'd still be on blood thinners, cholesterol medications, and two different blood pressure meds... perhaps even sedation and anti-depressants and an inhaler as well). Now, on this one-year anniversary, I have kept my word — and done better than I said I would. I said I would lose 100 lbs. I have lost 110.

I said I would present to a trainer at maintenance weight, five months before the contest, so contest prep had time for adjustments. It is six months out and I am maintenance weight and fit. Today, I begin the remaining journey to the stage again.

Matt and I have often been criticized for how often we talk on the phone (once, every single day) and the frequency of times we say

"I love you," but given that Matt almost lost his life 13.5 years ago, with seven months between Vancouver General Hospital coma and GF Strong Rehabilitation, *all the years* thereafter, for which he has no memory now — we are VERY cognizant of how quickly life and loved ones can be here one moment and FLASH gone in the next.

All the more reason to appreciate every single day and every single moment we can, particularly those spent with loved ones, family, and friends.

I'm always saying this because I am so attuned to the fact that we all have an expiration date... We're just not privy to what it is. TREAT EVERY DAY as though it will be your last, because one day — it will be.

MAY 15, 2015

When bad things are happening, we cannot see anything but the dark... but over my 60 years, I can honestly look back, in retrospect, and say the most horrific and traumatic experiences in my life... ALTERED my life and taught me lessons that ultimately made me a better person for my future.

It is all about how we fight back... how we respond, and how we learn from the trauma...

MAY 17, 2015

Mattie is home for a visit again. On awakening this morning, he said, "Oh wow — how can my legs be sore? We didn't train legs!?"

Me: "We did deadlifts, honey."

"Wow! And my ARMS are sore. Oh, wow — YOU GOT ME!"

"How's your back?"

Arching his back, "OH WOW (giggling) — this is GREAT! I feel huge!!"

Giggling, I tell him, "Outstanding, buddy — you did great" (poking at his chest)!

"Don't *do* that!"

"Why? Your chest shouldn't be sore."

"Well, it IS, and it's GREAT, but I don't want you to poke it! MOM, this is great — I'm suffering and I LOVE it! What are we training today?"

"Don't skip leg day."

"YAY, I want legs like my Mom!" Bless my buddy. Now, he's having cereal & almond milk before our outdoor power walk!

MAY 18, 2015

What a beautiful long weekend with my Matt. He's on his way back to the group home now, sore and exhausted — but a cheerful guy!

Saw the movie *Mad Maxx* today and loved it! Matt remarked it was "entertainment violence," adding it didn't bother him (he cannot endure violent programs; that bothers him deeply). We were on the "edge of our seats" throughout the entire movie!

I am worn out, too.

MAY 19, 2015

One of the many things Mattie and I did while he was down this past weekend was to choose some more music for both our MP3 players.

He chose a cardio song for me... must say it is perfect! Brittany Spears' "WORK BITCH!" After he chose it, he said, "But Mom — no disrespect intended... That "B" word in this one is about respect!"

JUNE 1, 2015

Some days you just have to focus on your blessings because cause other crap escalated out of control beyond your ability to affect it!

The washer makes a mess in the condo — twice. Water everywhere; every towel and bedspread used to soak it up... Landlord craps out; I blow a gasket in writing... Landlord apologizes.

My son gets assaulted by another patient in the group home and has to be taken to the hospital. The group home NEVER PHONES ME once to advise.

Blessings: my weight and conditioning are on track.

Blessings: I have friends who care about me.

Blessings: I am hungry as hell and I have food in the house!

Blessings: despite having no washer right now, I have a good roof over my head!

Although saying gratitudes may well soften the blow, I am persevering through a thickening plot now. It would seem the group home is not entirely a *safe haven* right now.

JUNE 2, 2015

It's a very sad state of affairs when Matthew feels he has to stay in his room in a fully funded group home, in order to avoid the irrational female patient in a wheelchair that assaulted him with a coffee cup yesterday and sent him to hospital.

Matt kept telling me over the phone tonight, "Mom, I need to live here... and at least I have two friends I love here... but I am really afraid because this place is going to pieces now. I just stay in my room so NOTHING can go wrong. That woman in the wheelchair is still trying to bother me. I was SO scared at the hospital yesterday; I was so worried that the woman had given me another brain injury. She told me she is gonna get me, Mom. She told me I was gonna be GONE — just wait and see."

Alas, such is the case for the disabled and the elderly in our entire country... living in fear while subjected to bullying and all the while being threatened with being thrown out of the home if they look the wrong way.

My heart aches. I am confident I am as afraid as he is.

JUNE 3, 2015

I am foregoing training tonight. The advocacy requirements for my son right now have me feeling that my bodybuilding is of significantly secondary importance, and the advocacy component has me absolutely drained.

When I see the shallow and insensitive occurrences in the bodybuilding community, it makes me second-guess why I am really doing this... the expense, the litany of cruel/mean and downright disrespectful people (despite there being many who are wonderful), the politics in the Bodybuilding Association... I'm just not feeling the love these last couple days.

Meals are still on time and my nutrition has been 100 percent clean. Tomorrow is another day, but I am *truly* not feeling the love of the sport right now.

JUNE 4, 2015

And finally, the Health Authority took control again! They teleconferenced with the group home temporary manager and laid down more "law." What a relief — I feel much better now that they have managed this without *me* needing to open my big mouth to group home personnel, which would be inappropriate and ineffective.

NOW, off to train legs. Don't want to do it, but it needs to be done. Hopefully, I can muster a shoulder workout in there at the end, as well.

Then, the plan is to resume 5 AM fasted cardio in the morning. My meals and nutrition are still on track.

I've become tired of eating Basa that I walked over to Safeway at lunchtime and got one of those wraps made from turkey breast luncheon meat. It tasted SO good! I know there's wheat in the wrap, but whatever... not much! I also got myself a banana!

There was an older, disabled gent in front of me in the checkout (clearly disabled, probably nearing 80). I had *no idea* what was in his little bag, but I felt moved to buy it for him. Bless his heart, he was so stunned! He must have thanked me about 20 times before leaving, and said no one in his life had ever done that.

Nice. It made my day and probably made his! I hope the memory of it makes him smile in the days and weeks ahead.

You know, I truly don't "get" why so many people are dedicated TAKERS when it feels SO good to GIVE...

JUNE 6, 2015

We all end up getting stunned by people's betrayals, whether on a massive scale or just overhearing someone we *thought* was a friend "unleash" on us... On those occasions it's happened to me and my son has laid witness, he always tells me that my good heart wants to see the good in people and ignores the bad that it probably knows is there. He tells me I always believe that people can change...

Last night, Mattie said, "Mom, unless someone has a brain injury or suffers a heck of a lot, they are not going to change. Most people don't change. You know that, *right?*"

Wow... Now, who's the parent, and who's the child? My son is a permanent child, but he has some incredible insights from time to time.

QUALIFIED RESPONSE

Today's honorarium for Throat-Punch Thursday goes to... MY LANDLORD! I emailed last night, politely asking for a status update on the replacement of the washer, which has been two weeks non-functional, now. This morning, I woke up to an email that said, simply "Fuck off." Truly, you can't make this stuff up.

There are so many things wrong with the property, the next time something goes wrong, it will be the same intolerable melodrama all over again... I considered buying my own washing machine and just taking it with me when I leave, but he entered my suite when I was not home. He took my dirty laundry last time (without asking) and I had to drive $10 worth of gas and 1.5 hours of my time to get it back (yes, dirty underwear in there)... He's three bricks short of a load, this one. It's time to cut my losses and move on (before I'm too close to my competition to lift boxes).

With the wrongful taking of my laundry, I felt violated. He refused to bring it back to me. I had to drive to his squalor of a basement suite in a sketchy neighborhood to pick up my dirty clothes! Initially, I tried to give him the benefit of the doubt, thinking *perhaps* he was trying to do a good deed... but NO, he never even apologized. This is far too much of an oddity — it's *freaky*, actually.

JUNE 14, 2015

I believe this and try to live it every day. Yesterday, after securing my new rental and feeling SO relieved and happy about it....on my way back home, I drove past a homeless man carrying a sign... and man, did he ever look down and out, humble and ashamed. So, I pulled over, walked over to him, and said, "If I give you money — what are you going to do with it? Even if you tell me you're gonna go buy a bottle, I'm still gonna give you money." With no hesitation, he told me, "Ma'am, I don't drink. I'm just hungry — haven't eaten anything for three days.

I said, "Hop into the car — I'll give you a ride." He did. He was completely silent. I asked, "What's your name?" He said, "Hugh."

I dropped Hugh at Superstore, got out and shook his hand, and gave him $20. He was clearly stunned. He spoke softly, with his head low, "Thank you so much. I can eat for a week on this." Then he walked away and never looked back. I watched him pick up a carry basket on his way into the Safeway store.

Now, my son had a fit when I told him this last night. "MOM, your good heart is going to get you killed one day. I wish you wouldn't take risks like that." Well, I guess *that* is another story for another day! But the fact remains: if I had not taken risks for my son and *with* my son, he would either be dead or in a mental institution today, rather than thriving, happy and loving as he is now.

We take risks just walking across a street, getting into our cars... biting into food. If no one took any risks in this life, where, in the name of heaven, would any of us be? SOMETIMES, we have to take a risk to help someone who truly cannot help themselves, and who will never give back, other than blessing our heart and soul for the compassion we felt compelled to share. But Matt is right; I am a risk-taker. Things could have gone woefully wrong when I let him enter my vehicle — but I followed my intuition. I was lucky I did not misjudge... or, maybe I was just lucky I had a guardian angel overseeing my well-meant compassion.

JUNE 13, 2015
I HAVE A NEW HOME! I moved in two days ago. What a fortuitous turn of events! It is a ground-floor suite in a lovely home, in a well-established neighborhood. The owners still have a small amount of construction to do (one wall installation and the new oven to come in). There are 12-foot ceilings and lots of light.

There are walking and biking trails a block away, and I am a mere seven-minute drive to my office. I will finally join Platinum Athletic Club, and then that is only ten minutes from my office. WHAT A RELIEF! I've also been able to view this as an incredibly amazing experiment to observe bodily response... I am experiencing raised cortisol levels now, of course, and I am holding water — but I do not look remotely like I did last night. The improvements are fascinating.

JUNE 20, 2015
So, while Mattie sleeps another 50 winks in my bed, I am doing my nails... then I will do a fasted walk.

Matt has already eaten two bowls of granola with cashew milk, and next, we are off to get him a fresh haircut, then to get some sun. I need to pre-tan for my competition and the vitamin D and sunshine will help with Matt's continuing acne. The group home staff has not returned to applying alcohol to his back, sadly. I do it here each time he visits, and he returns with improvements. But only he and I know that; no one else cares enough to ask — and he does not complain.

We are off to see *Jurassic World*! This is Matt's treat to me for "Father's Day!"

"Mom, you have been the best dad any son could want. You're a girl and a guy all in one package!"

We have so much fun together! I value every second I have with him, and vice versa!

JUNE 21, 2015

Weekend and sleep-in time. Right? NOPE! My body and my brain are conditioned now. Every morning, I am wide awake at 4:3, despite shutting off the lights at an unusually late 11 PM last night.

I tip-toed into the kitchen to make coffee... Matt, asleep on the sofa, whispers in such a gentle, soft voice (especially for a 6′3′ 250–pound man) "Good morning, Mom. How *are* you?"

"I'm great, buddy — go back to sleep. You need it."

"Thank you. I am SO tired but SO happy. Thank you for everything, Mom. Can I have a coffee with you?"

"Sure, buddy! Git 'yer coffee on!"

Then he gets up for his coffee, and says, "Holy shit, Mom! You're a freak! Look at your changes!"

"Why, THANK you, buddy!"

Then, I move one piece of the sectional sofa (which we slide around so big buddy has a larger space on which to sleep) and he says, "Sorry, Mom, I'm gonna swear, but you are fucking CRAZY! You have WAY more energy than I do and I'm only 36! I am so proud of you!"

JUNE 22, 2015

Every time Matt visits, the opportunity invariably arises that we discuss the "circle of life" (inevitable death)...

When I first began this with him, he did not want to hear it; he was not receptive. He would cry — and often walk out of the room (feigning another need to visit the washroom). But I have always, as an aging parent to a brain-injured son, felt it is my responsibility to prepare him for this in a healthy manner.

Yesterday, the subject arose again, and he now receives the discussion well. He said he would be very sad when I pass and will always miss me, but said these talks help him appreciate being with me every second he can right now. He said he will never stop talking about me when I pass and will talk *to* me every day. I have always explained to him I will merely be in another dimension — still a part of his life and waiting for him when it is HIS circle of life meeting mine again, and that my love and protection NOW, while I am living, is to fill him up so that he can hold on to that strength we are building together now. I told him the memories we make right now are what he will hold to remain close to me later.

YESTERDAY he told me he gets it, and he *likes* talking about it now because he understands this is the circle of life. People aren't meant to last forever. But he said he's not as worried because I am taking care of myself and because of that, he knows I am going to last longer!

I miss my buddy already, but he will be back in another three weeks.

JUNE 23, 2015

Another great day on the job... Such a relief that this one is actually a keeper! And my boss is ABSOLUTELY HILARIOUS — such a gentleman, but with such a wry and dry sense of humor behind the scenes.

I encountered an angry & disrespectful male client today. Whatever... I know the file history and he's a piece of work — a malingerer. So, I know to take it all with a grain of salt. When I had to tell the client, "Mr. _____, you can't speak to me in that tone." Of course, he went ballistic. Again, whatever. Professionally, I let him watch me walk away — HIS loss, my win.

I memo'd the file and when my boss returned from court, it was one of the first things he read and commented on with me personally.

In his dry sense of humor, with a totally straight face, he said, "What the hell? Does he not SEE and UNDERSTAND that you can break him like a fucking twig?"

I almost spit out my water on that one!

I told him I'd rather play dumb and just say, "It's okay, I don't understand; I'm just a secretary," to which my boss replied he liked his version better!

AUGUST 1, 2015

Matt has visited a couple of times, and all was wonderful. But now, the plot seems to thicken still again.

He was granted some short-lived freedom to walk to a nearby convenience store for coffee. This fared well for a few weeks, but now he has been told that the store owner doesn't want him back. This left me suspicious of my son's potential for inappropriate behavior, so I told him there has to be a reason. He cried and said he really didn't know.

I reminded him he still asks people for hugs... and big grown men just don't do that... People find it weird and sometimes even creepy. I used the analogy of me going regularly to a convenience store and someone asking me for a hug each time. He cried again...

"OMG, Mom... I get it. Thank you for bringing me back to reality. My brain is so fucked up. I am really a broken man."

I suggested he speak with a group home staff that he likes and trusts... letting them know he really wants to understand what went wrong — to make it an opportunity to learn and not just to feel rejected. He said he would do that. I hope he did.

Two days later, one of the group home staff told me Matt was asked not to return to the convenience store *because he was seeking marijuana, he was asking for handouts, he was intimidating others for cigarettes, and he was being inappropriate with women coming into the store.* So, I speculated accurately on the "hugging" syndrome, but I never suspected the rest of it.

Hopes of independence wane, as it becomes more and more apparent that he will require supervision and monitoring for the rest of his life. Hope truly makes us see what we want to see.

My heart aches again. And it's not the cardiovascular response I am seeking.

AUGUST 23, 2015

Mattie has returned to his group home. Everyone missed him, which thrilled him. He told me how bad the air quality is there right now due to forest fires. But being so tired, he couldn't communicate effectively. "Mom, there's so much smoke here we can't even see — what are they called... those tall things connected to the earth?"

Mountains — he was talking about *mountains.*

AUGUST 24, 2015
We're seeing more incredible and steadily consistent progress. This truly is a TBI tango, but we endure.

I tested him when he was down here this time... I had $4.35 in coins inside my car, $2.60 in a drawer in the kitchen, and in the trunk of my car, an old Visa card. He took NOTHING... When I sent him to the trunk of the car to retrieve something for me, he brought back the Visa card and asked me if I had lost it. WOW — good on him... FINALLY, this is enormous progress!

AUGUST 30, 2015
Well, I politely and moderately just "lost my shit" on a couple of folks in White Spot.

Power has been out at my place since yesterday around 1 PM... It's still disengaged this morning... I needed to eat, so I drove to White Spot. Line up outside... nothing moving. One by one, people gave up and left and I reached the front of the line... A harried female server rushed by and said "You'll have to seat yourself — we only have two servers for the whole restaurant."

NO PROBLEM. I cleared a table for myself, found some cutlery and a menu, and sat down. No one to take my order? No problem; I got up and grabbed a coffee cup at the server station and poured myself a coffee. One sweet gal (the 2nd server on duty) took my order when I asked if she could. Forty minutes later, my meal arrived. Fine. I'd helped myself to more coffee. No problem.

Other people with seats and no service kept leaving. Whatever — the staff was doing the best they could in the circumstances; by this time, they had no clean coffee cups, etc. Crazy.

A party of six and three VERY ill-behaved young children sat across from me... The women kept *demanding* they have service — insisting to know what was going on here...

The poor server burst into tears. I stood up and told this fat, miserable, ugly & nasty woman to either be patient or go back to Richmond where she could push her significant weight around, or I was going to snap her like a twig (diet brain recalls my boss' words recently). The men at her table (all half my size) sat stunned, and the miserable woman held her tongue... The server returned, and I told Madam Entitled she owed the gal an apology. SHE GAVE IT!

I will not sit idly by and watch good people, doing their best, be bullied (at least not in a safe environment where I am not putting myself in danger by doing so).

THEN, a man at another table bought my breakfast for me and said "Good on you for doing what I *wanted* to do!"

I never shared that story with my son.

Oh my! I hope power is on at the gym — today is leg day!

SEPTEMBER 6, 2015
I got sidetracked before heading for cardio today, avoided the

masses at SuperStore, and bought all supplies for a dinner party I am having for my bodybuilding team next Saturday! The man behind me told his girlfriend, "See... you can still buy real food and be fit," noting the ribs, cream cheese, and cheddar at my checkout! I told him this was for my off-season friends! I only get the lettuce and tomatoes!

The girlfriend smacked him on the arm and said, "SEE! Only YOU can stop super-sizing fries and call that a diet!"

SEPTEMBER 9, 2015

The new manager at my son's group home seems okay. I can't assess just yet; we're in a honeymoon phase again. The former temporary manager was so overwhelmed, doing her job and someone else's, and I'm sure she is relieved to go back to her own duties now.

Matt is happy and stable again. Certainly, if he were not stable, I could not do what I am doing in my own life. Chances are, I'd still be eating myself into an early grave. Despite the complexities that surround me, I continue to feel very grateful.

SEPTEMBER 10, 2015

Ugh... very limited sleep. Is "peace" a four-letter word? Is it too much to hope for?

My landlord had problems with their special needs 16-year-old daughter again. It was another long, violent, and angry night for the girl (and for all of us sharing this roof)... It is such a sad scenario and one to which I can relate. My heart sure goes out to this family. The daughter will become more and more unmanageable over time, I believe. It is and will continue to be a very sad reality for them. It is a sad reality for me as a tenant, as well...

"Don't go to sleep angry."

I believe in this... Fourteen years ago, I almost lost my son. I had not heard from him for ten days before his violent brain injury. He had been angry with me for telling him his life was off track and it was showing in his appearance... I am far more diplomatic these days, and I forgive more readily.

We're all lugging baggage of some weight... some of us just lift harder.

My landlords are lifting heavy right now.

PURSUING GOALS TO FRUITION DESPITE MURPHY'S LAW

W ell, given the continuing psychotic episodes occurring with my landlord's 16-year-old special needs daughter, and the reality that the environment is not one of safety for me or for my son during his visits each month, I spoke with a lawyer and was told I have a legal responsibility to myself and my family to remove myself from a dangerous situation. If I stay, I place myself at risk and jeopardy, when I knew or ought to have known that I was continuing in an environment with that knowledge.

As well, given my longstanding experience with these matters (e.g., with combined psychosis and learning deficits, and with consistently repeating violent/aggressive outbursts, I recognize the scenario only stands to worsen over time). I can relate to the logic, but it devastates me to face another move so soon.

I also know that the parents of this child are in denial, hoping each day that things will improve. But my thoughts are that once the girl attains the age of majority, with no Order of Committeeship in place, things are easily predicted to escalate. The girl presents a danger to her family and to any individual on the property.

I met with them, collected the information required, and drafted their Application to the Supreme Court for an Order of Committeeship — person and estate, including two affidavits to be sworn with a lawyer or notary before filing. I never knew if they sought Committeeship, but truly hope they did. If so, at least the materials I drafted for them would have saved them approximately $2,500 in legal fees.

OCTOBER 8, 2015
I now face an urgent need to move from my beautiful suite because of a special needs teenage daughter on the premises becoming violent and dangerous in psychosis. The Filipino family is so kind, so loving, and so respectful, however.

I texted them yesterday to let them know I would be vacated on October 10th. What does the wife text back? "Sarah, you are leaving five days early. We owe you money; we will give you a cheque."

Oh my. That brought me to tears. I was so incredibly touched by the kindness of people who feel responsible for my move when, in reality, it is no one's fault. It's merely circumstances complicated by a family member's health complications. Certainly, I understand that more than most. My text back to her was, "Maria, NO NO NO — you owe me nothing. Your kindness and empathy touch my soul, but I will not accept your money. Your friendship is all that matters to me, and our bond of having the struggle of children with brain dysfunction. Bless you."

Yesterday ended up as a recovery day, because of the PTSD triggered by another psychotic episode with my landlord's daughter. Her parents were out during the early evening, and she tried to collapse the door to my suite — shouting obscenities all the while, threatening me, body-slamming the door. I stood there silent and frozen in my stance, trembling and sweating. Actually, I was more fearful of what I might to do *her*, to protect myself, if she came through my door — than I was of what she might do to *me*. I did not phone RCMP, as I did not want to make more trouble for this lovely and overwhelmed family. The ordeal reminded me of Matthew in psychosis years ago. The voice that came from the daughter's throat was not her own. It was like watching a Linda Blair performance from the *Exorcist*. Matthew had been the same. This was dissociation into another psyche.

But alas, today's another day, and after two full sleeping pills last night, I managed some sleep. I have movers attending tomorrow morning at 9 AM; wholly ready for that.

Today after work, before unloading my car again at the new place, I will train full upper body. I missed quads yesterday, trapped in horror by the daughter in psychosis, but I figure tomorrow's jaunts up and down those stairs with moving will suffice as a light quad/ham/glute workout. Sunday I can commit to a hard-core lower body training.

OCTOBER 11, 2015
It's a relief to be out of the last rental; such a gorgeous place, but I didn't even realize how unsafe I felt until I got out of there.

Plus, the day before moving out, I learned (1) the psychotic girl that was terrorizing me (and her dear parents) had disconnected my sensor lighting in the back, which made it very difficult for me to find keys to get into my place and to traverse the steps back there in the pitch-black dark; and (2) she entered my suite through the door connecting (inside) to the main house... How do I know? Because I "booby-trapped" that door precisely for that purpose. I positioned a piece of 6-foot by 2-foot artwork up against the door, balanced and sturdy from my end, but if the door opened, the art would fall down. When I arrived home from work on Friday (after being told I could not come home early because the girl disobeyed her parents and returned home early unsupervised), the artwork had been knocked onto the floor. Lovely.

What did the girl hope to achieve by disengaging my outdoor sensor lighting? Did she have plans for me? Of course, I will thankfully never know.

I also learned, in a conversation with the neighbor across the street, that they have video footage of the girl exiting her bedroom window at night (from the 2nd floor of the house) and climbing up onto the roof. They also have video surveillance of her using a rope and entering and exiting the house late at night. HOLY CROW, that is so very disturbing. I can relate to the horror that her parents must endure, as I have felt the shame of Matthew's brain injury malfunctions so many times in the past.

The parents were so appalled and embarrassed by everything, but again, it's not their fault. I feel so badly for them. I know precisely what they are facing, and what they are feeling.

And I am more grateful than ever that Matthew is stable, well-supervised, and safe.

It's time to get back to the new place and finish cleaning and unpacking/organizing. I am determined to get it all done before bedtime tonight, hoping tomorrow I only have to hang rods and curtains before I train like a banshee, again!

Today will be a 2nd recovery day; my legs and glutes are sore from lifting and traversing multiple stairs with multiple loads yesterday.

OCTOBER 13, 2015
I don't know of anyone who would describe moving as "fun." It is always a financial assault of sorts, an affront to your physical endurance, and a grand inconvenience — at the best of times.

I hired a company operating under the name of "Metro Movers." They arrived over two hours late; the helper was an obese, unfit-to-carry-anything-over-20-pounds special needs man who only spoke Russian. The owner of the cube van (NOT a five-ton truck as described and promised) was verbally abusive to the special needs man, and what should have encompassed a less than two-hour move took 3.5 hours. I was overcharged. They stole my sleeping pills out of my nightstand, along with a $30 fresh bottle of "Green Away" for my competition prep, and a jar of coins with more than $70 inside... also in my nightstand. What did the man hope to accomplish with that bottle of "Green Away"? The coin-cache and the sleeping pills? That's easier to figure out.

What is "Green Away"? It's a product that one applies to the areas of the body that most prolifically sweat on stage (underarms, predominantly). The spray tan product that a competitor applies to their body for stage presentation will turn green with sweat. Green Away keeps the green away.

Hindsight is 20-20. A brief investigation, post-move, disclosed that the special needs mover was a self-reported alcoholic, and owner David? An OxyContin addict. Metro Movers: the bad news bears for an already stressful experience.

OCTOBER 16, 2015
What a wonderful day! I just received the quarterly report from Matt's group home, and we have even more good news. He is trying new outings (new freedom because his behaviors have been

consistently improving), and he's lost another six pounds this past month!

He is now in the 240s! His goal has always been 220, so he is now well on his way, — considering about 1.5 years ago, he was 368 pounds. This is an incredible accomplishment for anyone, much less someone with the apathy inherent with brain injury, double-vision that prevents his ability for many activities, frozen shoulders (residual from his injuries of 14 years ago), and numbness in his right leg and foot.

ONE PROUD MAMA!

OCTOBER 17, 2015

Well, an eventful morning. Does everyone's life bear some kind of melodrama often, like mine?

I witnessed a pedestrian accident this morning. The situation truly irritated me. The young chap driving tried to shirk it off, saying he shoulder checked, but I was right there. I tore a strip off him, took his photo, and photographed his car when he tried to drive away. He got out of the car and told me, "You can't take my picture." I said, "I just *did*, and the next call is to the RCMP and the Insurance Corporation of British Columbia. Want to wait around for that and make a proper reporting, or leave the scene of an accident with a witness and her photographs?" He left, and I photographed him leaving.

Poor Asian woman, likely in her 40s or early 50s, was hit broadside, knocked down hard, and struck her head on the pavement. She was in shock and bleeding at the scene, but she did not want to call the police... She didn't want any attention or trouble. I could not convince her otherwise. But I told her there would be an insurance claim number assigned for this, so if she finds herself in more pain later (and she will), to telephone the Insurance Corporation of British Columbia, report the location and date of the accident, and ICBC would have a claim number assigned — because I was phoning in to report and would provide photographs of the offending driver who struck her in the marked crosswalk.

If there's anything I know, it is personal injury law and the law concerning pedestrian/vehicular offenses, especially in a marked crosswalk where she had the GREEN light. King George Blvd at 102nd Avenue, 8:45 AM this morning.

Mattie has been earning some money for himself recently. Today he bought himself an easy chair for his room at the group home! Such progress. Until recently, he only wanted to buy cookies! The difference between this home and all others before is like comparing day to night!

NOVEMBER 4, 2015

I arrived one hour early to meet Mattie. I had a coffee, and I was prepared with a container of Basa and asparagus packed in my meal bag.

I will have a haircut today at 2 PM, and I will have my last workout today, too... Manicure-pedicure is done, and I will be the exfoliation and shaving queen tomorrow! My bags are packed for the hotel, and I am as ready as I'll ever be!

Two days to stage! This is my comeback to bodybuilding after facing health complications since 2004, and a birthday present for my son — planned for more than a year!

NOVEMBER 5, 2015

I am so grateful that Matthew can be here for this competition. Every time I woke up to pee last night, he had a sweet "I love you, Mom" for me. I can't be sure if he slept at all. Of course, he never complained.

Then, he had coffee with me at 4 AM!

He gave me a hug and broke into tears, saying how proud of me he was. "Holy shit, Mom... you changed again overnight!"

We have the most insightful and profound conversations... Despite his severe deficits, I am so proud of the depth of his character, and his commitment to positive change.

Tomorrow is his 37th birthday. This competition is my gift to him, and the planning and timing have been a very concerted effort!

He's the love of my life, and although I have zero regrets for the sacrifice made and grueling battles fought on his behalf, I am glad all turned out to be worthwhile and grateful the battles are seemingly in abeyance!

NOVEMBER 6, 2015

HAPPY BIRTHDAY, MATTIE! He keeps saying, over and over, "This is the best birthday, EVER!"

We have an elite group of competitors tonight! The promoters and volunteers have done an outstanding job, with much attention to detail. The athlete bags are crammed with incredible products, too!

I weighed in at 150 pounds! That means I have officially lost 118 pounds in 17 months! I am pleased with this, and Matt was so proud he cried more than once!

So wonderful to see the judges from my past shows, and I am flattered that the head judge remembered me from 2004!

Let's do this!!

Happy birthday to the love of my life! 37 years ago today, I drove myself to the hospital in early labor!

I took him to Starbucks this morning and handed him a cake pop and white chocolate mocha. Then, we were off to IHOP for his favorite breakfast (peanut butter & banana pancakes).

SATURDAY NOVEMBER 7, 2015
Competition Day
AT THE EVENING SHOW, as I walked out onto the stage to perform my 60-second routine, the audience was silent. Literally, one could hear a pin drop in the Hard Rock Casino theatre. Then (before my music started), in the dead silence, "I LOVE YOU, MOM!" The crowd of over 1,100 people, in unison, gave a loud "AWWW!" and my performance began.

And when I concluded my 60-second posing routine to music, the MC of the show handed me the microphone to speak — asking me to describe my journey to the audience! I was stunned but honored, and simply spoke of losing 120 pounds to return to a bodybuilding stage, getting my health back at 61 years of age — and adding that "It's never too late."

And my boss was also in the audience! When I finished my stage presentation, I returned to the audience to sit beside Mattie and with my team. He greeted me with a resounding, "That was fucking *awesome!*"

Mattie greeted me with tears of joy, adding, "Mom, I am in awe of your fearlessness." My buddy gets to add two trophies to his shelf, identical to eight others. Happy to see my young man so beamingly proud!

I am so grateful for my many friends who showed so much love and support, but I am equally glad this grueling endeavor has concluded now! Time to decide on the next goal and start making a plan to implement it!

Managing Stress with Humor & Sensitivity

The good news keeps on coming. What a refreshing turn of events after all the horrifically tough times in the first 12 years of Matthew's brain injury recovery...

Today, I got a request from the administrator at Matt's group home. In other times, that has always been my cue to take a deep breath and brace myself for the inevitable bad news coming — and to be ready for *anything*.

Not this time! Whew! She wanted to see how I felt about Matt having a wee bit more independence... just more baby steps. She said she believes he deserves it, adding that she could not be more pleased with his behaviors, cognitive improvements, and self-awareness. Of course, this is absolutely music to my ears.

SO, today Matthew takes a local bus for the first time, accompanied by one of his best friends there at the group home. This represents a very significant chance at independence for him — another step toward feeling more like a man than a child.

Were I in Matt's shoes all these years, with all the restrictions, I don't know if I could have fared as well as he has in these past two years. Again, I am reminded to be aware and grateful for the very measurable differences quality care accommodates.

I could not possibly be more pleased with his group home, with the health authority, with the staff, and with how Matthew was becoming the young man I always hoped I was raising.

NOVEMBER 24, 2015

It was refreshing to see a lighter moment in my office today. The firm administrator walked around, lawyer to lawyer (all men) asking them to help lift something. My boss says, with no hesitation, "Sher is right here; she can lift twice as much as I can — or any of these guys!"

Alas, they did not have me perform the lift, mumbling something about how that's a man's job... Hmmm. Chivalry is not dead, but these guys will assuredly have sore backs tomorrow!

NOVEMBER 27, 2015

On hearing how happy my son is now, I had another wee epiphany last night. I am in awe of the depths of his gratitude for 1.5 hours of freedom without staff supervision to go to the store by bus with his friend.

When he said "Mom, I can't believe how different life is for both of us," it occurred to me that when I made myself happier and healthier, he improved markedly. My declining health and social isolation made him feel immense guilt, feeling his needs had stifled *my* life. What a realization to know that he revels and thrives in my happiness now, as I do in his.

I am fortunate to have had that wake-up call for a return to health 18 months ago.

I came home to a lovely voicemail message. "Mom, I love you so much and I remember you have your work party tonite. I'm so proud of you for going out and socializing and hope you have fun. I'll talk to you tomorrow night!"

Wow... such progress that he even remembered I was to be out tonight. And progress for me too. I used to save every message he left for me, horrified I might never hear his voice again after almost losing him 14 years ago. Alas, I kept this message tonite, just because I could.

DECEMBER 5, 2015

I love waking up to a voicemail message from my son: "Mom, happy birthday! Just so you know, I got permission to call. I'm not breaking any rules. I sure hope I'm not breaking any of *your* rules!"

So proud of him for finally being so aware of doing the right thing...

DECEMBER 14, 2015

Ahh... the universe sends me greetings this morning! I've spent seven months walking on eggshells with our only office bully at the Surrey law firm. My most recent gift to her never elicited a thank you or response. She also "manages" the rental apartment I live in. I laugh at the word *manages*, as I am still heating my apartment with an open oven door, and I still have no key to the garbage bin (I take my garbage to Starbucks every morning).

I'm done with eggshell walking now, however; I am not the jackass whisperer. When I give up on someone, the door is permanently closed... for my health and well-being, they no longer exist for me. I will view her like a cockroach from this day forward.

But my random act of kindness to a stranger every Monday still continues! It invariably improves my Monday!

DECEMBER 15, 2015

The law of attraction. We all think of it simplistically as attracting what we put out. In the course of my over-thing and over-analyzing, I had another little epiphany this morning. The office bully has me further annoyed.

I ALWAYS ask myself, when others annoy me, WHY that is? I ask myself what part of that is on ME... my misinformation, my misinterpretation? I really want to take ownership, understand and move forward with positive growth.

I identified this woman on day two of my employment, eight months ago, as the solitary in-house bully, with two followers... I made it my personal project to do my best to turn her around, gifting insignificant items when she bitched and complained about having a need or a loss. But all that effort was to no avail, as I never once received a thank you... I absorbed her negativity to where our interaction became one of negative humor or ranting about traffic altercations, politics, and such. It all developed to where I became negatively triggered just by the sound of her voice or the sight of her. My internalized anger and frustration over her inability to be grateful for ANYTHING, including her health, her stable children, or the newly renovated bathroom our employer (her landlord) just provided. She lives on a property next door to the law firm. She had actually complained incessantly about the new tiles being "so white." In actuality, she had a beautiful opportunity to change decor simply with a new color of towels.

My ownership is to realize I must cut my losses when trying to uplift someone who pulls me down. It is my fault for participating in this lost cause for many months, but the lesson is not lost on me. Today is the day I allow myself to put blinders on and swim to shore for my own well-being.

We choose our paths... we choose our happiness and our thoughts.

DECEMBER 16, 2015
Five days until my Mattie is home! I miss him so much! I have a ton of fun stuff planned for him!

DECEMBER 20, 2015
I never hesitate to give my time freely to my son now. To listen intently... to HEAR & to laugh or cry together, but as a single parent with no support, there were times... years actually... that I had no time or didn't MAKE IT as often as I should have... It is my greatest regret in raising my son the first time... but I am confident I've made up for that by raising him a second time.

And my second-greatest regret? Not going to Israel from Japan when I had the opportunity. I cannot count the times I have wondered how life might have fared differently with that maneuver. I will never know, of course.

One of my new year's resolutions is to be cognizant of the day and grateful for it... not to be wishing for summer in winter... not to be anxious about folks not liking me... not to be wanting more, when I really have everything I need...

I want to live each hour doing the right thing... keeping my word... giving where I can... and loving every moment I have left with my son. And I want to feel nothing when a subversive mentality takes me to a place of self-doubt.

DECEMBER 21, 2015
Matthew has asked me several times what I would want if he could get me anything for the holidays. I told him he'd already given

EVERYthing I wanted. His stability is the greatest thing he has ever shown me. Without it, I could not have found my own...

DECEMBER 22, 2015

My buddy is feeling fresh after a new haircut and a pair of Nike runners! He's so happy he could burst! I actually love that when he sat down, he opted for a seat near a bearded Sikh gentleman.

Matt cannot make most of his own life decisions because of extreme brain injury, but he more often than not sees an alternate perspective in things that my brain overlooks. His off-color humor this morning was, "Mom, just cause she wants you to bend over doesn't mean you have to take one for the team!"

I laughed so hard... then his quick response followed. "Don't post that on Facebook! No WAIT! Just say *you* said it, and everybody will believe that!"

Oh, the depths of understanding and my Mattie's sensitivity... we're watching a movie called *Meet the Patels*. It is an Indian documentary & intimate portrayal of arranged marriage and the dilemma created in bridging Indian tradition and cultural assimilation in North America.

There were so many poignant, funny, and absolutely sweet moments in the movie, but the main character, a 30-year-old Indian male, just could not find an Indian wife.

My Mattie had to get up and go for a smoke, sobbing because identified so much with the fellow. WOW. 1 have such a deeply sensitive son... I'm incredibly proud. He defies those early psychiatric diagnoses every single day.

BE THE BETTER PERSON

No excuses. Despite almost no sleep last night, I was up for coffee with Mattie. I prepared oats with Nutracleanse and protein powder for him and then let him sleep again while I went out for fasted training that included heavy back, light shoulders, arms, and chest... and one set of dumbbell squats super setting with straight leg deadlifts. It was a good, modified full-body workout after four days off... I came home for meal 1 (greens and chicken breast) and now have the next round of meal prep in progress. I am qualified to compete at the BC Provincial Bodybuilding Championships, so I have started training for that. It is unlikely I will set a goal of doing the Canadian Nationals in 2017. The financial struggle with such a costly endeavor is one thing — but the toll taken on the body is still another. Anyone who says "age is just a number" is young.

I had to cook all Basa and my remaining chicken in the freezer, as it had all thawed. The landlord has not replaced my dead fridge; I've been three days without a fridge now. Wonderful. I was told he would pay someone $20 an hour to remove and deliver another used fridge. I chuckled and told his "manager" to be prepared for a minimum cash outlay of $100, or more. It doesn't help matters that his assistant, who "manages" his rental properties, is the woman bullying me in the firm.

I am viewing coach houses again today. It's a real conflict of interest renting a former commercial property from my employer. I am already 60 percent packed... There are so many unresolved issues here.

But I remind myself, that these are first-world problems. This is not a brain injury; I can view it as an opportunity to learn and to move forward.

DECEMBER 29, 2015
I am dreading my return to work today. My landlord is the managing partner of the law firm for which I work. Well, he's my landlord for two more weeks anyway... I've tried diligently to trust he would do the right thing for ten weeks but alas, he delegates management to

his assistant, the only instigator and bully in the office. I've now been without a refrigerator for five days. On the day the fridge died, his assistant told me I would need to help carry a fridge up and down 25 stairs. I said no. I'm 61, for starters, and no matter what, this is not remotely my responsibility. So, still no fridge. As an athlete, this is a valid issue for me.

The property is a commercial property. The apartment I have been renting from my firm's managing partner was formerly a medical office. I have been told that to adjust heat controls for my apartment, I must enter the office of the acupuncturist in the office next door, after hours. As that constitutes an illegal entry. I will not do it.

Police have knocked on my door twice in my brief residence here when a motion sensor was engaged in the chiropractor's office downstairs. Because there is no secured entry from the business offices and my suite, entering my suite would be a simple undertaking. To say that this is unacceptable seems to be the understatement of the decade to me. I sleep with a knife and a crowbar beside my bed. I wake up at least 30x each night. I am PTSD-triggered and my blood pressure has skyrocketed.

The business clients regularly usurp my assigned parking space. I cannot guarantee private parking on Sundays, either, as the Korean church patrons next door seem to be incapable of reading signage.

I still have no key to the garbage bin outside. I continue to take a small bag of garbage to Starbucks daily.

The conflict with being a tenant of the managing partner of the firm also places the lawyer for whom I work in a precarious position. He is an associate lawyer with the firm, and I am unable to discuss the issues with him. I need to remain professionally distanced and essentially act as though all is well.

My son and I spent days of our holiday searching, screening, and viewing coach houses for rent. THIS TIME I did not choose a rental based solely on desperate measures (fancy that not working for me over the past year)... I carefully analyzed each rental and its owner presentation, noting positives and negatives, and made an educated decision.

The expense and inconvenience of packing and paying for a truck/movers again will set me back even further financially. But I am determined to focus on what *is* going right, ensure my nutrition and training are optimal and keep my head on straight. All this, and a flare-up of my hemochromatosis and some measures needed to heal my inflamed liver, is a bit of a buzzkill, but I'm determined to find the lessons and opportunities in all this. I am so grateful that Matthew is stable. I have kept most of this distress from him. He is aware of the no-fridge issue, the heat issues, and the garbage issues, however. I have been careful not to "rant" about the disrespect and inconvenience, trying to let him see me "take it in stride" and move on.

I just have to pull up my big girl knickers now and adjust my ballistics, dress to kill, walk into that office with my head held high... do my job, and leave at 4:30.

DECEMBER 31, 2015

New Year's eve and the bullying continues. A fridge was to be delivered yesterday afternoon, then was rescheduled to the evening. I canceled my plans and stayed home to await delivery, and the bully texted me at 7 PM, alleging the driver bailed and the fridge would come the next day, after 1 PM. I've been over eight days with no refrigerator, and have lost about $150 in food supplies.

I predict insecure women will be the downfall of society as we know it. I am confident that the bully is purposefully perpetrating this scenario, simply because she can AND because she hopes I will ultimately resign and leave the firm. But, at the same time, the managing partner is not operating with integrity. I find myself in a precarious position, needing to maintain decorum in the workplace. It has made standing up for myself and what is legal and appropriate the wrong thing to do.

JANUARY 4, 2016

I am dreading the return to work today. I will have a discussion with our senior partner, advising I will not be paying rent for my final two weeks in the unacceptable rental.

JANUARY 5, 2016

I have found myself sinking into a depressive funk for several days now, particularly frustrated and disappointed with the turn of events in my office. I feel I have regressed back to where I was a couple of years ago, feeling trapped in my career but not yet able to retire. I am hopeful the relocation to a new home in ten days will provide relief.

One component of PTSD I face often is that with accumulated stress, triggers become more frequent. It becomes crucial to keep to logic and recognize this will pass with some effort and structured redirection. I can barely drive when triggered. I cannot multitask, and my tolerance for fools is almost non-existent.

JANUARY 7, 2015

Yesterday was a rough day with PTSD issues at every turn for me. I drove straight home after work, feeling felt my level of distraction was such that it was not safe for me to drive. I gave a quality work performance but any negative distraction triggered a brief brain shutdown. In times like that, I am probably dissociating. I seem to go into a fugue state of sorts. If I attempt to read my computer screen, I cannot understand the words or numbers. I cannot analyze, create or communicate. Today, I took the day off work to recoup.

I've been away from the gym for a week. I could not face people in my low mood. As Mattie would say, "nobody likes a complain freak." Today, however, I will use my headphones to work with some music in my ears, and I will crank out a much-needed full-body workout.

PTSD can trigger so much we're not prepared to deal with. I'm lucky to recognize that it is a temporary loss of logic that I can redirect. I've tried to use this circumstance as a springboard to learning something, and one epiphany I had was to realize that when the trigger takes me into depression, it's far easier to sink with it than to fight it. And my historical reality dictates that the gym is where the demons are to be extinguished.

JANUARY 12, 2016
The ordeal of so many consecutive bad rental decisions and costly, disruptive moves, conflict in the workplace, and a surplus of financial loss has me paralyzed with PTSD. Simply returning to the office found me triggered in short order. After my workday, I needed to drive straight home from work, as I felt it unsafe to travel elsewhere. I needed to collapse.

This week may be a write-off for training, but that's only a temporary setback. We all pursue goals while dodging "bullets" with life's unexpected struggles. The good news is that what might slow me down now would have seen me off work, or on medication if not for training. I am confident my enthusiasm will return once I have acceptable accommodation again.

It is now less than 27 weeks to stage... all over again!

JANUARY 13, 2016
I attended with my doctor yesterday and was told to take two weeks off work. I delivered the letter to my boss and administrator and was first greeted with ghostly faces because they thought I was resigning. I explained I would not be taking a full two weeks, rather only time as necessary. I was told I was "fully supported, health first," and that my job is secure... and...

Get this...

They gave me an impromptu raise in salary. Who says money can't make one feel a little better, at least temporarily?

I cannot help but wonder if they are *aware* of what the office bully has been perpetrating? Certainly, I have given no indications.

JANUARY 16, 2016
My buddy. Matt is 37 years old and maturing a little more every day now... but the fact remains that traumatic brain injury still has him presenting as a "man child." I have many recent creative craft projects made by him, only for me! I love and value these so much, but I'm facing a dilemma on where to put them while still maintaining minimalist decor!

Alas, Mattie is the son I always hoped I was raising, both times. I am so grateful for his continuing stability.

JANUARY 18, 2016
Now that residential stressors have stabilized, and I can hold a "devil may care" attitude toward the office bully, I have turned my mind back to rectifying health concerns. Investigations revealed that my liver enzymes were shockingly high. I'd had another trigger of hemochromatosis, which I've not experienced for nearly two decades. Mine is a genetic condition. About 20 years ago, I feared I might have chronic fatigue syndrome. They gave me a lecture about alcohol consumption when my liver enzyme levels showed a problem. When I told my doctor I didn't drink and had not consumed alcohol in years, additional testing revealed hemochromatosis. My body does not assimilate iron; rather, it stores it. I cannot eat foods with iron content frequently, and I cannot take vitamin supplements with iron. If I do, the ferritin (iron) accumulates

and places me at risk with little notice. Apparently, my liver is "nominally enlarged," with 8-12 being normal for my age and size. I am a 13. It's not alarming, but not to be ignored. An ultrasound disclosed the liver enlargement and a 1/ cyst on my left kidney.

So now, I undergo phlebotomy tomorrow to lower my ferritin levels and must abstain from red meat again.

As for the kidney cyst, I'm referred for a CT scan.

My ECG revealed an electrical arrhythmia in the heart, so it would appear the heart condition is again alive and less than well. Luck proved to be on my side, however, and I have a cardiologist consultation for this Thursday. Fortunately, I already had the day off work.

So there. I may act younger, and some say I don't look my age, but bottom line — 61 years of stressful living is bound to show some disruption in one form or another. I am glad I got my health back on track when I did and I am grateful to have kept that excess weight at bay successfully.

JANUARY 21, 2016

The cardiologist consult went well. There is no evidence of further damage and my heart rate was slightly slower because I'm fit! They commended me on weight, nutrition, and exercise. The biggest concern was hemochromatosis. He stressed the importance of having ferritin levels checked every eight to twelve weeks. He says it worsens with age and if left untreated, it kills. Thankfully, it's easily managed but I can't be lax with potentially serious health conditions. He added that this would be the reason for some liver enlargement.

They commended me for being successfully off all but thyroid meds for 18 months. He said it's very rare to see patients my age who were not on a variety of medications.

Now... off to train!

JANUARY 22, 2016

I gave an extra hour and 15 minutes to work for which I don't get paid. While I never gave it a second thought until the "fridge fiasco,, I am not doing much of that anymore. I am not enjoying my job these days, though I continue to have immense respect and admiration for the lawyer to whom I report.

BUT HEY, nobody likes a complain freak — so it's time to go to the gym and work off that frustration by lifting heavy stuff and putting it back!

Focusing on the good I could control, I had a 1.5-hour shoulder workout tonight and my nutrition was 100 percent on track, as well. I sauntered right past those donuts in the office!

I am still not emotionally 100 percent but a lot better... When Mattie phoned tonite, he expressed his concern again — since he could detect something "off" in my voice. But he quickly added he was so glad I'm pushing to train because "it's what's going to keep you stable and happy. Mom, I'm so proud of you. You're strong as a rock. You're MY rock. I'm glad we've both lived long enough to see each other stable and happy!"

Wow. My young man matures a bit more every day.

JANUARY 27, 2016

I am astounded at the continual improvements Mattie exhibits. He told me his best friend at the group home is going downhill more often than not, and yesterday this young man actually tried to goad Matt to fight with him — the friend being about 5-foot 6-inches and maybe 150 lbs and Matt being 6⬛3⬛ and weighing in at about 270 (again)... Three years ago, Matt would have decked him and faced another assault charge, followed by a lost residential placement and another sojourn in jail.

Matt described his response to his friend as being, "Man, I love you, but you've gotta leave me alone; I am *not* going to fight you. I would hurt you and maybe that's what YOU want, but I don't. I love you, man." And then Matt turned and walked away, and kept his distance from his friend for the balance of the day and night...

If this is not some sort of creative conjecture, covering a bigger collection of events, I am very proud of my young man. I want to accept this as truth, but the fact remains, that I must always be prepared for the next TBI tango.

JANUARY 29, 2016

Interesting how my friends, the group home staff, and even many of my gym acquaintances (folks whose names I do not know, but greet daily with a nod and a smile) asked if I was feeling better.

Not ONE individual in my office asked, despite my medical absence of four days. Silence is a loud response.

The realization helps in my decision to seek alternative employment and relieves the guilt I feel over walking away from a ridiculous and unrealistic workload. But alas, it's not my circus and not my monkeys, and the law firm will have an opportunity for additional management considerations.

FEBRUARY 6, 2016

I think most of us wake up pondering what we have to get done today, reviewing what sequence in which to best get it all accomplished. Well, I woke up this morning (Saturday), dreading my return to work on Tuesday.

Instead, I want to contemplate what might transform this day in front of me into excellence. Training has become my "go-to" medication for mental and physical health... to fight the limitations imposed by PTSD, depression, anxiety, and the feelings of never being enough. When I push myself physically, I calm the voices in my head from bad parenting that haunt me still 55 years after the fact. Yes, even at this age — my mother's negativity and disdain haunt me.

Today is leg day! There is no physical push to limitations greater than leg training (when done right)! And the more one pushes with training, the more cortisol is released!

FEBRUARY 8, 2016

I am back to work, have a job interview tomorrow, and have my bestie coming over for dinner tomorrow night. Tonight, I train my legs and shoulders again after work.

My meals have consisted largely of a carb-depletion variety, with my weight holding steady at 160 pounds.

I miss my son but look forward to the countdown to his visit home in nine days. Putting more time between us has been good, however. We still speak once a day by telephone and he often emails his cryptic all-caps one-liners!

I am dreading the work environment today but hopeful of being able to provide notice soon.

FEBRUARY 17, 2016

Kurt (the kind man that cleans our office property of all the trash left by local addicts and the homeless) remembered to buzz me after he finished cleaning today.

I brought him out two bags of veggies and he stood there and sobbed, saying it was the nicest thing anyone's done for him in a long time. We talked about how he needs to eat vegetables with every meal and particularly put celery into every meal he can (to lower blood pressure, reduce cholesterol, and more)... He told me he likes celery. Good.

The receptionist sat there stunned, especially after I told Kurt to come back in two weeks, and I'd have more for him. I often wonder if the owner of the firm is aware of how disrespectfully his staff treats this gentle chap? He is addressed in a tone that speaks to discrimination and prejudice, and he is the subject of gossip and ridicule in the office frequently. I find it sad and cruel. But of course, I have firsthand experience with the rampant cruelty and entitlement of many of the women in this firm — but I have also witnessed it elsewhere, despite this being the worst.

I told him I would try to help him for as long as I could, but just to know it might not happen every pay period, though I'd like to help whenever I can. I told him how I'd also been in "his shoes" with poor health and too much weight, less than two years ago. He seemed shocked.

Then, I went to Starbucks at lunchtime, and who do I see walking home with his two bags of veggies? Kurt! He gave me a Cheshire grin and asked if I was stalking him!

LOVE WHAT MATTERS

The wisdom of my dear son in the middle of TBI — some days it never ceases to amaze me. Some days, it stops me in my tracks.

Last night, he asked how things were in the office; I told him at least yesterday that the witches left me alone. He replied, without a second thought, "Mom, you just care too much. You've got to care less about people who don't matter. EVERYONE in this world doesn't matter. I know you always tell me we're all connected, but some people are just here, like cockroaches. They matter to their cockroach family, but not to anything else. You don't have a cockroach family; these people driving you crazy aren't in the same family as you. Try to be like me on one thing: I really don't give a fuck about people that don't give a fuck about me. They're just empty faces in a crowd and my double vision helps me choose to not see them."

Wow. CHOOSING to see or not to see. Life actually can be reduced to simple reality, sometimes.

FEBRUARY 19, 2016

It is so unbelievably wonderful to wake up to my son here... watching the news together. NO, wait – let me rephrase that! Make that talking incessantly with the news in the background! He made me coffee; told me not to DARE touch the three dishes in the sink from last night (bless him, he wants to do anything he can for me).

We're off to get him a haircut this morning; I asked him where he wanted to go. He opted for a barber he saw for YEARS when he was living at home with me. He stopped going because the barber offended him. Now, he wants to go back just to see how he feels about the guy, saying, "Mom, I'm proud of myself now; I've changed a lot. Maybe I will see him in a different way now. Maybe he's nicer again, and maybe he's *not*, and then I just won't go back. You taught me to give people ONE more chance, but I'm trying to teach YOU that one *second chan*ce is enough! But that rule doesn't apply to me — just everybody else in the world!" Ahhh, the insight...

And I notice his vocabulary has significantly improved... using words like *courage, diligent, obsessive, and concur.* For anyone WITHOUT a brain injury, others would not recognize it as remarkable. Case in point, this is a man who just three years ago said to me regularly, "I love you Babaloo; I love you more than pooh!" This is a man who recited "Brush teeth, comb hair, don't forget your underwear" to himself every time he got dressed, until two years ago.

And my young man will be my coach today at Platinum! I know he has no endurance for training, so I've asked him to promise to perform at least one set of every exercise I do, and then count, push me and help me unload and load weights today, as a good trainer does!!!

We will see a movie at some point this weekend. Mattie wants to see *Deadpool*, and check out our friend Billy's physique as the COLOSSUS character!

Great day ahead, and neither of us cares if it's raining!

The trip to Raf, the barber, went well this morning. I'm so proud of Matt for facing his fears, so to speak. He *chose* to place himself in a situation that could have hurt him emotionally but had the stones to face a situation that bothered him for almost four years.

Raf was happy to see us both. His mind was in a good place. Impressed with Matt's weight loss, he told Matt, "Man, you were at least 80 pounds heavier last time I saw you. And I can't *believe how much you've improved!* You have matured, you are shaking hands and being appropriate. This is really GREAT!"

Matt changed his hairstyle of three years, returning to the "Police Special" of a precision flat top... He also asked to have his eyebrows thinned and had a hot-towel, straight-razor shave!

I love seeing my young man taking pride in his appearance again!

FEBRUARY 20, 2016

When my son is home, I wake up to sweetness and love... This morning, I tiptoed out to the living room, where he was fast asleep on the sofa. I noticed he had himself wrapped like a big burrito in his blankets. He whispered "Good morning, Mom. I love you so much."

"I love you too, buddy! I'm so glad you're here. Are you cold, buddy?"

"A little, but it's okay."

"Oh no! Honey, why didn't you turn up the heat?"

"Mom, I would never disrespect your budget. You're struggling right now. You have a competition coming."

"Oh, sweetie! I don't pay hydro here!"

At that, he cracks up laughing! Says he'd freeze just to be with me...

That takes my breath away and makes my heart tug... such love in the face of adversity and never, ever one complaint.

Over our first coffee, Matt says, "Oh crap... did we train back yesterday?"

"Yeah, buddy. I'm proud of you! You lifted heavy!"

"I can't lift my coffee cup this morning. My arms are sore too!" Can I say we trained full body cause my legs hurt so much I can't get up off the sofa!

He finally gets up, giggling like a girl in a high-pitched voice! My gentle giant!

And he's already asked me what we're training for today! That sure makes a Mama proud!

Showered, teeth brushed, and exiting the bathroom, he remarks, "Wow! I forgot I got a great haircut. I feel proud of myself again."

I remark about how he never complains or asks for anything and he responds with, "Mom, sometimes I want to, but EVERYBODY complains and nobody likes to hear it... Everybody thinks their problems are the worst. And even IF my problems *are* worse, people still don't want to hear about them. Complaining only makes everybody feel like shit, especially me. So, I just try to focus on how lucky I am to be alive and safe, and loved."

FEBRUARY 21, 2016
Breakfast with my Mattie! Rice cakes instead of toast, egg whites, one whole organic free-range egg, and salad with lots of organic parsley! Same for me, but no rice cakes!

Mattie, February 21, 2016

My young man returns tomorrow morning and I go back to work! I certainly have enjoyed our time together, and I take pride in knowing he returns with every muscle group aching! He was quite the trooper for chest, biceps, triceps, and one set of hamstring curls!

I told him, again, how proud of him I am and shared a little poem:

> Say it before you run out of time.
> Say it before it's too late.
> Say what you're feeling today,
> Cause waiting is a mistake.

"Mom, I like that. That's why I always say 'I love you' when I leave, when I see you, when I talk to you, or when I pray for you. You taught me 'Love what matters.' I'm happy we still have time to tell each other how glad we are to still have each other. Thank you for loving me, really and truly. And thank you for never abandoning me, even when I deserved it."

"Buddy, I carried you then — I carry you now."

KNOW BETTER, DO BETTER

It's February 22nd. George Washington's birthday — my grandfather's birthday, RIP. He lived with full independence until his final year of life; by that time (age 106), he was "forgetting things." I always find it fascinating that dates can hold such significance over such distance and time. I remember birthdays attached to many who are no longer in my life — Matthew's father, my mother, my step-father, my half-brother... I suppose *connections* involve much more than we perceive.

I find myself missing Mattie already. After driving him to the Greyhound station this morning, and getting all the way to Abbotsford, he realized he left his jacket at my place — with his tickets inside the pocket! Yikes!

Thank goodness, out of an absolute fluke and mistake to print two copies when I purchased them online, I'd placed the extra copy into a file folder that was now in the trunk of my car. Well, there has to be something to celebrate in this turn of events!

He won't have a down-filled jacket in the Okanagan for a few days, but he at least has a suede jacket he never wears. It will be time to excavate that from the back of his closet!

He cried this morning, going back, not because he doesn't want to return home, but because he's worried about me. I haven't had a good night's sleep in five consecutive days now and it's wearing me down again. He also knows my job causes me significant anxiety, and he keeps praying (out loud) that I find an alternate position elsewhere.

FEBRUARY 29, 2017
Funny thing, until I purchase the next tickets for my son's visit, I feel anxiety. It is almost as though I fear I will never see him again. I ask myself why, and the only answer I can proffer is that it must be due to almost losing him on multiple occasions. I have always feared that an "I love you" said today could be our last. I just purchased his next Greyhound tickets. Feeling better now!

MARCH 3, 2016

Have you ever had a moment where you almost cannot stand to hear a person's negativity (or even the sound of their voice) another moment? A moment where you almost LITERALLY feel your cortisol rising — conditioned solely by experience and that voice?

Welcome to my workplace, where 50-something women behave like mean girls from the movie of the same name. Change is imminent. I just don't know whether a change of career is afoot, or whether simply I can have a good work ethic without the politics of insecure women at every turn.

MARCH 9, 2016

My dear son. Of course, I always look forward to talking to Matt every single night; if I am busy and unable to take his call, I invariably look forward to the consistently sweet and positive voice-mail message he always leaves for me.

Many times, our chats are almost like a pre-recorded rendition of what was said in countless other telephone conversations. That is the nature of brain injury. On most days, he cannot remember what he ate an hour ago, cannot remember anything he did in the course of his day. On other days, he has significantly better clarity and insight.

Last night was a conversation of clarity and insight that left me reeling with emotion, reflecting on what is *truly* important, all over again. I am still pondering those thoughts this morning.

He said, "Mom, last night when we talked, I held the phone in my room, hugging it, 'cause I felt like you were still attached to the phone. I know you're not but I just need to be close to you. I am worried about you. Your job is changing you; every night I hear you sad, stressed, and frustrated, but I am amazed that you still help people and still keep your training going. I am so very proud of you, and I'm really worried about that circle of life thing we always talk about. Every time I talk to you, I worry it could be the last time. I just want you to be happy - wherever you find it."

And if THAT was not enough to stop me in my tracks, he continued (and this part is hard for me to type out, even now), "Mom, I know you don't see yourself as anything special. I wish you could — 'cause you are REALLY special, and not just to me. I know you think I feel that because I'm your son but it's more than that. I wish you could see how others see you. I wish you could see how your shine makes people that aren't shining feel UNCOMFORTABLE [he said this loudly]. They want to bring you down because they aren't on your level. They want to see you miserable because they are miserable. This is what bullies do, Mom. You taught me that. I used to be a bully and I now know it was because I didn't love myself. I wanted everyone around me to hurt, to be sad, to want to die — just like I did."

"Mom, promise you will remember I love you more than anything in the world. I hope that makes a difference for you."

MARCH 9, 2016

My son just phoned me, in tears. At first, my heart sinks —
worrying that something has gone awry at the group home.

"Mom, you've been telling me for years this was gonna happen and
I guess I knew it but I thought it wouldn't happen to me. I always
think nothing is going to happen to me when I hear warnings."

Alarmed, I asked, "Buddy — what's wrong? Is everything okay
at the group home?" Thankfully, all is well in residential paradise.
Whew. My heart sank. We are always "subject to change without
notice."

He is borderline diabetic now. The doctor impressed upon him
that this would *kill* him if he didn't get his act cleaned up...
. a sedentary lifestyle, an excessive and obscene amount of sugar
consumption, and as much "bad fat" in the mix.

In his newly realized self-redirection to positive thinking, he says,
"I'm so lucky I got a wake-up call. I'm gonna do better, Mom. I'm
so sorry. You *told* me so. But I am gonna do better. I know you are
going to ask 'When am I starting?' I already started — right after the
doctor told me that."

I told him, with a soft smile attached to my voice, that I am going to
kick his arse when he's down for Easter... there will be gym training
and two walks a day... and I'm teaching him how to make oatmeal
cookies with Stevia and coconut oil...

I am grateful to have *my* health back. It's important that I keep
setting good examples for my young man.

MARCH 11, 2016

Last night, I had to admonish Mattie for eating a pack of cookies,
just the day after being warned of the threat of diabetes. I told him
if he kept eating cookies, just take a break from phoning me. "All
our lives boil down to choices, Matt — and brain injury or not, you
know right from wrong. If knowing your lifestyle choices can kill you
doesn't give you enough memory to abstain, then perhaps not being
able to talk to me might help your memory."

He, of course, sobbed and apologized, meekly saying, "I
understand, Mom. You're right. Mom, I love you very much. I
promise to do better, Mom. I really promise. I'll prove it to you. I
know talk is cheap."

Then I cried hard after hanging up that telephone last night.

So, I just gave him a quick call at the group home from work, and
he was thrilled to hear from me. I told him I felt he deserved an
apology, but it didn't give him the go-ahead to have another cookie!
He laughed uncontrollably! I told him I was a bit harsh on him, but
I only apologize for hurting his feelings, and not for the message,
adding that the harshness merely comes from a place of the greatest
love and concern for him.

He didn't miss a beat: "MOM, you NEVER have to apologize to
me. You love me SO much and have so much RESPECT for me... I
know this is because you love me. I needed it. I got this, Mom. Thank
you so much."

And again, he's crying, but because he was so happy to hear my
voice. Seems my young man is slightly more emotionally fragile
these days. I think the reality of aging and his limited future is

perhaps sinking in for him, maybe for the first time at this depth of understanding.

In less than two weeks, he will be here with me again. We will walk twice a day, RAIN OR SHINE! If it rains, I'm going to teach him the experience of letting go and enjoying the rain!

MARCH 15, 2016

Today, I listened to a woman at work complaining about her two entitled daughters... one 23 and one 26, both living on their own, owning their own condos, but every week asking Mom for groceries, or to fix a blown transmission in their car, complaining when Mom makes them breakfast and refusing to eat "that kind of bread" as toast, adding that the eggs are just not cooked right.

Then I thought of my Mattie. Believe me, there were what seemed like 100 years in there where he, too, behaved and reacted like a privileged little rich kid. No doubt that was because I loved him so much and spoiled him, buying for him and letting myself go. I just wanted to find any means possible to reduce the suffering he experienced with traumatic brain injury and the inability to have much control over his life. But, I can state in emphatic honesty, NOW, if I take him out to eat, he invariably and consistently says, "Mom — I don't want you to waste your money; you work so hard." Or "Mom, I wish I could do for YOU cause you've always taken such good care of me and still are." I heard these words spoken with unmistakable sincerity on countless occasions. Matthew was truly cognizant and grateful, but perhaps, also feeling a little guilty. I didn't realize that until a few years into the future. I was too occupied with maintaining stability, for him and for myself, in my employment, advocating left, right and center, and staying prepared for any encounters with the law that might need to be addressed.

Indeed, he has such love in his eyes now, and he looks at me every time like he's won the lottery, like every single second with me is valued and NEVER, EVER taken for granted.

The terror and trauma of brain injury, rehabilitation, and inalienable change have been hard on us both, but there is not a day that passes that I ever lose sight of how very blessed I am to still have him alive and breathing, and now stable.

MARCH 18, 2016

I fell asleep on the sofa last night and missed Matt's call... The endearing message I heard this morning was, "Hi Mama bear! Hope you had a great day and hey whatever holiday it is today, I can't remember what it is or what color you're supposed to wear, but happy unknown holiday! Happy is the key. You always taught me holidays don't mean much, they're just another day, *but* to remember to be happy!"

That's my boy! This time next week we'll be having oats and egg whites together!

The holiday was St. Patrick's Day, and the color was green.

MARCH 20, 2016

Day One of official competition prep (16 weeks out)! Four months to step-it-up, polish, and refine my conditioning and drop another five percent bodyfat!

MARCH 22, 2016

My buddy Mattie. I bought him a wonderful green and grey shirt to go with his grey track pants... He has a lot of trouble matching his clothes and has been seen to walk out wearing brown and yellow with the grey. We know he's not color blind, but it's always been unclear why he cannot coordinate colors. Maybe it's simply not important to him, or perhaps he is so excited to venture out for socialization that he just dresses in the first items that his hands pick up!

He has never remembered the names of colors, either. When we spoke of green, I had to remind him it was the color of summer grass. Grey has always been "wannabe black" to him. Red was his favorite color, and that was the only color he could quote accurately. I never knew why.

So, I reminded him to pack his grey track pants. At the end of our conversation, I remind him, "I love you, buddy... GREY TRACK PANTS!"

"I love you too, Mom!"

Me: "GREY track pants!"

Sixty seconds later, the phone rings. "So sorry, Mom. Which track pants?"

So... We're going with "Wannabe black!" He gets that one!! It's what he's called GREY for 14.5 years now!

He brought the grey track pants on his next trip down!

Training to Be More

We just returned from training at Platinum Athletic Club in Surrey. It was an awesome back & arms workout for me. Matt took part and really tried some back work, but he has almost zero endurance. Yet, the pride is in the *trying*! He enjoyed chatting with Ben, one of the young competitors on my team, and others in the front lobby while I finished all my sets. I am thrilled that he had the chance to meet some of my "FitFam" at the gym, and vice versa. Most of my bodybuilding teammates are younger than Mattie.

Because he wanted to feel he was in competition prep with me, we ate our meals in the car, immediately post-workout (real food, not a protein shake)! "Mom, this is so cool — this is the life!"

He has participated in full prep with me all day. I am very proud. He's stayed on track for meals, meal preparation, training, fasted cardio, and water intake (peeing his brains out, bless him)! We also got him a haircut... no flat top this time. He asked the barber to shave his head and says he is growing a mustache & goatee now.

"You go, buddy! You are 37. It's your hair, it's your choice!" I asked, "Hey, what about a Mohawk?"

"Mom, I think I am too mature for that now!"

It's unlikely we will get a second walk accomplished today, despite being blessed with a lovely sunny day today. He is sound asleep on the sofa right now (this being his third nap sneaked in there while I'm on the computer)! He's absolutely POOPED! Competition prep is brutal!

My weight is 162 pounds today, inching steadily back down! I am pleased with the results of the hard work.

MARCH 23, 2016
Is this my son's bus? Yes indeed, there's my towering Giant with a grin that could light up the night! These are the moments I live and breathe for! Home for the Easter weekend, my grown child has already asked me if there's an Easter basket for him! Bless his heart... some arrested development there, but I do enjoy the moments of

innocence (in between the rest of the struggles). And no, there was no Easter basket!

MARCH 25, 2016

Teaching Mattie some nutritional basics today. Meal One, oats with flaxseed & NutraCleanse with a little protein powder (Mattie got seven raisins (he chose that quantity because seven is his lucky number, lol — a little OCD going on there, but hey, OCD can be part of good nutrition, and it is definitely part of bodybuilding!))... Six scrambled whites are to go down now (still part of Meal One)!

We did fasted-cardio together this morning! The sun was out, so we walked outdoors, around a paved track just three blocks from my home. There's a little duck pond in the center of the circular track, positioned in a safe neighborhood, and there is a small incline and decline on the walk. So, it is great for hitting a few different leg muscles! He also used the technique I taught him — focusing on his glutes with every step. He told me, "Mom, my butt is sore already; this is gonna be great!"

The next lesson on the agenda for him is meal prep. He will be my assistant on that (weighing and putting portions into the containers, different color containers for training day meals, as opposed to non-training day meals!) Brain Injury and PTSD require some seriously consistent conditioning on seemingly inconsequential things, so we work well together on this learning process! He has welcomed the opportunity.

Then, we're off to train back and arms (and abs for me, while Mattie relaxes with a high-fiber protein bar and a lot of water!)

So long as this sunshine holds up, we're committed to a second walk after Meal Five today! That one will be slower, so as not to incapacitate him and prevent him from training & walking tomorrow!

After one week on my coach's plan, I am feeling tighter, leaning down, feeling a difference in my waistline, and seeing more separation in my quads. I am totally psyched for this prep season, and committed to making the last one, the BEST one!

MARCH 26, 2016

My young man is SO exhausted this morning! But on arising, he said, "Mom, I didn't wake up ONCE last night — that hasn't happened in, well, I can't REMEMBER when" (he suffers from chronic restless sleep or complete insomnia). I explained to him that, until now, he had not been sufficiently active, and that when we don't move our bodies in the way and frequency they need, at night our bodies expect more movement and refuse to sleep (a bit of a simple analogy, but he got it).

And he still did three laps of fasted cardio with me (I did four), and ate his egg whites and oats (raisins & pecans added for him, with a half scoop of Beyond Yourself Maple Syrup Pancake whey protein powder in there)!

He is asleep on the sofa again (but before he nodded out, his last words were, "So, we're gonna do another walk later today?") Atta boy!

And, my weight is 160 lbs this morning. I had a visible overnight weight release and am ecstatic! That is the motivation I need to pursue the next round of cardio. It's futile to deny that I can meet training goals "*sans*" cardio. Much as I detest the process, cardio is a must!

Now, it's time to watch a movie at home with my young man, and get ready for the next walk after that!

MARCH 27, 2016

It's a brand new day, and a brand new week! Today is leg day, which translates to "let there be suffering!"

Leg training, then off to see *Star Wars* with Mattie at the theatre!

Having Mattie here presents SO MANY opportunities for heartfelt conversations... It amazes me how deeply into life's intricacies we dig, and more so each time we're together. He's improving on a functional level so much that I am absolutely astounded.

"Mom, you're not afraid of aging now, are you? I think you are embracing your age." WOW. Did he just say that?

And if I take a minute to contemplate that, he's right. I spent many years ignoring the fact that we start dying from the moment we're born and I was living like I considered myself immortal. I never considered the consequences of my poor choices, which included sleeping pills, tranquilizers, horrific eating habits, Yo-Yo dieting (up and down by over 100 lbs on three occasions)... then horrific depression with the battle to save my son after brain injury.

What I seek now, in every single aspect of my life (work, training, friendships, family, grocery shopping) is PEACE. I want an absence of drama.

And I want that for my son, too. We train to be more.

POSITIVE SACRIFICE

A couple of days ago, Mattie opted to have his entire head shaved... asked me if I would be embarrassed that his full scar from the brain surgery would be showing. I told him absolutely no way it would embarrass me — I told him it is his trophy of survival from something that kills most.

He said "Yay. Thanks, Mom, cause that's how I feel about it. My scars tell my story. They remind me of how life broke me but made me a better man. I am a better man for the brain injury, Mom."

Then, this morning, as we were ready to exit for the gym, he stopped. "Sorry, I have to go comb my hair first — OH, WAIT! I don't HAVE any hair! AWESOME!"

Then after just discussing that he would grow a beard, he emerged from the bathroom as smooth as a baby's behind, clean-shaven. I said, "I thought you were gonna grow a beard!"

"Oh crap, I forgot. Guess I'm conditioned. Don't worry, you'll see it growing again in a couple of hours!"

Then, a few minutes ago, he asked, "Do you think I could grow a beard like Hardip?" Hardip is a friend from my "FitFam," a few years younger than Matt. He has a generous, long, and thick Sikh beard. I said I didn't know if his beard would come in that thick, but all he could do was try!

He then said, "I love that guy, Mom. I'd like to be more like Hardip."

Ahhh, my Mattie. Like his mom, when he loves, he is ALL IN (or all out).

We did fasted-cardio together outdoors again! After that, we had Meal One sitting on a park bench, enjoying more random, deep conversations, and people-watching a bit. One young man walked by, and I said (once he was out of earshot), "He looks calm."

Matt says, "Wow! I think he looks *miserable*!"

Clearly, our profiling protocols differ! Then my hilarious Mattie adds, "But hey, ONE of us is right!"

I could not be more proud. He has eaten wholly clean this entire trip down, almost five days. He had a 1-inch square of an oversized chocolate bar that was given to him, and he's saving the rest of that enormous bar to give to his friend in Kamloops! It's been sitting out in open view the entire time and he has consciously chosen to not touch it. This represents amazing progress from my sugar addict!

He has also done fasted cardio with me every single day and twice we did double walks in a day. He trained with me once too, and is still sore from that!

We have enjoyed a wholly positive visit, with no conflict, no marijuana seeking, no over-smoking, and no lies. It has been incredible getting to know the transformed adult my son is becoming, and equally amazing to have him get to know me on a different level as well.

MARCH 30, 2016

While missing my Mattie, things he said and did over our incredible five days together keep creeping back into my mind...

I try to condition him to think about fitness and to recognize how small matters count so much, with almost every word spoken... So when I needed to get up and get something, before he could offer, I jumped, and said, "I get the calorie burn!"

After one day of that, HE was jumping to get whatever I needed, saying, "I'M TAKING THE CALORIE BURN!"

It's SO small, but is the START of bigger things to come — just transitioning his mind to thinking and realizing that MOVEMENT counts! Apathy kills! Baby steps add up to a huge transformation, and I am proud to have set that example for him and have it taken to heart by my young man.

MARCH 31, 2016

My Mattie is progressing in some capacity every single day, it see ms... He told me he washed off the patio today for a female staff he doesn't like. They gave him a pack of gum for his efforts, but the *real* lesson was in recognizing he would feel good doing something for someone, even if he didn't like the person. That is some kind of progress.

He says I taught him to do that. I don't remember teaching that lesson. I don't think I do things for people I don't like... He told me I am always doing it in my job — being the better person, going the extra mile. Wow, thanks for noticing the lesson, buddy.

I have no words to express how proud I am that my young man is transforming into an individual I would be proud of if he were *not* my son.

It's nice, for a change, to "take ownership" from a different perspective than usual. I am thrilled that he is transitioning so well and has these incredible opportunities to socialize in safety with supervision!

APRIL 8, 2016

FITNESS SABOTAGE on a subconscious level!

I woke up this morning, per my usual routine, and noticed on the sofa an open box of HONEY NUT CHEERIOs, half spilled on the sofa.

I did not even RECALL that there was still any cereal in the cabinet from Matt's last visit — and these would have been there from two months ago. This past visit, I did not permit him any sugar content because of his pre-diabetes warnings.

HOW DID MY SUBCONSCIOUS mind recall those nutrition-free pellets of crap in the cabinet? And how could I open that box, sit down, eat G-D knows how much, and then spill half of it on the sofa, get up and go back to bed?

Then, I recalled a memory from my intensive training in 2000. Matt had just visited, and there was still a box of toaster waffles in my freezer. My discipline was "on point," however, and I was not tempted to consume those empty carbohydrate calories. But I awakened one morning, two days before the BC Provincial Championships that year (which I won) — to find one toaster waffle in my bed, with one bite out of it! This is what we call "diet brain!"

The remaining cereal is no longer in the house, and today is also garbage day, in case my over-active "DIET BRAIN" opts to go outside to the garbage can at night.

APRIL 10, 2016
I spent another weekend with my son. We had no outings other than to take our walks but enjoyed lots of conversational bonding, lots of perspective, and insights. He is growing emotionally now, trying more and more diligently to curtail his childish comments and behaviors.

He spoke a lot about how he observes me slowing down... that I am much calmer and more patient than I was six months ago.

And I am fascinated with his focus on having an emergency protocol in place, should we ever face an impending crisis. All the political ruckus in the news has him distressed, and he is obsessing over wanting to make sure we are together if there is a disaster. Bless him, no one could love me more.

> Enjoy the little things in life, for one day you will look back and realize they were the big things. ~Unknown Author

APRIL 20, 2016
Talk-of-the-moment in my workplace environment: "FAT BLOCKERS" and being ready for summer swimsuit season. Heaven help me.

I was asked by a group of three (women, of course) this morning, all HOT TO TROT over how these pills are going to reset their life while they can STILL eat & drink anything they want (including alcohol), what my opinion of the product was. I said with a cautious smile, "Not a good one!"

Then, I hear the same group chatting again about an hour later (DON'T THEY HAVE WORK TO DO?) about how "the sound of her [MY] voice, all happy and positive and shit, annoys the piss outta me."

I rest my case: put three women together in any law firm, and you have office politics with which to contend!

APRIL 21, 2016
It's a new day! And for me, this is a profoundly new day, the beginning of another transition toward my future — focusing on goals of being closer to my son, into a peaceful and drama-free work environment, and living in a community that is just sufficiently slower to keep my mind more at peace as I enter my wind-down years.

Another day in the office has concluded. I gave notice to my employer this morning. Last night, I came home to an email from a law firm confirming it had selected me as the new paralegal for a sole practitioner's personal injury practice in Kelowna.

On tendering my resignation this morning, my boss was stunned. He actually asked if there was anything he could say or do to change my mind (sweet, such a nice guy), and I said no, this was as much for Mattie as it was for me. He understood and thanked me for three weeks' notice as opposed to two. I did not discuss the office politics with him, the bullying, the alienation, or the history of rental infractions and negligence I had endured. As an associate lawyer, he had enough on his plate — and politics was not his purview.

APRIL 22, 2016
I feel like a load has lifted now with the fortuitous turn of events going forward!

When I told Mattie the evening of the day I got the news, he sobbed like a baby, then said, "Mom — PLEASE tell me the truth: is this even a LITTLE for you and not just for me? If it's for ME, you know I thank you, but *really*, all I want is *your* happiness." My buddy sure has come a long way.

I told him this is for me, that leaving the Surrey firm had been a "long time coming." I told him, too, that close-second, this was for him, too. Actually, "This is for *us.*"

"I love us," he uttered in a high-pitched voice, with tears streaming down his cheeks.

Yeah, buddy — I love us, too.

APRIL 28, 2016
Throwback Thursday thoughts. I was thinking about the sacrifices that have to be made in order to compete in bodybuilding and how financial struggles proliferate all our lives in this sport. Fitness competition is not an inexpensive endeavor, by any means imaginable.

Sure, this prep is tough, but adding to that a major relocation, selling almost everything I own still again, moving to a city where I have very few friends going in, and all the financial setbacks that go with such a relocation, I am going to feel the effects of my decision for about six to twelve months.

BUT, when I think back to my BEST CONDITION EVER, prepping for BC Provincials and then Nationals in 2000, I survived some difficulties and made immense sacrifices to get through that time, as well. I was living in the (then) Ambassador Hotel, at Granville

& Davie Street in Vancouver, for my entire pre-contest prep. I had no vehicle and rode a bicycle everywhere. Further, the Ambassador was a downtown residence for mostly alcoholic pensioners or welfare-recipient males. Yes, I was the only woman in there. I had to walk down a long, poorly lit hallway to a public shower room to shower and toilet! There was a mini-fridge in my small room, a television, a dresser, and a bed. I carried my bicycle, every day, up a long flight of stairs to my room, and carried it down the next morning. I cycled to work, and I cycled across the Cambie Street Bridge to train at the Fitness Quest Gym in False Creek!

I'd completely forgotten about all that until my son reminded me last night. It is amazing he holds such a detailed memory from a time pre-dating his TBI, yet today, he cannot remember what he ate ten minutes ago. I think *love* is the glue that holds so many of our memories for us. For me, without comprehensive journaling/writing, I would never be capable of keeping the rapid-fire events straight.

And hardship? We remember tough times and the victory we had over them! So, perhaps I can use this wee hardship for 2016 BC Provincials prep to propel me toward pursuing goals to fruition! Turn that frown upside down!

But, here's to making new goals for my future that require a lesser sacrifice. Cheers.

MAY 2, 2016

I enjoyed another incredible whirlwind of a weekend with my beloved son. I swear, every time we have a couple of days together, our quality time is better and better. He was exhausted, as we had back-to-back appointments all weekend long, but we achieved everything on the big list! He kept telling me how I amazed him, doing so much at my age.

I said, "What? I'm younger than YOU, buddy!"

"Mom, I feel a lot older than I am, but I sure am glad you feel younger!" I wish I had asked him to elaborate on what he meant when he said he feels older, but I wanted to keep the conversation light and on a positive upswing.

We had two people ask us if we were a couple this weekend! That must be the grey in Matt's goatee and the fact that "Lady Clairol" keeps my grey at bay. I found it rather odd, however — but Matt loved it!

Mattie got to meet more of my friends, too, which was nice. He actually said to me, "Mom, thank you for not being embarrassed by me."

WOW. There was a time (pre-brain-injury and a few years post-TBI) when I *was* embarrassed, but only because his behaviors were so alarming, inappropriate, and often shameful in public... There has been no trace of that for some time now.

He worries I am embarrassed by his appearance — the lazy eye, the slight dragging of the right foot, the scars on his head, his poor memory, trouble with word-finding, or difficulties with depth perception — but I assured him I have never once been concerned by what the community thought about any of that. Rather, I viewed all of that as victories he has endured and overcome.

MAY 6, 2016

Example of the continuing childishness in my office, in my last week here. Two women here have been the "bane of my existence" from the first few weeks of arriving in this office. Let's call them Frick and Frack.

INTERESTING SIDEBAR: The noun bane refers to anything that is a cause of harm, ruin, or death. But we often use it for things that aren't that bad, just feel like it. You might say mosquitoes are the bane of your existence. The source of this word is Middle and Old English *bana*, meaning "destroyer, murderer."

SO, after a year of sucking up to Frick and Frack, TRYING to get a semblance of a smile in passing and spoken pleasantries of "good morning,"

or "Have a good night," not all that effort is once again for naught!

Frick — Team Leader and Queen Biotch, though I have another name for her that is incredibly less than polite — as of yesterday, began giving me dirty glares in passing again. There are no circumstances or reasons for this, other than the fact that she dislikes me and feels threatened by me. I responded by turning my head and speaking happily to someone else nearby.

Frack, the follower who will say or do anything Frick suggests, has not spoken to me (without me speaking first) for months. THIS MORNING, she

cheerfully walked by EVERYONE's desk (e.g., made a circle around our floor) and said a loud good morning to everyone, by name, except me! Ya just can't make this stuff up. It is even more unfathomable to me that these females are well over the age of 16 — heck, they both have *children* older than that.

All the while, management (and the lawyer to whom I report) is oblivious to the petty and childish disruption. At least at the Kelowna firm, management was aware of the melodrama, though legally at a loss to make it stop. When staff has maintained employment past a 20-year-endurance, it's almost impossible to effect reprimand. They've grown roots in the firm and are there until they decide to retire.

These are women in their late 40s/early 50s. It is sad to see them so unhappy with themselves that they feel a need to ostracize and bully someone who is tuned into health, discipline, and an absence of alcoholism!

I will be a happy camper to vacate this scenario, never to return, in one week.

No Good Deed Goes Unpunished

I had an interesting occurrence and lesson with Mattie this weekend. As anyone who knows me and Mattie well is aware, he was not always the angel he is now. Pre-brain-injury (and for several years post-TBI), he was manipulative...

We went to see a movie on Saturday; we got there too early, but bought our tickets and opted to go inside and watch the end of the movie, anyway. Going in, we talked about how early we were.

At one point, per his usual, Mattie had to go to the washroom. He told me this story when he returned. When he went to the washroom, he received an apology from the ticketing clerk, who said, "I am SO sorry — I should have told you and your Mom that the movie was not starting for another hour. I have never done that before and I've worked here for five months; I'm SO sorry."

WELL, a part of Matt's "old nature" (just under the surface, and he's still working on controlling that) came through. He asked the young man, "Well, is there anything management can do for us?"

My heart sank. When he related his story, he seemed proud of getting something in compensation from management potentially. I quickly told him how wrong that was, to think about it... that young man working all his weekends here for minimum wage, and being SO thoughtful and remorseful, when ALL THE WHILE, he and I knew FULL WELL we were early and it was OUR DECISION to see the end of the movie before watching the full movie for which we paid.

He sat there and thought for a second, bowed his head, and cried. He said, "Wow, that's old-Matt. That is SO bad. I made a victim out of him." He got up immediately, went out to see the young man, and apologized.

Lesson learned... ALWAYS do the right thing. ALWAYS. And he realized he had victimized someone. That shows a real depth of understanding.

"Buddy, we're a team. Whatever you lack, I will try to see you have what you need. Minor setback? We will pursue a major comeback.

Bad day? I will do my best to get you to a better night, and a still better next morning. As long as you appreciate me and keep trying to do the work, I am here. As long as you want the help, I am here trying."

Sobbing through tears, he tells me, "Mom, I sure don't deserve you. Thank you for still loving me. I know I am a handful."

MAY 4, 2016

Training continues to be on track. It's also the grand countdown for my relocation now. One week from tomorrow marks my final day at work here in Surrey. One week from Friday, I will drive that Coquihalla Highway again with my loaded car, accompanied by a friend with her truck, and we're off to K-Town! The plan is to get unloaded, visit for a minute with friends, and then train at the Steve Nash gym in Kelowna!

My new job begins on Monday, after the move! I am feeling grateful for a good life, filled with opportunities!

MAY 15, 2016

I told Mattie last night that my life feels like I'm dreaming...like even talking to him could be a dream... Without missing a beat and with a wry chuckle, he chortled, "Thank goodness I'm not a nightmare anymore!"

Still another blessing... When I signed my rental agreement yesterday, I read the document (of course). Noting an error, I told her there was an error on the rent amount, written as $600 rather than the rental price of $650 plus $50 for hydro.

She smiled and said they raised the rent for the advertising, but because they liked me, they are renting for the same price paid by the former tenant. So, $650 all in for a private, furnished bachelor HOUSE! ($600 plus $50 for utilities!!) I have driveway parking access, air conditioning and even my Wi-Fi is included!

Unheard of! My guardian angel needs a raise!

JUNE 6, 2016

One month in, and my reminder–lesson of the month? No good deed goes unpunished. I need another job and fast. They summarily dismissed me without warning this morning and it's all legal, as I'm still in a probationary period within 90 days of hire. So much for giving away almost all my possessions to be here in three weeks for employment.

No more mom-and-pop law firms for me... Mom can always decide to work in the office again, and that is precisely what just happened here. I was stunned to see the lawyer's wife walk in, dressed in a suit and heels this morning. Within two minutes, the lawyer had called me into his office (three feet away from the reception desk that I occupied as a paralegal). It's funny (well, not truly funny), but I never liked him from our first meeting. He was what my grandfather would have called "Caspar Milk Toast," with his limp handshake and beady eyes that never made eye contact when speaking. Without even suggesting I sit, he looked me in the eye this time. "We've decided to go a different direction here. Karen will take over reception and filing and keeping the office clean, and

I will do the work I would have delegated to a paralegal. Here's your cheque and your Record of Employment. Just leave your keys on the reception desk."

Yes, they had me answering phones, scheduling appointments, vacuuming and dusting the office, and occasionally typing dictation from the lawyer, for work I typically delegated to my own assistant in other positions. It was not a good job; it did not give me validation and a sense of pride, and I had no opportunity to use the skills honed over decades of education and experience — but it had been a paycheck.

If I'm not working elsewhere by next Monday, my contest is no longer an option for me. What a shame, as I am sitting in the best condition of my life since 2000. I feel utterly devastated.

JUNE 7, 2016

I am not letting this get me down just yet. Conflicted between wanting to lie down and bawl and wanting to avoid creating a victim mentality for myself, I have not even cried. I am numb.

One day at a time — that's all I can do for *Mattie*, and now it is all I can do for myself. There are no jobs advertised in Kelowna that I haven't already applied for (in my field), so I will examine possibilities *outside* my field, starting tomorrow. I was earning $80K per annum, then dropped to $55K, then dropped to $50K. Interesting to note that making a lower income is not representative of increased peace in employment. Thankfully, I need less in my life, and Mattie needs far less, now that he has enjoyed stability over the long term for some time. So, $15 hour may well be my next "good job," but I have yet to find even that. I cannot survive on minimum wage and I am hoping the Universe does not intend for me to be homeless.

Today is a day of rest and training; I need that as I sit back and hope for replies to those applications forwarded. For now, I am grateful to have competition training as an outlet and a healthy distraction. I also count my blessings amid this turmoil. I have a lovely and affordable rental. I am healthy (well, pneumonia is now subsiding, at least), I have food in the fridge and I am positioned closer to my son (and he will be here on the weekend for a visit).

If I lose the car, so be it. If I cannot compete, so be it, but I certainly am putting forth my best effort to secure another job on the heels of the last disaster.

JUNE 10, 2016

Well, it's a good thing I had the luxury of resting today; seems my lungs are still clearing. Stress does not contribute to healing.

My big buddy arrives in an hour, so I'm off now to get coffees from Tim Hortons. It's been "our tradition" for a while that I always have an extra-large Timmies waiting for him when he gets off that bus (always decaf, and he never knows the difference)! He usually says, "UMMMM, that's so good, and thanks for not getting decaf!" Even at this age, we still have parent & child "games" ongoing, but that's my job!

Sure hope we get some warmth and sunshine for tomorrow. It would be a shame to be stuck in my tiny coach house and not get some pleasant walks in, but one day at a time! We have two umbrellas, so we may well opt for a nice walk in the rain through Mission Park!

And I should be able to get some progress photos taken; when I saw my coach last Sunday, I was exhausted and still sick and didn't even think about progress pics until I was about 15 minutes down the road!

JUNE 11, 2016

Oh my; my poor buddy. Mattie is sad to see me so stressed over finding myself unemployed... He's just sobbed and said, "Mom, I wish you could be as proud of yourself as I am; you're in the best condition of your life right now and you're probably not going to go to the stage after all this — but I am SO proud of you."

It's not looking good for my making it to stage. With no job prospects in this small town, I'm facing a bit of a quandary.

Bless his heart; I love my big buddy so much. Matthew is also facing issues with numbness in his right leg again this morning, which also has him freaked out. He forgets this is a recurring issue, and no one has ever explained why it happens intermittently. On those rare occasions when he has a flare-up like this, he fears he is dying.

THE PURSUIT OF INDEPENDENCE

Four weeks to the stage! British Columbia Provincial Championships — for the ultimate time!

It's time to get that fasted cardio in! I'm in slow motion this morning, feeling utterly drained and exhausted! But, if I didn't feel that way this close to competition day, I would have been remiss in my training and diet down to stage!

Matt made interesting observations this morning. "Mom, you're so hard on yourself; I am so proud of you and you are making crazy progress. You haven't been this small — SORRY, lean, in 16 years. But one thing I don't like to see: the better you get, the more you pick on yourself. I don't think this is good for your mind!"

Bless his heart, he hit the nail on the head... Competition is hard (really hard) on our bodies, and perhaps harder on our minds. At four weeks out, I have ALWAYS hated doing this (with a bittersweet effect, of course)... "You think you're never good enough; you compare yourself to friends who are 30, which is SO SILLY! You are 61!."

Yes, this is what competitive bodybuilding does to anyone who pursues it. The journey is not for the faint of heart (oh; I suppose there's a pun intended with that comment). We feel we have failed, despite our best efforts, despite our many sacrifices. We feel our best efforts are ludicrous and we just want to eat a burger and fries, maybe even with some gravy.

But then we put on clothes and find they're looser than the day before, and we push through to train again and again! It's an absolutely fascinating endeavor, but it never gets easier!

JUNE 13, 2016

And for now, I have a wee hole in my heart with my Mattie headed back to his home. We had such a lovely visit, despite some difficulties on Day One. Still believing ALL adversities are opportunities to learn and grow, I have witnessed Mattie thinking that way, too. He said to me, more than once over the past two days, "Mom, I'm so glad we are a real family. We work through things and make it all right again...

You love me even though I have a lot of problems, and you never quit trying — with *everything.*"

I miss him so much already; my little carriage house seems so empty (well, it was quite full with two people living here for three days)!

His last words to me today were "Mom, go get some rest and then train hard; don't worry about anything cause it won't help; remember I love you and think of you all day long. And thank you for another great weekend. Have fun at your competition and remember: it's about YOU and not a trophy! Can I call you tonight?"

I am blessed to have such a loving son.

JUNE 18, 2016
I have a grocery-store tale from yesterday to share. I dropped into Safeway after training. At the checkout, the lady in front of me kept turning around and smiling and trying to sneak a look at my shoulders (cute!), then she said, "You look like someone I should ask for an autograph!"

THEN, the cashier says, "Didn't you have blonde hair a couple of weeks ago?" I chuckled, "No — not me!"

She says, "Well, this woman bodybuilder was in here with blonde hair a couple of weeks ago; thought that was you. But I have to say, you're impressive."

OH MY HEAVENS! That certainly made my day, as I seem to be invisible most of the time!

But as much as those comments can make our day, the mirror and our diet brain all conspire against us, moment by moment! Four weeks ago, I felt I was ahead of my target. Now, at 3 weeks out and in the middle of a cortisol spike that's going to last G-D-knows-H OW-long... I am feeling behind... but it is what it is, I am doing what I can do and not about to push past my health limitations... so we'll see what three weeks offer! One hundred percent I could step on stage right now without cutting water and look better than I did on November 7th, so that's good enough in one sense! And for sure I will improve further over the next three weeks, so whatever comes up from here forward is just a bonus in my thinking. Gravy, if you will!

JUNE 21, 2016
Formal announcement: I am leaving the Okanagan. I really have no choice.

Humiliated and devastated, but with my head on straight and feeling positive, I am leaving next week. There are no jobs here for me in Kelowna, and working for minimum wage here in some other mundane capacity is absolutely not an option — not when there are many positions in Vancouver in my field, paying $60-$80K. It's certainly not that I am "too good" or too proud to work for minimum wage, but I ran the math and cannot survive on such a lowered income at this stage of life; I would lose my vehicle in short order, and in the Okanagan, a vehicle is a need — not a luxury. So, despite being 2.5 weeks away from my bodybuilding competition, and my brain function not WHOLLY manifest, I have discussed this with several trusted friends, and each one unanimously agrees this is the thing to do... One sent me a couple of general employment adverts, but on contacting them all, minimum wage or commission jobs accommodate my responsibilities to myself, much less for Matthew. So, now that I've checked the water, it's time to jump in.

It's been a LONG TIME since I found myself this trapped (decades), but I have a place to stay temporarily (no need to sleep in my car, but I'm not too proud to do that if I have to), and I have culled even more of my personal effects, so one carload is all I need. I need to be living life on the most simplistic terms possible now!

Why do I post this to the public? BECAUSE, I really want everyone out there to understand that SO MANY OF US fall prey to people who do the WRONG thing, hurt us, and have no remorse for the real-life consequences they often leave for us. It is crucial that we approach such betrayals with an educated and logical mind, and think clearly about how we respond, and how we detach from it to plan a move forward. I spend so much of my time strategizing such responses to Matthew's advocacy; I forgot I must take the same approach for my own forward movement.

Cue another compulsive-list extravaganza!! I created five columns on paper: pro, con, potential solutions, advice from whom, and the last column for decision commentary, and made qualified decisions with that initial strategy. Yeah, I'm Type A, OCD all the way; and actually think those are positive traits, within reason and with some flexibility in the mix!

I am helping my landlords find a suitable replacement tenant; they are SUCH incredible people, somewhat innocent despite them both being my age... and I do not want to see them hurt by a prospective tenant experienced in pulling the wool over their eyes.

The departure drive date will be the 29th or the 30th (next week). Then I have nine days to contest, ten days to an eating frenzy, and *hopefully*, 11 days to resume my nutrition plan & training while starting a new job. It certainly would be nice to secure a position in which I could work from here to retirement. I still have a good five to six years in the workforce and have always loved what I do!

Onward and upward.

JULY 24, 2016

After strategizing for days, I philosophized on another lesson I've learned from my adversity in Kelowna.

I have FOR YEARS been a Type A, driven, OCD, anal-retentive multi-tasker. I have missed a lot of life's golden, simple moments, always hurrying, never making time for spontaneity, never taking the time "to stop & smell the roses," so to speak.

My landlord knocked on my door today, just to chat — to tell stories. At any other time in my life, I would have been looking at my watch or saying sorry, I had to be somewhere. Today, I took the time to recognize that I need to make efforts to break that habitual pattern of five decades.

I sat there and fought my desire to run and multi-task, and we had THE best chat — THE best laughs! Story after story (he has more stories than I do)!

And the lovely thing is that I think he's found a replacement renter. A First Nations man from Vancouver viewed the carriage house tonite and I'm glad I got to meet him, so I could assess & privately give my opinion (which my landlord sought and appreciated). He was a lovely, calm, and kind man. The last of his four kids recently moved out. All kids are now stable adults. He started working a new job in Kelowna and has been living in a hotel for two weeks. Like me, the first thing this man noticed about the neighborhood was the HORSES half a block away, the green belt behind the property, and the wetlands park/bird sanctuary two doors down. I am so relieved and pleased that this is such a good fit for my landlords (and the incredibly nice First Nations man) and that my landlords will not suffer a day of lost rent!

It was such a small sequence of events, but contributed to such a profoundly "nice feeling" in my day! It's the little things that contribute to the bigger picture.

AND, a touch of good luck! I just received word that they have accepted me to rent the suite I wanted. After three hours of searching ads, sending emails, and viewing two more suites that were unsuitable today, the good news just arrived!

I will move in on August 13th, starting off with an inflatable bed, which will go into the guest bedroom after I purchase a better bed for myself.

AUGUST 8, 2016
Another excerpt from my conversation with my son last nig ht... first he proudly tells me he washed a van and earned $10. Outstanding!

Then, "and Mom, I bought you a present!" (Me: Buddy, you're supposed to be saving your money (trying to sound emotionless)).

Matt (emotionless): "Mom, it was $1.50."

"Okay buddy; thank you for thinking of me, I love you."

"Mom, can I read it to you?" He's like a child — unable to wait or hold a surprise! It was a phrase from Walt Disney "Growing old is inevitable, but growing up is optional."

Bless his heart, we've talked a lot lately about the circle of life. I really want him to be prepared; we have to talk about that because he is "special needs," and it could affect him differently than another person. Clearly, he gets it and his sense of humor shines through.

AUGUST 14, 2016
Too many people don't know the joy of walking in the rain. I recently insisted that Mattie walk with me in the rain and he thought I'd lost my mind. Begrudgingly, he came along but didn't want *any* part of it. Once he got wet and we relaxed (with hair dripping), he laughed and said, "Wow - Mom, you're crazy, but this IS fun!"

I have missed so many of life's little gifts and want to take the time to live more "in the moment." I want that even more for Mattie. If we ever found ourselves hospitalized, or G-D forbid incarcerated/robbed of our freedoms, walking in the rain and touching trees and grass, appreciating the moon in the night sky - would become our most valued moments!

AUGUST 13, 2016
Another proud moment with my son. Mattie lives in a near-constant

state of apathy, needing to be directed & encouraged to do anything but watch movies, smoke cigarettes and eat, bless his heart. Traumatic brain injury makes anything more complex and tedious, and double-vision 24-7 sure doesn't make things simplistic, either. But, bottom line: he has to learn to push forward through that and to find any level of motivation. It's been a challenge identifying motivators for him.

He's had opportunities at the group home to wash cars or mow the lawn and has messed up — utterly crapped out. Finally, they gave him another opportunity to try again. He's washed a vehicle once a week for the last two weeks. Two nights ago, he told me he was going to ask to wash TWO vehicles. Oh, and his motivation? He asked me two nights ago, "Mom, if I can earn the money to pay for my Greyhound ticket down there, can I come to see you sooner?"

"Yes, of course, sweetie," was my response. I realized my young man actually needs to feel like a man, somewhat earning his own way.

SO, here's our email exchange from this morning!

"Well, buddy, I hope you got to wash TWO vans this morning! Fingers crossed!"

"ME TOO MOM!! AND I WASHED 3 CARS 2DAY!! 2 OF THE HOUSE AND 1 OF THE STAFF!"

I found myself in the middle of a "proud Mama" moment, also proud that I was moving forward to pursue *my* independence, while my son tried his best to envision his.

An infant's laugh singing Happy Birthday
sunsets ♥ paying it forward
Old love God's love singing it forward
you're Cancer free surprise parties Teachers
Watching your child sleep Family ♥ Nurses
Beach sand on your toes

LOVE ♥ WHAT ♥ MATTERS

The bond between family and dog Sunrises you're going to be a dad
puppies acting like children Sunrises
New love Good meals with good friends
Random acts ♥ of kindness a bride's dance with dad
you're going to be a grandfather A soldier's return
Kids playing in the snow
Beach sand on your toes
Dancing in the rain ♥
"I do"
♥♥

ALL THINGS WITH LOVE AND RESPECT

W ell, the good news and the bad news... Always start with the good — *that being* that I brought home another trophy and a 1st Place Women's Heavyweight Bodybuilding medallion from the BC Provincial Championships. More for Mattie's collection — and this one, likely the last!

268 lbs to 145 lbs, age 61

AND, more good news — Mattie is definitely arriving for the weekend, this Friday! YAY!

The bad news is I have to take that ghastly prednisone for another five days. Turns out I am not in as good a recovery position as I had hoped. Am to report for an x-ray tomorrow as well; the doc says he does not like what he hears inside my lungs, mostly on the left side. Lovely (not).

AUGUST 28, 2016
I made soup for Mattie (and me) this morning for breakfast. At first, he begrudgingly took a bite, questioning the efficacy of *soup* for *breakfast!* I told him he needed a healthy meal before he boarded his bus to return home - and Honey Nut Cheerios was not a healthy option!

He took the first bite and his eyes widened, bless his heart. I heard at least 10x this was the best soup he'd ever had. He completely forgot this has always been his favorite since he was a child!

Lemon chicken soup in a coconut cream base, with cinnamon, cayenne, bok choy, celery, and brown rice.

He's been SO much help to me here this weekend; we've had so many incredible deep conversations, but he has grave concerns about my health, as do I. He has also given me a GRANDIOSE reminder of what is important in this life... And his comment a few minutes ago was, "Mom, I told you that some of your friends aren't really friends. I hope you pay attention to who hasn't been here for you at all since you've been sick. You've been sick for almost a month now. I hope you stop giving people so many chances. You're wasting your time on a lot of those people. You always tell me to 'love what matters' and I think you need to take your own advice! OH! Sorry, Mom — no disrespect intended. You know my mouth has its own controls!"

And yes, I am paying attention. Some things broken can never return to where they were, but that's just the consequences for actions ill pursued. Mattie faces his consequences, and I face my own.

The coughing and breathing impairment is getting worse. I hope that another full day of bed rest will help me heal... as it is back to work tomorrow. My x-ray results will arrive later in the week.

AUGUST 29, 2016

I was so incredibly proud of my Mattie this morning, as I stood beside him, waiting in line for him to board the Greyhound bus. Two white-bearded Sikh men were in line behind him; Matt turned and smiled, and gently said, "Uncle, please go first."

WOW. I was stunned and so proud... and the two Sikh gentlemen were stunned as well. Both nodded to me as though to affirm I'd done a good job.

My Mattie has learned so many incredible lessons through his hardship and limitations. I am so grateful to have lived long enough to see it come to fruition.

SEPTEMBER 4, 2016

We just returned from watching the movie *Jason Bourne*! I've read all the books, and I've seen all the previous movies (at least 3x each) - and THIS ONE was the absolute best yet! NON-STOP action, crazy storylines, and first-rate entertainment! And it leaves one hanging — hoping for another sequel!

On exiting the theatre, a sad and disheveled man was sitting with a sign, head-down. The sign said, "Hungry. Will work for food."

Matthew did not hide his displeasure and kept walking as I stopped to chat. I know he was trying to keep from becoming irritated. Now, Matt was standing beside my car.

"Hey there. What's your name?" He told me it was 'Chris'. I took a moment to listen to the man, who told me his best friend died three days prior of a fentanyl overdose, and he cried — actual tears, looking down and trying to hide his emotionalism. I reached into my wallet and gave him about $10 in change. The man sobbed and said thank you, and "G–D bless you."

I clicked the remote to unlock the car doors, and Matthew and I got in. He told me, "Mom — you have a good heart, but sometimes, and I am SORRY for this, but SOMETIMES, you're a sucker, Mom." I said, let's follow the dude and see where he goes.

Thrilled with the potential of proving me wrong, Matthew was all too happy to conduct some surveillance. We exited the car and discreetly followed the man as he crossed the street and went straight into McDonald's. He came out with two bags of food and sat down on the curb. He carefully opened the bag of food, opened his coffee cup and set it down beside him on the asphalt, and ate his Egg McMuffin. It became apparent he was a man of manners, as he carefully folded his bag and the wrapper from his breakfast sandwich. He sipped his coffee slowly, as though to savor every drop. Matt then said, "Okay Mom, you win. How did you know? I was *SURE* he was going to go into the liquor store — not McDonald's."

"Buddy, I didn't know, but his story and his tears touched me, and given he was not high, did not smell of alcohol and he looked like a man truly down on his luck, I thought he could use a hand up today." I explained to Mattie that we can't harden our hearts and *sometimes* we have to take a chance on giving someone the benefit of the doubt. I reminded him that LOTS of people had done that for me, including recently, and lots of people had done that for him, too.

"But Mom — you're broke, too."

"But there's no denying that I am far better off than that fellow and that $10 of change is not life-altering to me, but it sure looks like it is him."

With tears streaming down both his cheeks, Mattie spoke in a high-pitched whine, "I love you so much, Mom. People walk all over you and you still stay kind and want to help. I don't know how you do that."

I love my young man's incredible sensitivity. And to think, "they" diagnosed him as a sociopath years ago. A sociopath is incapable of empathy or compassion. It simply is devoid of their psyche. Mattie may have some authentic challenges and issues, but he is not a sociopath.

SEPTEMBER 5, 2016

I rested a lot after Mattie left this morning - slept through the high-octane action-thriller movie, *Shooter* if you can imagine THAT! But I am relieved to feel incredibly improved from what I've felt over the last five weeks. I am still, however, not 100 percent... still experiencing some breathing dysfunction, but definitely on the mend and won't push too much just yet, and won't be training for at least another two days, but we'll see how it goes. Hoping to start some yoga next weekend (fancy that - a totally new undertaking for me), I also intend to get a couple of walks in this week.

After this recent health scare, I am not pushing myself for anything until I know I am healed.

SEPTEMBER 9, 2016

Today presented another learning opportunity and a wake-up call. I had to email my son.

Matthew, I am STUNNED that you wasted money after all the conversations we have had recently (for two consecutive months or more) that you need to earn money and save money to help with your own expenses, including your bus fare to visit me.

I absolutely cannot send money to you anymore. The comfort monies you receive only cover one carton of cigarettes; there is not even enough left for you to pay for your Melatonin. In fact, the $95 per month that you get does not even cover the cost of your cigarettes. I will NOT send money to top that up. You will need to earn that now.

I have no money for bus fare for you now, either. You have been wasting your money at every turn, and you need to grow up and realize that life is tough.

I don't know when your income tax return will arrive, but when it does, I will send that to Westsyde for their management. I am going to take a step back from your financial management so that you can learn some adult skills. You always talk about how you want your independence, and managing your money is part of that, buddy. I feel you are taking advantage and becoming apathetic again, and I don't have the energy to keep doing things for you when you can do so much more for yourself. After all, you're almost 40 years of age.

I don't know when you will visit me down here again. I am truly saddened by that - but I am exceedingly disappointed that you seem to think people will just bail you out at every turn - that you assume I will keep covering your extra expenses. It's now important that I take a step back, buddy. Can you understand that?

You know the rock-gut cheap instant coffee I drink here? That's one way I find the finances to pay for your Greyhound tickets. I also buy marked-down meats and vegetables for myself, and I buy my clothes at thrift shops. There has been no pedicure or professional manicure for two years or more now, either. I choose the sacrifices so that I can see you and help you, yet you cannot hold on to even $10 to pay your share to come and visit?

Your actions show me your intentions and your priorities. I have to face the fact that you think of yourself before you think of sacrificing to come and see me. I don't believe you mean it maliciously, but I believe you take a lot for granted.

Matt, I want you to think about this. In a few days, we will talk again, but I really feel I need to distance myself from all this — for my own mental and physical health, right now. I love you.

SEPTEMBER 10, 2016
Email from Matthew at 11:49 AM

I TRULY THANK YOU, EVEN-THO I PISSED U OFF, U STILL LOVE ME!! YOU ARE THE BEST FRIEND AND MOTHER!! AND THOSE WERE SOME GREAT THINKS U SENT ME! THANKS TO

U FOR CARING ENUF TO DO THAT! MUCH LOVE
TO U!

He accepted the lesson, and we did not throw the baby out with
the bathwater! I also note that instead of writing "things," he used
thinks — but that is likely to translate as "things I thought about"
— but "thinks I thought about" gives me a chuckle, as well, and I
wonder if he *meant* to state his phrase that way? Ahhh, my buddy.

My health recently took a downturn, first, with strep throat that
escalated into double pneumonia... While I'm feeling incredibly
better now, and slowly coming back to some reduced stamina, x-rays
and a subsequent ultrasound discovered a quarter-sized mass on my
left lung... and it's apparently why I continue to have some breathing
dysfunction - notable when I speak and when I walk, or traverse
stairs (up or down). It's also preventing me from solid sleep at night
and is likely responsible for some of the vivid nightmares over the
past few weeks.

I'm on a waitlist to have it surgically removed, as it's sufficiently
large enough to warrant that, apparently. Could happen in three
weeks, or six months. We'll see how the ORs are stacking up. Not
an urgency, per se, but definitely a necessity.

SO, we have to count our disguised blessings when they come to
us — this one being my contracting pneumonia again. I've known
I've had permanent lung disease for a while, as I was a heavy
smoker in my youth, and I smoked marijuana for many years as well.
Consequences will reach out and touch us every time.

Take care of your health folks; don't go through life as I did for
years, thinking you're exempt from any of this happening to you...
NONE of us are immune; we just live in denial until mother nature
smacks us in the jaw.

Find the blessings in the trauma, folks... and get to a doctor at the
sign of any illness that's with you beyond three days.

SEPTEMBER 13, 2016
SO, last night I had to tear another strip off my son, for wasting
hard-earned money on buying stronger cigarettes (representing a
difference of $25 per carton). I've been sending funds to cover
monies for his community outings and for his $50/carton Rez
cigarettes and wondering why he runs out of cigarettes so frequently
(he smokes 1.3 cartons per month). THEN I learn, he's been wasting
my money. ARGH! I felt bad, but he had to hear some harsh truth
last night (as in, "Because you've wasted money, there's no money
now for you to have a Greyhound ticket to visit over Thanksgiving,
and it is what it is").

He cried, said he was sorry and wasn't thinking... but nothing
changes the fact that we can't pull money out of an apple tree. And
frankly, he is just too "sharp" to have been "not thinking." He wanted
what he wanted, he made his play for it — and now, there needs to
be a consequence for the action.

So, I wake up to send my email of the morning to him... "Good
morning, buddy. Sorry I tore your head off again last night. You have
been buying the more expensive cigarettes with my money, and I

was just shocked. I realize you love the Marlboro's a lot more than the Rez smokes, but hey — I also prefer a T-Bone steak to a can of tuna, but I know I cannot afford the T-Bone, so I can't have it. If I give in to instant gratification and have the steak, then I have to sacrifice something else, because that money can't be plucked off an apple tree."

"I get it, Mom; I really do. Sorry — I really mean that. You are always here for me and some days, I just don't deserve it."

"Buddy, I carried you then — I carry you now." And he cried...

Unconditional love. LOVE WHAT MATTERS, FOLKS. I know I sure do.

PROGRESSING TO THE FUTURE

I t's September 21, 2016. I've had some opportunities to revisit the power of positive reinforcement.

Everyone knows I've changed jobs, and is aware of the stress, anxiety, and decline in emotional & physical health suffered as a result.

Everyone knows I have ongoing challenges in trying to find ways & means to trigger positive growth and change in my son. Well, I had another little epiphany yesterday.

Having tried to get my son to journal (in the most elementary of ways) for 15 years of brain injury, we have never been successful. He forgets, despite daily reminders from me by email. I cannot lose sight of the fact that he has had incredible improvements in multiple areas and has demonstrated a complete 360-degree turnaround in the past three years... But journaling, noting his appointments and responsibilities, is important to his future given his memory loss. I have scolded, threatened to not let him come to visit, desperately seeking anything I could say or do to drill the importance of this into his head. Yesterday, I even designed a daily page for a three-ring binder, with prompts (questions) on what to write. Completion takes five minutes or less... BUT NO! He phoned last night, and no journaling had been done. I told him to go do it and call me back. He did, feigning memory loss... Okay.

I had been considering, earlier, how grateful for I am for my current employment conditions. In this position, I receive commendations for work well designed, performed, and strategized. I am left thinking of what I can do better and more efficiently after I return home each day. That is the work ethic I've enjoyed with several good lawyers through the course of my career, and it gives me great pride in a job well done. I am looking forward to the next day, every day, and sleeping well at night with pride in a job well done and recognized, again.

Then, it occurred to me! Mattie needs to feel this commendation — this spirit of a job well done. He even told me last night that the manager of his group home called him into the office (he was worried almost to the point of "puking" as he described it, not knowing what he had done wrong). She and another staff told him how proud of him they are, how much he has improved, and how they have hopes of him going further. He cried. She gave him a hug. She commended him further and articulated *all the things he had done right.*

HOLY CROW - that realization stopped me in my tracks.

I need to stop reprimanding him for efforts missed and reserve that for the rare occasions where he commits an act with real consequences. I need to remind him of how proud of him I am, how much I love him, how I *remember* how far he has come and what a wonderful job he is doing on all the levels where he excels. He needs to be reminded that we ALL have room for improvement. I want him to understand that these are the moments that create decent humans, with every single day presenting another opportunity to improve something from the day before.

So today, I added to his journal pages, "THINGS I WANT DO TO BETTER TOMORROW."

And a lesson to remember, beyond all this: we are ALL children. We just have varying levels of experience being the child.

SEPTEMBER 25, 2016

About a week ago, I wrote about my continuing frustration with Mattie's apathy for any daily journaling/keeping a daytimer. For 15 years, we've been trying to instill this in him, as he has no short-term memory capacity — which translates into no long-term memory for his future.

After much cajoling, a little angered frustration, then giving in and just letting it go, telling him bottom line, this is his life — his decision, after all, he is an adult. No one is trying to punish him, so if he wants to approach it as a child would, refusing to even try, so be it. Bottom line, I told him, "Buddy, I will always love you and promise to do my best to NEVER lose sight of how far you have come. There may come a day you cannot go further, and this could be it... but my love will *never* change. I want you to always know I have loved you from before you were born, and I will love you until my final breath. I told you when you were born, 'Nobody is going to take you from me', and here I am, still meaning that to the same degree."

And just like that — for four consecutive days, he has journaled. He has been oh so proud to read his entries to me every night on the phone! The staff at the group home is astounded and proud of him as well.

AND TODAY, he opts to put on dress clothes out of the blue! Says he wants to take more pride in his personal appearance!

Miracles never cease... BAH HUMBUG to those who said he had a two-year, then a five-year, then a ten-year-max window of opportunity after this level of brain injury. LOVE, a positive environment, patience, appropriate medication & medical treatment, and an extra dash of love for good measure, can go a LONG way to overcoming the impossible. Add to that a good measure of some personal self-worth, and even though the sky might not be the limit with brain injury, slight improvements can be astronomical.

Mattie on life support,
November 2001

So proud of my young man... and bah humbug to all who told me to give up and let the "state" handle it (as in permanently institutionalizing him, since they said he could not rehabilitate). "They" had assessed his life to have no value, which is among the most disheartening characterizations anyone could hear — about themselves, or about their child.

OCTOBER 10, 2016
Mattie is here for another full day and night. Turns out we have a "happy accident" in the mix, as I erred when purchasing his Greyhound ticket online and selected a TUESDAY return instead of Monday! Heck, back when I purchased that, I was still at my former job and might have been thinking, "'FTN', I'm enjoying my time with my son!" In any event, we are both grateful for the extra day together! Nonetheless, a happy accident also considering that I will only be 30 minutes late for work! All good.

We started our morning with coffee and a Netflix movie... then I cut his hair. I asked if he was going to trim the beard he's opted to grow or was he good with that? He gave me a sheepish glance. I told him he looked like a warrior from Afghanistan, but that was great if that was the look he was going for!

Then, he asked for scissors and again gave me *the look*. "Mom, so sorry, but I don't know how to trim my beard. I've never had luck growing it out this far before. Can you teach me?"

Wow. Still another one of "the little things" that no one has picked up on in all these years. One just assumes a big, grown man like Mattie knows how to trim a beard, myself included. Sigh. Poor guy — being criticized for inattention to grooming, and all the while not knowing what to do with the facial hair mother nature allowed him to grow!

Well, that not being in my realm of experience, I didn't quite know what to say. He tried by using a comb and combing upward and preparing to cut. I suggested that was going to make the beard VERY short, and he said, "OH, okay! If I make a mistake, it will grow again. But I'd rather learn how to do it right the first time!" Finally, we came up with what seemed like a logical plan, of combing the beard downward first, then upward so he could see all the uneven growth (which rendered a loud "WOW" from him)! I left him to it, and he came out proud and smiling five minutes later, tastefully well-groomed!

I was so proud of him for ASKING for help and for expanding on his grooming protocol.

Ahhh, the many things I've had to teach my son since raising him again as a full-grown man. I don't always get it right, but we both try (and try again) with more than a modicum of love!

I certainly feel a "hats off" is due to all the single moms out there, and to all the Dads and Uncles who teach their sons these things! There is nothing easy about raising young men to become gentlemen with a sense of honor, to have pride in their appearance, to know the importance of loyalty, to know and act appropriately on the differences between right and wrong — and to respect the subtle boundaries between the two. We can only do our best, take educated guidance from wherever we can get it, and do it all with profound and unconditional love.

OCTOBER 20, 2016

I enjoy the repeating revelations that my son continues to improve in multiple ways with every passing week. For almost 15 years, I have managed his small monies provided every month for emergencies, because he has been incapable of managing those funds.

NOW, today marks still another milestone, with me relinquishing those duties to the group home. They will now assist him with cashing his cheque and budgeting his funds each month. Even one year ago, we could have never speculated he would come this far.

What's more, he is still proudly journaling his day — every day. The staff has commended him, astounded by his sudden change in motivation and for bringing himself more into adulthood.

Miracles never cease... Despite my health not being optimal for several weeks now, and despite my own struggles with aging, tolerating imbeciles without "going ghetto," and more, it is never lost on me the blessings I have with my son's incredible progress and transformation.

OCTOBER 21, 2016

For three full weeks now, Mattie has consistently journaled his day and kept track of his minimal future appointments in a daytimer. It is truly remarkable progress, and I nearly weep with delight to hear his voice shining with pride as he reads his entries to me each night over the telephone. I don't think he even realizes how the journaling is helping his penmanship and his reading abilities as well!

I noticed he never journals about anything negative in his day. I mentioned that to him, and his response was, "Mom, I don't want to remember the negative things, and if I don't write it down, it won't be in my brain. That's the good thing about brain injury for me. If I put that negative stuff back in, more negative is gonna come out - and nobody wants that. I sure don't need it. I want to love my life." Wow.

NOVEMBER 3, 2016

Well, time to hit the road. Mattie arrives in a little more than an hour! I will continue our "tradition" and pick up an extra-large Timmy's for him (he never knows it's decaf, LOL — he's just happy to have the warm beverage when he gets off the bus!) and a fresh pack of Marlboros. Yes, it's his ONLY vice, and he is unlikely to quit, but he has disciplined himself down to smoking seven to eight cigarettes daily (ONLY) for the past two years. I am so very proud of him for that, particularly since there was a time post-brain injury when three packs a day wasn't enough. In those days, he would venture out, pick up cigarette butts off the ground (ANYwhere) and smoke them. He's horrified to remember those times now; brain injury takes so much from a person, but he is so fortunate and blessed to have reconnected a litany of neurons.

Hoping for some rain-free weather over the weekend so we can do more bonding chats over some walks through nature, and around that nice padded, paved track at Bear Creek Park!

Tomorrow we will see a movie IF there is one worthy of a $30 expenditure! Thank goodness, Matt also understands the value of a dollar now, and refuses to let me pay for a movie if it's only a "possibility of enjoyment!"

I get more excited than a child at Christmas, every time my young man is coming down for a visit. My "WHY" for living. My Mattie.

NOVEMBER 5, 2016

I woke up at 4:30 this morning to hit the washroom and return to bed; tip-toed out quietly, but Mattie is typically a light sleeper! "Good morning, Mom — I LOVE YOU! It's time for ME to get up, too! I'll make our coffee!"

WOW! We never stopped talking from that moment forward — all day long!

SO enjoying every moment with my young man; so many words of uncanny wisdom from him -- his improvements are just remarkable. He's extremely worried about my health and my stress levels; keeps telling me to let him handle things while he's here....to ask him for ANYTHING. less his heart.

He also keeps telling me to talk to him about anything and he will help me decide. And 'ya know what? He HAS given me perspectives that my brain did not perceive. He HAS helped me make many decisions far more rapidly than I could have on my own.

It's utterly amazing. So grateful to live in the moment. SO grateful for what I have, right in front of me. So blessed to have my son still with me, despite all this tragedy.

Cannot WAIT to see the look on his face when he sees his suit! He has NO IDEA!

Stress makes us forget little things... I had forgotten this jewel of an experience shared with my Mattie on his last night here at the time of his prior visit.

We spent some time on Facebook together while he was here; he read the various posts, and my replies... some people came up often and he asked me how I knew them, and I told him. Many were people I'd never met face-to-face, but some of whom had become good friends through Facebook. He ended up remembering Mark B's name because it came up so much. He was impressed with the various posts and how it "felt" like we knew one another personally.

When Mattie said his prayers here the final night, he actually added Mark into his ask for blessings. In the middle of speaking with his head down and eyes closed, he said, "Mom, what's that lawyer's name in Florida who is your friend?" I said Mark, and he asked G-D to bless Mark and his family and all his dogs and everyone he cared about!

I love the kind and perceptive heart my son exhibits these days.

NOVEMBER 6, 2016
Happy birthday, buddy! 38 years today! I reminded him that he is now, officially, three years past his "expiration date."

"Expiration date? Mom, what in the world does that mean? I'm not a carton of milk!"

"Buddy, back in 2001, your neurosurgeon predicted your life expectancy to be age 35 or less."

"Wow, you know how I like proving people wrong!" He hesitated for a couple of seconds and added, "Mom, if not for you — I would be dead now. THAT is a fact."

NOVEMBER 16, 2016
Fifteen years ago today (around 10 PM tonight), I got the call informing me that my son had just undergone brain surgery. That photo I've shared is not even the worst that I saw (that pic taken days after his surgery). They beat him intending to end his life, and he spent a long time in a coma. Between VGH and GF Strong Rehabilitation, he was there for seven months. I was told he would not survive; then, I was told to prepare myself — that he could end up a "vegetable" (not the neurosurgeon's choice of words, of course — but that was what he meant); then I was told he would not live past 35, then I was told he would never have the ability to learn, then for more than a decade, I fought to keep him away from institutionalization.

Well, I am grateful to be living in the modern age! I cannot imagine what we would have done without the live-camera footage over the Coquihalla Highway — BC's very own "Highway to Hell!" The roads are not bad right now, and it's a lucky turn of events that there was no snowfall overnight.

Coffee, bath, and ten minutes of news, and I am "on the road again!" The car is loaded and once I hit Timmy's for two coffees, I will begin my creep to Kamloops (since there can be no 140 kph stints along the way)!

NOVEMBER 17, 2016
We moved another load to my Kamloops storage unit today. I'm getting good at navigating that Coquihalla Highway now! I am so very grateful that the roads have been clear, only seeing some minor slush in a couple of areas. My car, however, looks like a bush pig it's so filthy — but all good!

We are taking another load to Kamloops tomorrow. I will make a nice meatloaf stuffed with mozzarella cheese, some bok choy & mushrooms, and yams for the family for whom I will be working. We will drop that off and let them meet Mattie, then return to Surrey.

Matt's here for another ten days! We are really enjoying our time together, the incredible bonding in the course of this "adventure" (he says it's our vacation). We've had an incredible day, both of us utterly exhausted, but in a good way. And for me, it is a welcome change to vacate that exhaustion after a stress-from-a-crappy-office-experience scenario!

In one of the beautiful moments shared with Mattie today, as we made our third trip by car to Kamloops to move another load of my belongings, it became even more apparent to me how consciously and remarkably observant he is.

As we neared Hope, on the way back, he noted something in my body language. "Mom - my city is going to be so good for you; I noticed when we were there today, that you relaxed; I loved seeing that. Right now when we're getting closer to the lower mainland, you are tensing up again. I see it in you. It's like your shoulders want to touch your ears! You need to relax. I am so glad you are getting out of here. This is not good for you."

Wow... and then I realized again how important it was to live MORE "in the moment," cognizant of how fortunate I am to have my son and these next extended ten days with him!

NOVEMBER 18, 2016
Even for our last days here in Langley, I am now boycotting Gate Pizza. I have loved the food from Gate (pizza, Indian food, wings) for a long time. I've been a loyal customer in every location they own, but the Langley store just messed up for the third time and I am done. Last night's order was delivered with three phone calls asking for directions (this is Surrey — easily identifiable addresses, logical numbers; mine is no exception). By the time the rude female staff snapped to ask our address again (which was identical to what I provided twice before) and the driver phoned three times to ask how to get to us, the pizza arrived cold. Mattie insisted on handling the situation (I'm sure he was afraid of what might escape my lips).

I was so proud of him as I stood outside within earshot of him. First, the driver walked away with $4.75 owing in change; Matt asked for the money. The man said, "That's my tip." Matt said the pizza was cold, so there was no tip. The man said he would not return the change, and Matt said, "Uncle — you WILL return the change. That is not your money." Matt stood there OH so patiently while the man pretended to search for the money, and ultimately produced every cent. Matt never lost his temper, never resorted to profanity or rudeness, and remained patient.

It's not the first time I have watched/heard him call an East Indian man "Uncle." Perhaps he picked that up from my friend Romi? It makes me very proud, and it is not something for which I can take credit!

He told me, "Mom, I think I handled that one better than you would have" — and I had to absolutely concur!

I am just delighted and proud of my young man. A mere five years ago, he likely would have decked the man. And ten minutes ago, I would have made an angry fool of myself! A very real and measurable!

NOVEMBER 19, 2016
Holy crow, a whirlwind move maneuver out of town like this is really a drain on the body and mind. So grateful to have Matt's help; he has been invaluable both physically and emotionally — and has been a guardian angel watching over me (which has proven quite necessary over the last couple of days). After four trips to the Okanagan to put full carloads into storage, I am wiped out. I kept saying we had taken three loads, but NO, it was, in actuality, four. Matt counted it out for me. Holy crow.

There is SO much to finalize before leaving, and only five working days to get it all accomplished, but I have a list/a strategy. We ventured out to the mall earlier today and my PTSD was so triggered that I kept thinking I was at the Kelowna mall. I was in Langley. I kept saying, "This is so different; I don't know why I can't find my way around." Matt was SO worried, as he sees the toll this has taken on me. I felt so disoriented; it is even difficult for me to drive right now. Matt has had to follow behind me to make sure I turn the burner off the stove when I warm up our food. I am truly hoping for some downtime at home for a couple of days.

What a whirlwind, driving seven to eight hours each day for three consecutive days. Poor Mattie woke up around 1 AM with a sore throat and sniffles. I gave him two vitamin C and two vitamin D, and a Hall's throat lozenge. We've done so much, pushing past our comfort zones with every drive, and I honestly don't know how well I would have fared without him here helping me. That Coquihalla Highway, even with clear roads, is treacherous, with so many irresponsible, risk-taking drivers. We saw SO many could-be-serious disasters in the making. In hindsight, I wonder if that made him nervous, or aggravated his PTSD at all? He never complains unless things become unbearable for him (like years ago when one of his workers took him for a drive around the track in a race car, as well as the time I took him go-kart riding). I wish, somewhere along the way, some group home personnel or medical staff warned either of us that these activities could cause less than optimal outcomes with brain injury.

On arising this morning, both of us said, "Wow — glad we have a day off today!" Well, as in not making a round-trip to Kamloops, but still so much to accomplish. This Mama has to go to Value Village and find a winter coat. Living in Kamloops will not be well-served from December to April with the windbreaker I've worn all winter for the past two years. Yesterday, temperatures were -3 degrees (+7 degrees in the lower mainland).

Then, my dear young man tells me this morning, "Mom — you're 62, and I cannot believe how much you do. There is NOTHING lazy about you. I see how you push, and push, and push until you can't push anymore. I sure hope you learn to relax!"

Wow, that's a recurring theme from my boy — but it is incredible to be loved that much, and to realize how observant and perceptive he is. Bless him, he cannot remember what he did two hours ago most days, but he sure puts in concentrated focus where I'm concerned.

I am exhausted, but feeling very blessed.

NOVEMBER 20, 2016

Whew, I certainly need a few hours today to recharge, and so does Mattie, bless his heart. He has not pushed himself this hard since before his brain injury; he's been so exhausted he just does what we now call "the nod." I can be in the middle of a deep discussion with him or a loud movie can be on television — and it doesn't matter; unilaterally and without warning, his head drops and he's OUT. It's only for a few seconds, but it's morbidly fascinating and a little "scary" to witness. Poor guy. He has helped me SO much, but this "nod" has been ongoing for a while now. I'm wondering if there is something more — something warranting investigation, however. He will often ask, "How long was I out?"

Tonight, he made light of it all (as nobody likes a *complain-freak*), and chuckled, "I guess I'm *Noddy by Nature*" — a clear pun on the rap group that he enjoyed so much in his youth!

Making another trip up tomorrow to the storage unit; the trunk is now full, the back seat will take a few more items as we go out in the morning; have to return to Kamloops to pick up more meds for him, since we've extended his time down here with me.

Then, we are in town finalizing multiple important errands until we leave next Monday morning (early) with the last load of computer, printer, bed linens, and final kitchen items.

We have rain in the forecast today. I've always welcomed and enjoyed rainy days, but today I am hoping to at least get out for a walk. I truly need that exercise in my regimen again consistently. Today marks Day One of full-on clean eating again, too. My blood pressure has been stupidly high lately and I need to smarten up with that since I do have a heart and stroke condition just under the surface. 165/90 and 162/92 are not good. Sure, things could be worse, but that is a danger zone set of numbers right there. I need to return to celery and asparagus with every meal again, four liters of water daily, vitamin consistency again, and exercise by any means necessary, every single day, even if it's "only" some stretching at home.

Well, as we sit here listening to the high-velocity winds outside, we're grateful we have no commitments until 11 AM this morning!

Bless his heart, he has done so much. He's had so much over-stimulation this past week and is utterly exhausted. It's 8 AM now, and he is still sleeping (despite having gone to bed at 7 PM last night)! He has not had this much activity since he played football as a running back for John Oliver back in the day! Heck, this relocation prep probably has lasted as long as his John Oliver "football career." Sad to think in those terms, but life changes on a dime with Mattie — which means life changes on a dime for MOM, as well.

I, myself, again slept from 7 PM until 4:30-5 AM...truly exhausted in every sense of the word. But the winds of change are upon us now; two more days here to finish saying goodbye, to get some last walks through nature in the lower mainland, and then to venture toward the next chapter of my life - proximate to my son. This is how and where I intend to finish my years — close to what is most important to me. No more dreams to chase, no more wondering where my life is going. Just go with the flow, give as much as I can to those around me, and find my peace and balance at last.

2016 has been a wild ride, with circular arguments, trauma and blessings, and unforgettable lessons at every turn. 2016 saw me compete in bodybuilding for the last time, and the year found me in need of a new direction in stress relative to my career. With all those winds of change, I probably need to build windmills! But now, I progress to a new future — for myself, and with my son just a little more proximate!

EPILOGUE

A fter traumatic brain injury, survivors are seven times more likely to develop symptoms of mental illness. After penal incarceration, 60 percent of those released after sentence completion emerge with mental health issues. Add two parts of addiction complications to the mix, and we can witness a succinct circle of disaster creating medical, psychological, and advocacy response emergencies on additional levels.

And the cumulative issues take on a life of their own from there. Families and caregivers grieve the loss of jobs, apartments, and friends — and mourn the loss of the normalcy that they no longer recognize, in its new form. We don't just relate to the emotions and needs of a survivor, we feel them.

But we also lose sight of the fact that our *survivor* is also mourning all of this as well — perhaps in an even greater capacity than those of us acting as advocates and providers. After all, we are overwhelmed.

One fleeting moment can change who we are and where we are headed. We can drift like smoke in the wind from a position of stability and peace to one of unbridled chaos.

It's the little things that can make or break us. For Matthew, the little things that experts never saw coming, and caregivers only witnessed once, it was "too late". His triggers to disaster included:

- Cigarettes
- Cannabis
- Cookies
- Sedation medications
- Benzodiazepines

We came to refer to those as the "good boy" addictions and compulsions — invariably taunted by a majority as less disconcerting than opioids or stimulants.

But in the years from Matthew's TBI in late 2001 through to where we next venture in this journey — to *Hell House* — we saw strangers, a medical doctor, landlords, a probation officer, and other clients inside a group enabling a marijuana addiction, simply because it was merely considered a "good boy addiction" with no consequences perceived other than the one of raiding the refrigerator.

Then, add alcohol to the recipe, as occurred in the Langley group home, and one achieves an expedited route to full-blown disaster and decompensation. Case in point, if a reformed alcoholic crosses the line, we *all* understand the downhill vortex that flows from there.

It took brain injury experts a lot longer to clue into lesser addictions, which created the "appetizer recipes" that propelled a survivor to catastrophic decompensation. In Matthew's case, twenty years ago, a family physician prescribed cannabis for sleep in a patient with a severe TBI. One would like to believe this practice is no longer in place today, given our understanding that cannabis induces seizure activity in survivors of stroke and TBI, and the fact that it will intensify a smoking addiction, as well.

There were no caregiver support groups twenty years ago, either. As a primary caregiver, advocate, and dedicated parent, there is no doubt such support would have provided me with better strategies and more educated responses. One can only speculate, but hindsight *has proven* to be 20-20. The effects of TBI or stroke impact an entire family – not just the individual who survived the injury. Family dynamics and relationships are challenged by the changes in communication, roles, and responsibilities that shift alongside the cognitive and behavioral transitions. Managing and adapting to these changes is daunting — and requires education, time, effort, finances, and dedication to achieve stability for all.

Mattie was trapped in the spider's web, and I was advocating from a sticky predicament. We are all hostages to what we love, but the limits to which we will travel as reluctant heroes are seemingly infinite.

ABOUT AUTHOR

 Canadian writer Sarah Martin has lived in diverse cultures such as Japan, Korea, Thailand, and Central America. No stranger to trauma and a self-described recluse now because of it, she writes from home with the inspiration of water and mountains in every view. She is known to regularly take refuge on a park bench, chatting about freedom, peace, and undying love with her son, Mattie.

A Tale of Two Psyches

1 CHAOS FOR THE FLY
2 HELL HOUSE
3 BEFORE THE MASK SLIPS
4 DEATH SENTENCE
5 FREEDOM

Non-Fiction

THE AMYGDALA RESPONSE:
Dissociation as a Survival Mechanism

Made in the USA
Middletown, DE
26 May 2022

66216060R00179